Kenneth H Scott

Newcastle United

League Division 2 – Season 1893-94

Record of the 1893-94 season when Newcastle United entered the Football League for the first time in their history

Season One

Published by KayLynM Publishing
Newcastle upon Tyne

Copyright © 2021 Kenneth H Scott

Cover design courtesy of PinkTea Vanity

ISBN: 978-0-9934201-8-4

Table of Contents

Preamble… 5
    League Football comes to St James's Park 5
    Finalisation of the Division 2 clubs… 6
    It's all about the money! 7
    Finally, some words of caution… 9

Football League Division 2 ~ Season 1893-94 11
    Final Table 11
    Results Matrix 11
    Division Miscellany 11
    Complete Games Listing: Football League Division 2 ~ Season 1893-94 12
    Football Association Test Matches: Season 1893-94 17
    Football Association Challenge Cup (FA Cup) : Season 1893-94 18

Match Reports 19
    Game: 1 ~ Saturday, September 2nd, 1893   vs. Woolwich Arsenal 20
    Game: 2 ~ Monday, September 4th, 1893   vs. Trafalgar 21
    Game: 3 ~ Wednesday, September 6th, 1893   vs. Sunderland 23
    Game: 4 ~ Saturday, September 9th, 1893   vs. Middlesbrough 24
    Game: 5 ~ Saturday, September 23rd, 1893   vs. Burton Swifts 25
    Game: 6 ~ Saturday, September 30th, 1893   vs. Woolwich Arsenal 27
    Game: 7 ~ Saturday, October 7th, 1893   vs. Lincoln City 28
    Game: 8 ~ Saturday, October 14th, 1893   vs. Notts County 30
    Game: 9 ~ Saturday, October 21st, 1893   vs. Ardwick 31
    Game: 10 ~ Saturday, October 28th, 1893   vs. Small Heath 33
    Game: 11 ~ Saturday, November 4th, 1893   vs. Liverpool 35
    Game: 12 ~ Saturday, November 11th, 1893   vs. Sheffield United 37
    Game: 13 ~ Saturday, November 18th, 1893   vs. Northwich Victoria 38
    Game: 14 ~ Saturday, November 25th, 1893   vs. Liverpool 39
    Game: 15 ~ Saturday, December 2nd, 1893   vs. Dipton Wanderers 40
    Game: 16 ~ Saturday, December 9th, 1893   vs. Notts County 41
    Game: 17 ~ Saturday, December 16th, 1893   vs. Small Heath 43
    Game: 18 ~ Saturday, December 23rd, 1893   vs. First Royal Scots 44
    Game: 19 ~ Monday, December 25th, 1893   vs. Middlesbrough Ironopolis 45
    Game: 20 ~ Tuesday, December 26th, 1893   vs. Walsall Town Swifts 46
    Game: 21 ~ Wednesday, December 27th, 1893   vs. Crewe Alexandra 48
    Game: 22 ~ Saturday, December 30th, 1893   vs. Burslem Port Vale 49
    Game: 23 ~ Monday, January 1st, 1894   vs. Lincoln City 51

Game: 24 ~ Tuesday, January 2nd, 1894　　vs. Middlesbrough Ironopolis	53
Game: 25 ~ Saturday, January 6th, 1894　　vs. Ardwick	54
Game: 26 ~ Saturday, January 13th, 1894　　vs. Northwich Victoria	56
Game: 27 ~ Saturday, January 20th, 1894　　vs. Rotherham Town	58
Game: 28 ~ Saturday, January 27th, 1894　　vs. Sheffield United	59
Game: 29 ~ Saturday, February 3rd, 1894　　vs. Burslem Port Vale	61
Game: 30 ~ Saturday, February 10th, 1894　　vs. Bolton Wanderers	63
Game: 31 ~ Saturday, February 17th, 1894　　vs. Rotherham Town	65
Game: 32 ~ Saturday, February 24th, 1894　　vs. Grimsby Town	67
Game: 33 ~ Saturday, March 10th, 1894　　vs. Walsall Town Swifts	69
Game: 34 ~ Saturday, March 17th, 1894　　vs. Burslem Port Vale	70
Game: 35 ~ Friday, March 23rd, 1894　　vs. Crewe Alexandra	71
Game: 36 ~ Saturday, March 24th, 1894　　vs. Burton Swifts	73
Game: 37 ~ Monday, March 26th, 1894　　vs. Leicester Fosse	75
Game: 38 ~ Saturday, March 31st, 1894　　vs. Middlesbrough Ironopolis	76
Game: 39 ~ Thursday, April 5th, 1894　　vs. Sunderland	77
Game: 40 ~ Saturday, April 7th, 1894　　vs. Dundee FC	79
Game: 41 ~ Saturday, April 14th, 1894　　vs. Grimsby Town	80
Game: 42 ~ Saturday, April 21st, 1894　　vs. Sunderland	81
Game: 43 ~ Monday, April 23rd, 1894　　vs. Willington Athletic	82
Game: 44 ~ Wednesday, April 25th, 1894　　vs. Shankhouse	83
Game: 45 ~ Saturday, April 28th, 1894　　vs. Middlesbrough Ironopolis	83
Game: 46 ~ Monday, April 30th, 1894　　vs. Sunderland	84
The Players	85
Newcastle United: Appearance & Goalscoring Statistics	86
Mass Dismissal	87
Sacked or accept wage reduction.	87
About the Author	100
Bibliography	101

Preamble...

League Football comes to St James's Park

Newcastle United enter the Football League as they accept an invitation to join the fledgling Football League Second Division, the division itself only entering its second year, and Newcastle had refused an invitation to join it in its inaugural season. This after their application to join the First Division was rejected. A decision made in a fit of pique by the Newcastle committee perhaps? One will never know. Now realising the benefits of joining the league, they accepted this second offer.

However, before our journey through the trials and tribulations of the season begins, we need to ask ourselves, how did we get here? Having already rejected an offer to join why were they now invited to join? The answer to that question lays back in May, with the Annual General Meeting (AGM) of the Football League.

Held on Friday, 26th May at the Crosby Hotel in Manchester, under the chairmanship of Mr McGregor there were a large number of delegates present, and the agenda was a full one.

Of those agenda items there were two which were of particular interest to us.

The first of these concerned the First Division, but the ramifications would undoubtedly affect the Second Division. The matter arising was a one concerning the number of clubs that constituted the First Division.

- It was proposed by Sheffield United that the number of clubs in the division be increased to twenty instead of the current sixteen. The motion was seconded by Everton. However, upon being put to ballot, it was defeated by a single vote.
- Newton Heath then brought forward an amendment that the number of clubs be eighteen. This amendment was supported by both Bolton Wanderers and Small Heath, citing that the increase would dispense with 'unprofitable' friendly matches.
  This however was objected to by Blackburn Rovers and Preston North End. They in turn citing that it would increase expenses for more players. On being put to the ballot the amendment did not reach the required three-fourths majority needed for alterations to rules, so it was also defeated.
- Upon this Preston North End withdrew their proposition that the division be reduced to only twelve clubs.
- A further motion, which would have had no effect upon Newcastle United, but I include it only as a matter of interest, was proposed by Blackburn Rovers, this being that the division be divided into a 'Northern' and a 'Midlands' section. It was also defeated.

So now to the Second Division, which holds most of our interests.

- The four 'retiring clubs' from the Second Division, i.e., the bottom four from last, *the inaugural*, season 9th Lincoln City, 10th Crewe Alexandra, 11th Burslem Port Vale, 12th, and last, Walsall Town Swifts were all re-elected.
- It was then that Grimsby Town proposed by that the Second Division be increased from the present 12 clubs to 16. The motion was carried unanimously. Rotherham Town and Newcastle United were elected to two of the newly available positions whilst it was decided to advertise for applications for the other two. The applications to be in time for the meeting of the divisions at Anderson's Hotel, Fleet Street, London.

So that, dear reader, was that, and Newcastle United were now a bona-fide member of the Football League! Who however was to join them in the second division?

As per the Football Association rules at the time the bottom three clubs in Division 1 played test matches, the equivalent of the Play-Offs we have today, against the top three clubs in Division 2. These were simple 'one-off' games at a ground neutral to both opponents. The fixtures, and results, were as following:

Results: Test Matches (Season 1892-93)					
Date		Score		Venue	Gate
22/04/1893	Sheffield United	1-0	Accrington	Town Ground, Nottingham	6,000
22/04/1893	Darwen	3-2	Notts County	Hyde Road, Manchester	3,000
22/04/1893	Newton Heath	1-1	Small Heath	Victoria Ground, Stoke-on-Trent	4,000
Replay					
27/04/1893	Newton Heath	5-2	Small Heath	Olive Grove, Sheffield	6,000

Those results meant that Sheffield United and Darwen became the first-ever 'promoted' clubs, whilst Accrington and Notts County became the first-ever 'relegated' clubs.

Meanwhile Newton Heath retained their place in the First Division and Small Heath retained their place in the Second Division.

We now need to jump forward a week to find out who would be filling those two spare slots and be joining Newcastle United on their journey.

Finalisation of the Division 2 clubs…

Here we are, Thursday, 1st June 1893, and we are safely ensconced at the aforementioned Anderson's Hotel in Fleet Street, London. The management committee of the Second Division needed to, *amongst other items*, resolve the vacant positions now that the division had been increased to 16 clubs. Of the applications received they decided that the successful candidates for the positions were:

- **Liverpool:** having only formed prior to the 1892-93 season, and who had an application to join the division dismissed 'out of hand' at last year's meeting, were duly elected to the division.

- **Woolwich Arsenal:** Upon their election they became the very first 'southern' club to enter the Football League. The name "Woolwich Arsenal" was brand new to the club. Formed as Dial Square Football Club in 1886 they quickly (within a month of their first game) became "Royal Arsenal" and then in June 1893 had to change their name again as they wanted to become a limited company.
Within the United Kingdom no company can have the word "Royal" in their title without special dispensation.
As the club were once again based in Woolwich it was an obvious choice. Their full title now being "The Woolwich Arsenal Football and Athletic Company, Limited".

It should be mentioned that applications had also been received from Doncaster Rovers and Loughborough Town; these however were rejected. The composition of the Football League Division 2 was thus:

Accrington	Grimsby Town	Rotherham Town
Ardwick (now Manchester City)	Lincoln City	Small Heath (now Birmingham City)
Bootle	Liverpool	Walsall Town Swifts
Burslem Port Vale (now Port Vale)	Newcastle United	Woolwich Arsenal
Burton Swifts	Northwich Victoria	
Crewe Alexandra	Notts County	

Or was it?

What we now thought was the finalised composition was thrown into complete turmoil by two significant events before the ink was even dry on the fixture lists, the first was quite easily rectified, the second was unfortunately irreconcilable.

- Accrington, who had lost their Division 1 status, held a special meeting on July 26th. At this meeting the main question discussed was whether they could remain within Division 2 or opt to apply for membership of the Lancashire League. It was explained at the meeting that the club could not possibly hope to continue in the Second Division without raising the club's debt from £200 to £1,000. It was ultimately decided the club could not afford such debt and therefore resigned from the division. Middlesbrough Ironopolis were invited to take their place, an invitation that was accepted.

So, that was the "easily rectified" event out of the way now, and so to the other event.

- The event which could not be reconciled was the rather surprise resignation of Bootle, in August, from not only the division but the Football League itself and the directors decided that as they could not compete with their major Merseyside rivals, Everton and Liverpool, that the club was to be disbanded forthwith. This occurred too late for remedial action to be taken as other leagues had already made their fixture lists, and the "knock-on" effect would have been too great. So, for this, only its second year in existence, the Second Division did not have the desired 16 teams, but only 15 teams instead. Such is life in football.

Now, at last, we have the final composition of the division.

Ardwick	Lincoln City	Notts County
Burslem Port Vale	Liverpool	Rotherham Town
Burton Swifts	Middlesbrough Ironopolis	Small Heath
Crewe Alexandra	Newcastle United	Walsall Town Swifts
Grimsby Town	Northwich Victoria	Woolwich Arsenal

Supplementary Notes…

- Ardwick changed their name to Manchester City in 1894
- Burslem Port Vale liquidated at the end of the 1906-07 season and were reformed as Port Vale
- Small Heath changed their name in 1905 to Birmingham FC and adopted the "City" suffix in 1945
- Woolwich Arsenal dropped the 'Woolwich' prefix in 1914

Still, we are not ready to continue our journey yet, for there appeared some very dark clouds and some very worrying developments at Newcastle United and it was slowly revealed how close we came to not having first-class football within the boundaries of our fair city.

It's all about the money!

Yes, very little changes in football regarding finances. Just as we have today, some clubs have the money, and some clubs don't. Unfortunately, Newcastle United fell into that second category. Indeed, they were only £200 away from folding! Here we will follow a series of events that almost saw our great city have no professional football team at all…

We are made aware of the dire straits of Newcastle United in a letter which was published in one of the major local newspapers of the day, the Newcastle Daily Chronicle. The letter, from a reader who identifies themselves simply as "Play Up United" from Heaton, the old home of Newcastle East End, reads:

> To the Editor.
> Sir.- I am sorry to inform you that a report was circulated in the city during the last week that this club were not going to have a team next season, owing to being in debt. Might I suggest to the energetic secretary of the club, Mr Walter H. Golding, that a meeting be held at St. James's Park next Saturday afternoon at 3p.m., to take into consideration the best means of clearing the debt off, and that a collection be made during the meeting for the benefit of the club. Thanking you very heartily for the above space in your valuable paper. – yours, &c.,

Two days later another letter was printed in the same publication, this from "A Lover of Football", and it read:

> To the Editor.
> Sir.- Permit me, through the medium of your paper, to endorse the practical suggestion of your correspondent in to-day's issue. As a lover of football, I should be glad to see a good football club formed in the city. But why is there not? The officials cry about the debt that is hanging over their heads. But what are they doing to decrease the magnitude of this debt? Nothing at all. The fact is that four committee meetings have been summoned since the meeting in Northumberland Hall, and only two members of the committee, along with the secretary turned up. What about the subscription lists that were got up in aid of the club? With the exception of those of the secretary and one humble member of this committee, no other lists are heard of. How, then, with these facts staring us in the face, can we look for any good and solid work being accomplished to further the grand game of football in Newcastle? Wake up, ye slumberers, and do your duty. Thanking you in anticipation. – yours, &c.,

As can be gleaned from these letters matters concerning finance and the management of the club a cause of grave anxiety to some. The questions begin to become answered in a series of meeting held by the *somewhat shamed* committee. Here is an abstracted 'calendar' of said meetings.

July 13th.
On July 13th, the day of the Annual General Meeting (AGM) of the Newcastle United shareholders the following snippet appeared in various local newspapers.

> FOOTBALL.
> Association.
> Newcastle United.- The annual general meeting of the shareholders in this club will be held at Turnbull's Assembly Rooms, Chillingham Road, Heaton, at eight prompt to-night. We understand the balance sheet, which will be read, will show a loss of about £300 on the season's workings. There is very important business to be transacted, including the election of a new committee, and the appointment of a new secretary in the place of Mr Golding, who has resigned.

It turned out the deficit was worse than the press had speculated. A synopsis of the meeting was provided and read as such:

> NEWCASTLE UNITED FOOTBALL CLUB ANNUAL MEETING
> Last Night, at Mr W Turnbull's, East End Hotel, Heaton, Newcastle, the annual general meeting of the above club was held, Mr Alex Turnbull presiding over a fairly large attendance. The secretary read the annual report of the committee, which stated that with regard to the playing of the team he could not congratulate the members upon consistent play during the season. He hoped that next season the committee would see that their players went through a proper course of training. The result of the season's play has been as follows :- Matches played 46, won 28, drawn 5, lost 13: goals scored, for 139, against 77. The club had signed on Ramsay (late of Stockton), J Miller, J McKain, W Graham and H Jeffrey. For the position of outside-left the committee had settled W J Burke, of Notts County, and formerly of 3rd Lanark. There were several good men open for the remaining positions.
>
> With respect to the financial aspect, he regretted to state that the result of the season's working had been a loss of £384 8s 9d, the deficit being due to the heavy guarantees given to the visiting teams, bad weather, and poor support they had received through bad trade. The total receipts had been £2,185 19s 5d and expenditure £2,570 8s 2d. As he (Mr Golding) had served as secretary for three years, and owing to increased business engagements, he had to tender his resignation. He thanked the members for the way in which he had been treated by them and could only express his regret that his efforts had not been more successful. - The report was adopted.
>
> The election of officers resulted as under:- Committee, Messrs Alec Turnbull, J Neylon, J Black, J Bell, D Macpherson: auditors, Messrs Nevin and Dalrymple. The Chairman said he was sorry that they could not persuade Mr Golding to continue in office. Mr Golding had worked in excellent style for the club, and he was sorry that the club was not in such a position that they could give their late secretary some tangible recognition of the invaluable services which he had rendered to the club. He proposed that they pass a hearty vote of thanks to Mr Golding, and this was carried enthusiastically.- Mr Golding returned thanks, and said that he was sorry that he was unable to continue in office. He hoped that they would be able to tide over their difficulties, and have a most successful season.
>
> After some discussion it was decided to hold a meeting on Tuesday, the 25th inst., when the directors wish all those who took lists at the last meeting will give in their accounts of success or otherwise which has attended their labours.

Finally, some words of caution…

Attendance: Where the gate, (*attendance*), is quoted for a game you will have to bear in mind that these can vary enormously dependent upon which reports are read. A perfect example of this is in our very first game against Woolwich Arsenal. The gate for this game is anywhere between 1,200 (*Newcastle Daily Chronicle*) and "fully 10,000" (*Kentish Mercury*).

This can be further confused by some figures being pure "gate" figures, i.e., what the attendance was calculated simply from the money taken at the gates together with, *or sometimes without*, "ticket" sales. In general, there is a consensus but in the cases of the hugely different figures the ones presented here favour the 'local' newspaper reports.

So, going back to our first game against Woolwich Arsenal the figure I present is from the Kentish Mercury, it being the nearest available 'local' paper to Woolwich.

Line-ups: You will also come across variations as to what the team line-ups were. Whilst these are not as common as the differences in attendance figures they still exist. Wherever possible the line-ups listed within are biased towards 'local' newspapers, local that is to the 'home team'. Consensus is also a determining factor, but again bias would be towards the local outlets.

Players names: Much more common is the variations in the spelling of players names. For example, dropped, *or added*, "p" in names such as Thomson/Thompson, "ai" as opposed to "ne" in Cain/Kane, etc. A perfect example of this being provided above where the newspaper article refers to "McKain" as opposed to "McKane". Another noteworthy example to this may be the inclusion and/or omission of a "d" in a name, i.e.. "Roger" instead of "Rodger" and the pluralisation of such Rogers/Rodgers. Both are highlighted in the 1893-94 season team "picture postcard" which is reproduced within the "Players" section. These are minor of course as it should be easy enough for you to distinguish these anomalies in any further research you may wish to undertake.

Familiar Linesmen: You will often see linesmen being quoted as affiliated to one of the clubs, again using our first game as an example the linesmen are "Woolwich: A. Brown and Newcastle: J. Pearce". That is simply because they were attached to those clubs, J. Pearce being a trainer for Newcastle United.

The reason is that prior to 1891 each side would put forward an individual to act as an "umpire" to make decisions when contentious moments arrived in a game. The umpires would discuss the matter between themselves and try to come to an agreement, if they could not agree then the issue was raised to the referee, who was basically at this juncture little more than a timekeeper, and he would have the deciding vote.

In 1891 the Football Association agreed a re-structuring of the Rules of the Game and referees took centre stage when it came to decision making and the umpires were turned into linesmen, their role however was still more akin to that of the umpire as to that of a linesman as we know it today, and they were still selected by the two teams involved in the game.

Unfortunately, in the majority of cases these 'officials' are not even named in newspaper reports so you will not find them within these pages.

Record of Season

Football League Division 2 ~ Season 1893-94

Final Table

			Home					Away					Total						
Pos.	Team	Pld	W	D	L	F	A	W	D	L	F	A	W	D	L	F	A	G.Avg.	Pts
1	Liverpool	28	14	0	0	46	6	8	6	0	31	12	22	6	0	77	18	4.2778	50
2	Small Heath	28	12	0	2	68	19	9	0	5	35	25	21	0	7	103	44	2.3409	42
3	Notts County	28	12	1	1	55	14	6	2	6	15	17	18	3	7	70	31	2.2581	39
4	Newcastle United	28	12	1	1	44	10	3	5	6	22	29	15	6	7	66	39	1.6923	36
5	Grimsby Town	28	11	1	2	47	16	4	1	9	24	42	15	2	11	71	58	1.2241	32
6	Burton Swifts	28	9	1	4	52	26	5	2	7	27	35	14	3	11	79	61	1.2951	31
7	Burslem Port Vale	28	10	2	2	43	20	3	2	9	23	44	13	4	11	66	64	1.0313	30
8	Lincoln City	28	5	4	5	31	22	6	2	6	28	36	11	6	11	59	58	1.0172	28
9	Woolwich Arsenal	28	9	1	4	33	19	3	3	8	19	36	12	4	12	52	55	0.9455	28
10	Walsall Town Swifts	28	8	1	5	36	23	2	2	10	15	38	10	3	15	51	61	0.8361	23
11	Middlesbrough Ironopolis	28	7	4	3	27	20	1	0	13	10	52	8	4	16	37	72	0.5139	20
12	Crewe Alexandra	28	3	7	4	22	22	3	0	11	20	51	6	7	15	42	73	0.5753	19
13	Ardwick	28	6	1	7	32	20	2	1	11	15	51	8	2	18	47	71	0.662	18
14	Rotherham Town	28	5	1	8	28	42	1	2	11	16	49	6	3	19	44	91	0.4835	15
15	Northwich Victoria	28	3	3	8	17	34	0	0	14	13	64	3	3	22	30	98	0.3061	9

The top three teams, Liverpool, Small Heath, and Notts County were to face the bottom three teams in League Division 1 in 'one-off' Test Matches. *The results of these are given at the bottom of the "games" listing.*

Results Matrix

Home / Away	ARD	BPV	BS	CA	GT	LC	LIV	MI	NEW	NV	NC	RT	SH	WTS	WA
Ardwick		8-1	1-4	1-2	4-1	0-1	0-1	6-1	2-3	4-2	0-0	3-2	0-1	3-0	0-1
Burslem Port Vale	4-2		3-1	4-2	6-1	5-3	2-2	4-0	1-1	3-2	1-0	2-3	5-0	1-2	2-1
Burton Swifts	5-0	5-3		6-1	0-3	1-3	1-1	7-0	3-1	6-2	0-2	4-1	0-2	8-5	6-2
Crewe Alexandra	1-1	1-1	1-2		3-3	1-1	0-5	5-0	1-1	3-0	0-2	2-0	3-5	1-1	0-0
Grimsby Town	5-0	4-0	2-1	3-2		2-4	0-1	2-1	0-0	7-0	5-2	7-1	2-1	5-2	3-1
Lincoln City	6-0	2-2	1-1	6-1	1-2		1-1	2-3	2-1	4-1	0-2	1-1	2-5	0-2	3-0
Liverpool	3-0	2-1	3-1	2-0	2-0	4-0		6-0	5-1	4-0	2-1	5-1	3-1	3-0	2-0
Ironopolis	2-0	3-1	2-1	2-0	2-6	0-0	0-2		1-1	2-1	0-0	6-1	3-0	1-1	3-6
Newcastle United	2-1	2-1	4-1	2-1	4-1	5-1	0-0	7-2		3-0	3-0	4-0	0-2	2-0	6-0
Northwich Victoria	1-4	1-5	1-1	1-2	0-1	0-3	2-3	2-1	5-3		0-1	1-1	0-7	1-0	2-2
Notts County	5-0	6-1	6-2	9-1	3-0	1-2	1-1	3-0	3-1	6-1		4-2	3-1	2-0	3-2
Rotherham Town	1-3	0-1	2-5	1-4	4-3	2-8	1-4	4-1	2-1	5-4	0-2		2-3	3-2	1-1
Small Heath	10-2	6-0	6-1	6-1	5-2	6-0	3-4	2-1	1-4	8-0	3-0	4-3		4-0	4-1
Walsall Town Swifts	5-2	0-5	3-4	5-1	5-0	5-2	1-1	1-0	1-2	3-0	2-1	3-0	1-3		1-2
Woolwich Arsenal	1-0	4-1	0-2	3-2	3-1	4-0	0-5	1-0	2-2	6-0	1-2	3-0	1-4	4-0	

Home team score listed first.

Division Miscellany

Top Scorer: 23 Frank Mobley [Small Heath]
Most Goals: 13 Burton Swifts 8–5 Walsall Town Swifts (24/02/1894)
Biggest Win Margin: 8 Small Heath 10-2 Ardwick (17/03/1894) *and* Notts County 9-1 Crewe Alexandra (17/02/1894)
Champions, Liverpool, go all season without defeat, winning 22 and drawing 6.

Complete Games Listing: Football League Division 2 ~ Season 1893-94

Date	Home	Score	Away	Venue	Gate
02/09/1893	Burslem Port Vale	4-2	Ardwick	Corbridge Athletic Ground	2,500
02/09/1893	Crewe Alexandra	0-2	Notts County	Alexandra Recreation Ground	2,000
02/09/1893	Grimsby Town	7-0	Northwich Victoria	Abbey Park	3,000
02/09/1893	Lincoln City	1-1	Rotherham Town	John O'Gaunt's	3,000
02/09/1893	Middlesbrough Ironopolis	0-2	Liverpool	Paradise Ground	2,000
02/09/1893	Walsall Town Swifts	1-3	Small Heath	Wood Green Oval	5,000
02/09/1893	**Woolwich Arsenal**	**2-2**	**Newcastle United**	**Manor Field, Plumstead**	**10,000**
04/09/1893	Small Heath	4-3	Rotherham Town	Coventry Road	300
09/09/1893	Ardwick	6-1	Middlesbrough Ironopolis	Hyde Road	4,000
09/09/1893	Liverpool	4-0	Lincoln City	Anfield	5,000
09/09/1893	Northwich Victoria	1-2	Crewe Alexandra	Drill Field	1,500
09/09/1893	Notts County	3-2	Woolwich Arsenal	Castle Ground, Nottingham	6,000
09/09/1893	Rotherham Town	4-3	Grimsby Town	Clifton Grove	3,000
09/09/1893	Small Heath	6-1	Burton Swifts	Coventry Road	2,000
09/09/1893	Walsall Town Swifts	0-5	Burslem Port Vale	Wood Green Oval	3,000
11/09/1893	Ardwick	1-4	Burton Swifts	Hyde Road	1,000
11/09/1893	Northwich Victoria	0-1	Notts County	Drill Field	1,000
11/09/1893	Woolwich Arsenal	4-0	Walsall Town Swifts	Manor Field, Plumstead	3,000
16/09/1893	Ardwick	0-1	Liverpool	Hyde Road	6,000
16/09/1893	Burslem Port Vale	4-2	Crewe Alexandra	Corbridge Athletic Ground	2,000
16/09/1893	Grimsby Town	2-1	Burton Swifts	Abbey Park	5,000
16/09/1893	Lincoln City	4-1	Northwich Victoria	John O'Gaunt's	2,000
16/09/1893	Rotherham Town	0-2	Notts County	Clifton Grove	12,200
16/09/1893	Small Heath	4-0	Walsall Town Swifts	Coventry Road	2,000
18/09/1893	Burslem Port Vale	4-0	Middlesbrough Ironopolis	Corbridge Athletic Ground	3,000
20/09/1893	Burton Swifts	5-0	Ardwick	Peel Croft	3,000
23/09/1893	**Burton Swifts**	**3-1**	**Newcastle United**	**Peel Croft**	**3,000**
23/09/1893	Lincoln City	1-2	Grimsby Town	John O'Gaunt's	6,000
23/09/1893	Liverpool	3-1	Small Heath	Anfield	8,000
23/09/1893	Middlesbrough Ironopolis	2-0	Ardwick	Paradise Ground	800
23/09/1893	Northwich Victoria	1-5	Burslem Port Vale	Drill Field	1,000
23/09/1893	Walsall Town Swifts	5-1	Crewe Alexandra	West Bromwich Road	3,000
25-09-1893	Burslem Port Vale	5-0	Small Heath	Corbridge Athletic Ground	1,000
25-09-1893	Woolwich Arsenal	3-1	Grimsby Town	Manor Field, Plumstead	8,000
26-09-1893	Walsall Town Swifts	3-0	Rotherham Town	West Bromwich Road	2,000
30-09-1893	Ardwick	0-1	Small Heath	Hyde Road	5,000
30-09-1893	Burslem Port Vale	3-2	Northwich Victoria	Corbridge Athletic Ground	2,500
30-09-1893	Burton Swifts	4-1	Rotherham Town	Peel Croft	2,000
30-09-1893	Crewe Alexandra	5-0	Middlesbrough Ironopolis	Alexandra Recreation Ground	3,000
30-09-1893	Grimsby Town	5-2	Walsall Town Swifts	Abbey Park	1,500
30-09-1893	**Newcastle United**	**6-0**	**Woolwich Arsenal**	**St James's Park**	**2,000**

Record of Season

Date	Home	Score	Away	Venue	Gate
30-09-1893	Notts County	1-1	Liverpool	Trent Bridge	6,000
02-10-1893	Burton Swifts	6-2	Northwich Victoria	Peel Croft	2,000
05-10-1893	Notts County	3-0	Grimsby Town	Trent Bridge	4,000
07-10-1893	Ardwick	8-1	Burslem Port Vale	Hyde Road	4,000
07-10-1893	Crewe Alexandra	1-2	Burton Swifts	Alexandra Recreation Ground	4,000
07-10-1893	**Lincoln City**	**2-1**	**Newcastle United**	**John O'Gaunt's**	**2,000**
07-10-1893	Liverpool	6-0	Middlesbrough Ironopolis	Anfield	6,000
07-10-1893	Northwich Victoria	1-0	Walsall Town Swifts	Drill Field	6,000
07-10-1893	Small Heath	5-2	Grimsby Town	Coventry Road	2,000
14-10-1893	**Notts County**	**3-1**	**Newcastle United**	**Trent Bridge**	**5,000**
14-10-1893	Small Heath	3-4	Liverpool	Coventry Road	8,000
21-10-1893	**Ardwick**	**2-3**	**Newcastle United**	**Hyde Road**	**4,000**
21-10-1893	Burslem Port Vale	2-3	Rotherham Town	Corbridge Athletic Ground	1,000
21-10-1893	Burton Swifts	1-1	Liverpool	Peel Croft	3,000
21-10-1893	Crewe Alexandra	1-1	Lincoln City	Alexandra Recreation Ground	4,000
21-10-1893	Grimsby Town	5-2	Notts County	Abbey Park	3,000
21-10-1893	Small Heath	4-1	Woolwich Arsenal	Coventry Road	3,000
21-10-1893	Walsall Town Swifts	1-0	Middlesbrough Ironopolis	West Bromwich Road	2,000
26-10-1893	Notts County	6-1	Burslem Port Vale	Trent Bridge	3,000
28-10-1893	Ardwick	0-0	Notts County	Hyde Road	4,000
28-10-1893	Crewe Alexandra	3-0	Northwich Victoria	Alexandra Recreation Ground	3,000
28-10-1893	Grimsby Town	2-4	Lincoln City	Abbey Park	4,000
28-10-1893	Middlesbrough Ironopolis	2-1	Burton Swifts	Paradise Ground	1,200
28-10-1893	**Newcastle United**	**0-2**	**Small Heath**	**St James's Park**	**3,000**
28-10-1893	Rotherham Town	0-1	Burslem Port Vale	Clifton Grove	2,000
28-10-1893	Woolwich Arsenal	0-5	Liverpool	Manor Field, Plumstead	9,000
04-11-1893	**Liverpool**	**5-1**	**Newcastle United**	**Anfield**	**8,000**
04-11-1893	Notts County	3-0	Middlesbrough Ironopolis	Trent Bridge	5,000
11-11-1893	Lincoln City	2-5	Small Heath	John O'Gaunt's	1,000
11-11-1893	Middlesbrough Ironopolis	2-6	Grimsby Town	Paradise Ground	2,000
11-11-1893	Rotherham Town	2-5	Burton Swifts	Clifton Grove	1,000
11-11-1893	Walsall Town Swifts	1-1	Liverpool	West Bromwich Road	5,000
11-11-1893	Woolwich Arsenal	1-0	Ardwick	Manor Field, Plumstead	4,500
13-11-1893	Woolwich Arsenal	3-0	Rotherham Town	Manor Field, Plumstead	3,000
16-11-1893	Notts County	1-2	Lincoln City	Trent Bridge	2,000
18-11-1893	Ardwick	3-0	Walsall Town Swifts	Hyde Road	2,000
18-11-1893	Burton Swifts	6-2	Woolwich Arsenal	Peel Croft	2,000
18-11-1893	Liverpool	2-1	Notts County	Anfield	8,000
18-11-1893	**Northwich Victoria**	**5-3**	**Newcastle United**	**Drill Field**	**1,000**
23-11-1893	Notts County	6-1	Northwich Victoria	Trent Bridge	1,500
25-11-1893	Burslem Port Vale	1-0	Notts County	Corbridge Athletic Ground	1,009

Newcastle United 1893-94 – Season One

Date	Home	Score	Away	Venue	Gate
25-11-1893	Middlesbrough Ironopolis	3-0	Small Heath	Paradise Ground	200
25-11-1893	**Newcastle United**	**0-0**	**Liverpool**	**St James's Park**	**2,000**
30-11-1893	Notts County	6-2	Burton Swifts	Trent Bridge	2,000
02-12-1893	Crewe Alexandra	1-1	Walsall Town Swifts	Alexandra Recreation Ground	1,500
02-12-1893	Grimsby Town	4-0	Burslem Port Vale	Abbey Park	2,000
02-12-1893	Liverpool	3-0	Ardwick	Anfield	4,000
02-12-1893	Rotherham Town	2-8	Lincoln City	Clifton Grove	1,000
02-12-1893	Small Heath	8-0	Northwich Victoria	Coventry Road	1,500
04-12-1893	Burslem Port Vale	6-1	Grimsby Town	Corbridge Athletic Ground	500
06-12-1893	Small Heath	6-1	Crewe Alexandra	Coventry Road	500
09-12-1893	Ardwick	4-1	Grimsby Town	Hyde Road	3,000
09-12-1893	Burton Swifts	0-2	Small Heath	Peel Croft	1,500
09-12-1893	Crewe Alexandra	1-1	Burslem Port Vale	Alexandra Recreation Ground	4,000
09-12-1893	Liverpool	3-0	Walsall Town Swifts	Anfield	3,000
09-12-1893	Middlesbrough Ironopolis	6-1	Rotherham Town	Paradise Ground	600
09-12-1893	**Newcastle United**	**3-0**	**Notts County**	**St James's Park**	**3,000**
09-12-1893	Northwich Victoria	2-2	Woolwich Arsenal	Drill Field	2,000
16-12-1893	Burslem Port Vale	3-1	Burton Swifts	Corbridge Athletic Ground	4,000
16-12-1893	Middlesbrough Ironopolis	0-0	Notts County	Paradise Ground	2,000
16-12-1893	**Small Heath**	**1-4**	**Newcastle United**	**Coventry Road**	**3,000**
23-12-1893	Lincoln City	1-1	Burton Swifts	John O'Gaunt's	5,000
23-12-1893	Small Heath	2-1	Middlesbrough Ironopolis	Coventry Road	2,000
23-12-1893	Walsall Town Swifts	3-0	Northwich Victoria	West Bromwich Road	2,000
25-12-1893	Lincoln City	6-1	Crewe Alexandra	John O'Gaunt's	4,000
25-12-1893	**Middlesbrough Ironopolis**	**1-1**	**Newcastle United**	**Paradise Ground**	**2,000**
25-12-1893	Woolwich Arsenal	4-1	Burslem Port Vale	Manor Field, Plumstead	10,000
26-12-1893	Ardwick	3-2	Rotherham Town	Hyde Road	4,000
26-12-1893	Grimsby Town	3-1	Woolwich Arsenal	Abbey Park	3,000
26-12-1893	Lincoln City	2-3	Middlesbrough Ironopolis	John O'Gaunt's	3,500
26-12-1893	**Walsall Town Swifts**	**1-2**	**Newcastle United**	**West Bromwich Road**	**3,000**
27-12-1893	**Crewe Alexandra**	**1-1**	**Newcastle United**	**Alexandra Recreation Ground**	**2,000**
28-12-1893	Crewe Alexandra	0-5	Liverpool	Alexandra Recreation Ground	4,000
30-12-1893	Ardwick	0-1	Woolwich Arsenal	Hyde Road	4,000
30-12-1893	Burton Swifts	0-2	Notts County	Peel Croft	2,000
30-12-1893	Liverpool	2-0	Grimsby Town	Anfield	3,000
30-12-1893	Middlesbrough Ironopolis	1-1	Walsall Town Swifts	Paradise Ground	1,500
30-12-1893	**Newcastle United**	**2-1**	**Burslem Port Vale**	**St James's Park**	**3,000**
30-12-1893	Rotherham Town	5-4	Northwich Victoria	Clifton Grove	500
30-12-1893	Small Heath	6-0	Lincoln City	Coventry Road	1,000
01-01-1894	Liverpool	2-0	Woolwich Arsenal	Anfield	5,000
01-01-1894	Middlesbrough Ironopolis	3-1	Burslem Port Vale	Paradise Ground	4,000

Record of Season

Date	Home	Score	Away	Venue	Gate
01-01-1894	**Newcastle United**	**5-1**	**Lincoln City**	**St James's Park**	**4,000**
02-01-1894	**Newcastle United**	**7-2**	**Middlesbrough Ironopolis**	**St James's Park**	**3,000**
06-01-1894	Burslem Port Vale	2-1	Woolwich Arsenal	Corbridge Athletic Ground	900
06-01-1894	Middlesbrough Ironopolis	2-0	Crewe Alexandra	Paradise Ground	1,000
06-01-1894	**Newcastle United**	**2-1**	**Ardwick**	**St James's Park**	**1,200**
06-01-1894	Northwich Victoria	0-7	Small Heath	Drill Field	500
06-01-1894	Rotherham Town	1-4	Liverpool	Clifton Grove	500
06-01-1894	Walsall Town Swifts	3-4	Burton Swifts	West Bromwich Road	2,000
11-01-1894	Notts County	4-2	Rotherham Town	Trent Bridge	1,500
13-01-1894	Burton Swifts	5-3	Burslem Port Vale	Peel Croft	2,000
13-01-1894	Crewe Alexandra	3-5	Small Heath	Alexandra Recreation Ground	1,000
13-01-1894	Grimsby Town	5-0	Ardwick	Abbey Park	1,000
13-01-1894	Liverpool	5-1	Rotherham Town	Anfield	4,000
13-01-1894	Middlesbrough Ironopolis	0-0	Lincoln City	Paradise Ground	1,500
13-01-1894	**Newcastle United**	**3-0**	**Northwich Victoria**	**St James's Park**	**2,000**
20-01-1894	Crewe Alexandra	3-3	Grimsby Town	Alexandra Recreation Ground	2,000
20-01-1894	Northwich Victoria	0-3	Lincoln City	Drill Field	1,000
20-01-1894	Notts County	2-0	Walsall Town Swifts	Trent Bridge	2,000
20-01-1894	**Rotherham Town**	**2-1**	**Newcastle United**	**Clifton Grove**	**1,000**
27-01-1894	Ardwick	4-2	Northwich Victoria	Hyde Road	3,000
27-01-1894	Crewe Alexandra	2-0	Rotherham Town	Alexandra Recreation Ground	1,000
27-01-1894	Liverpool	3-0	Grimsby Town	Anfield	8,000
27-01-1894	Middlesbrough Ironopolis	2-1	Luton Town	Paradise Ground	1,400
27-01-1894	Notts County	1-0	Burnley	Trent Bridge	8,000
27-01-1894	Small Heath	3-4	Bolton Wanderers	Coventry Road	6,000
27-01-1894	Woolwich Arsenal	1-2	The Wednesday	Manor Field, Plumstead	15,000
03-02-1894	**Burslem Port Vale**	**1-1**	**Newcastle United**	**Corbridge Athletic Ground**	**2,000**
03-021894-	Grimsby Town	2-1	Middlesbrough Ironopolis	Abbey Park	2,000
03-021894-	Lincoln City	3-0	Woolwich Arsenal	John O'Gaunt's	2,000
03-021894-	Liverpool	4-0	Northwich Victoria	Anfield	3,000
03-021894-	Notts County	3-1	Small Heath	Trent Bridge	6,000
03-021894-	Rotherham Town	3-2	Walsall Town Swifts	Clifton Grove	1,000
06-021894-	Rotherham Town	1-1	Woolwich Arsenal	Clifton Grove	2,000
10-02-1894	Burslem Port Vale	1-2	Walsall Town Swifts	Corbridge Athletic Ground	1,500
10-02-1894	Burton Swifts	1-3	Lincoln City	Peel Croft	2,000
10-02-1894	Burton Wanderers	1-2	Notts County	Derby Turn	6,000
10-02-1894	Grimsby Town	7-1	Rotherham Town	Abbey Park	1,500
10-02-1894	Liverpool	3-2	Preston North End	Anfield	18,000
10-02-1894	Middlesbrough Ironopolis	0-2	Nottingham Forest	Paradise Ground	7,000
10-02-1894	Northwich Victoria	1-4	Ardwick	Drill Field	2,000
10-02-1894	Woolwich Arsenal	3-2	Crewe Alexandra	Manor Field, Plumstead	4,000
12-02-1894	Walsall Town Swifts	1-2	Woolwich Arsenal	West Bromwich Road	3,000

Newcastle United 1893-94 – Season One

Date	Home	Score	Away	Venue	Gate
17-02-1894	**Newcastle United**	**4-0**	**Rotherham Town**	**St James's Park**	**6,000**
17-02-1894	Northwich Victoria	0-1	Grimsby Town	Drill Field	1,000
17-02-1894	Notts County	9-1	Crewe Alexandra	Trent Bridge	200
17-02-1894	Woolwich Arsenal	4-0	Lincoln City	Manor Field, Plumstead	3,000
24-02-1894	Bolton Wanderers	3-0	Liverpool	Pikes Lane	20,000
24-02-1894	Burton Swifts	8-5	Walsall Town Swifts	Peel Croft	1,200
24-02-1894	Crewe Alexandra	1-1	Ardwick	Alexandra Recreation Ground	1,000
24-02-1894	Lincoln City	2-2	Burslem Port Vale	John O'Gaunt's	2,000
24-02-1894	Middlesbrough Ironopolis	3-6	Woolwich Arsenal	Paradise Ground	500
24-02-1894	**Newcastle United**	**4-1**	**Grimsby Town**	**St James's Park**	**4,000**
24-02-1894	Nottingham Forest	1-1	Notts County	Town Ground	15,000
03-03-1894	Crewe Alexandra	0-0	Woolwich Arsenal	Alexandra Recreation Ground	2,000
03-03-1894	Grimsby Town	2-1	Small Heath	Abbey Park	3,000
03-03-1894	Liverpool	3-1	Burton Swifts	Anfield	8,000
03-03-1894	Middlesbrough Ironopolis	2-1	Northwich Victoria	Paradise Ground	500
03-03-1894	Notts County	4-1	Nottingham Forest	Trent Bridge	12,000
10-03-1894	Burslem Port Vale	5-3	Lincoln City	Corbridge Athletic Ground	2,000
10-03-1894	Grimsby Town	3-2	Crewe Alexandra	Abbey Park	1,500
10-03-1894	**Newcastle United**	**2-0**	**Walsall Town Swifts**	**St James's Park**	**1,000**
10-03-1894	Northwich Victoria	1-1	Burton Swifts	Drill Field	1,000
10-03-1894	Notts County	1-0	Blackburn Rovers	Bramall Lane	20,000
10-03-1894	Woolwich Arsenal	1-0	Middlesbrough Ironopolis	Manor Field, Plumstead	5,000
12-03-1894	Walsall Town Swifts	2-1	Notts County	West Bromwich Road	2,000
15-03-1894	Notts County	5-0	Ardwick	Trent Bridge	2,500
17-03-1894	Burton Swifts	7-0	Middlesbrough Ironopolis	Peel Croft	2,000
17-03-1894	Lincoln City	1-1	Liverpool	John O'Gaunt's	4,000
17-03-1894	Small Heath	10-2	Ardwick	Coventry Road	2,000
23-03-1894	Lincoln City	0-2	Notts County	John O'Gaunt's	6,000
23-03-1894	**Newcastle United**	**2-1**	**Crewe Alexandra**	**St James's Park**	**10,000**
23-03-1894	Rotherham Town	2-3	Small Heath	Clifton Grove	1,000
23-03-1894	Woolwich Arsenal	6-0	Northwich Victoria	Manor Field, Plumstead	5,000
24-03-1894	Lincoln City	6-0	Ardwick	John O'Gaunt's	1,000
24-03-1894	Liverpool	2-0	Crewe Alexandra	Anfield	3,000
24-03-1894	**Newcastle United**	**4-1**	**Burton Swifts**	**St James's Park**	**3,000**
24-03-1894	Small Heath	6-0	Burslem Port Vale	Coventry Road	4,000
24-03-1894	Walsall Town Swifts	5-0	Grimsby Town	West Bromwich Road	1,500
24-03-1894	Woolwich Arsenal	1-2	Notts County	Manor Field, Plumstead	13,000
26-03-1894	Rotherham Town	1-3	Ardwick	Clifton Grove	2,000
26-03-1894	Walsall Town Swifts	5-2	Lincoln City	West Bromwich Road	2,000
28-03-1894	Northwich Victoria	2-3	Liverpool	Drill Field	3,000
31-03-1894	Ardwick	0-1	Lincoln City	Hyde Road	3,000
31-03-1894	Burton Swifts	6-1	Crewe Alexandra	Peel Croft	3,000

Date	Home	Score	Away	Venue	Gate
31-03-1894	Grimsby Town	0-1	Liverpool	Abbey Park	4,000
31-03-1894	Northwich Victoria	1-1	Rotherham Town	Drill Field	1,000
31-03-1894	Notts County	4-1	Bolton Wanderers	Goodison Park	37,000
31-03-1894	Woolwich Arsenal	1-4	Small Heath	Manor Field, Plumstead	6,000
07-04-1894	Ardwick	1-2	Crewe Alexandra	Hyde Road	2,500
07-04-1894	Burslem Port Vale	2-2	Liverpool	Corbridge Athletic Ground	5,009
07-04-1894	Burton Swifts	0-3	Grimsby Town	Peel Croft	2,000
07-04-1894	Lincoln City	0-2	Walsall Town Swifts	John O'Gaunt's	1,500
07-04-1894	Northwich Victoria	2-1	Middlesbrough Ironopolis	Drill Field	1,000
07-04-1894	Small Heath	3-0	Notts County	Coventry Road	6,000
09-04-1894	Rotherham Town	1-4	Crewe Alexandra	Clifton Grove	4,500
14-04-1894	**Grimsby Town**	**0-0**	**Newcastle United**	**Abbey Park**	**2,000**
14-04-1894	Liverpool	2-1	Burslem Port Vale	Anfield	5,000
14-04-1894	Rotherham Town	4-1	Middlesbrough Ironopolis	Clifton Grove	1,000
14-04-1894	Walsall Town Swifts	5-2	Ardwick	West Bromwich Road	1,700
14-04-1894	Woolwich Arsenal	0-2	Burton Swifts	Manor Field, Plumstead	2,000

Football Association Test Matches: Season 1893-94

As indicated above the top three teams from Division 2, these being Liverpool, Small Heath, and Notts County, would meet the bottom three teams from Division 1, they in turn being Preston North End, Darwen and Newton Heath, in 'one-off' test matches. *These being the precursor one could say to the 'play offs we have today.*

The draw was such that the Division 2 champions, Liverpool, were to play the Division 1 *'wooden spooners'*, Newton Heath. Small Heath, as Division 2 runners-up, played the Division 1 second bottom side, Darwen, and third top, Notts County were to play third bottom side Preston North End. All three games were to be played at neutral venues, the results being:

Test Matches					
1894-04-28	Darwen	1-3	Small Heath	Victoria Ground, Stoke	3,000
1894-04-28	Liverpool	2-0	Newton Heath	Ewood Park, Blackburn	5,000
1894-04-28	Notts County	0-4	Preston North End	Olive Grove, Sheffield	8,000
*Liverpool elected to League Division 1					
*Small Heath elected to League Division 1					
Preston North End retain their League Division 1 status					
Darwen Relegated from League Division 1					
Newton Heath Relegated from League Division 1					
Notts County retain their League Division 2 status					

*Even though they had won their test matches promotion for Liverpool and Small Heath was still by means of election, it was not an automatic process. It may have been a forgone conclusion, but it was still not automatic.

Football Association Challenge Cup (FA Cup) : Season 1893-94

FA Cup: First Round					
Date	Home	Score	Away	Venue	Gate
27/01/1893	Aston Villa	4-2	Wolverhampton Wanderers	Perry Barr	22,981
27/01/1893	Derby County	2-0	Darwen	County Ground	7,500
27/01/1893	Leicester Fosse	2-1	South Shore	Filbert Street	6,000
27/01/1893	Liverpool	3-0	Grimsby Town	Anfield	8,000
27/01/1893	Middlesbrough Ironopolis	2-1	Luton Town	Paradise Ground	1,400
27/01/1893	**Newcastle United**	**2-0**	**Sheffield United**	**St James's Park**	**8,000**
27/01/1893	Newton Heath	4-0	Middlesbrough	Bank Street	5,000
27/01/1893	Nottingham Forest	1-0	Heanor Town (AET)	Town Ground	3,000
27/01/1893	Notts County	1-0	Burnley	Trent Bridge	8,000
27/01/1893	Preston North End	18-0	Reading	Deepdale	2,000
27/01/1893	Small Heath	3-4	Bolton Wanderers	Coventry Road	6,000
27/01/1893	Stockport County	0-1	Burton Wanderers	Green Lane	4,500
27/01/1893	Stoke	1-0	Everton	Victoria Road	14,000
27/01/1893	Sunderland	3-0	Accrington	Newcastle Road	4,000
27/01/1893	West Bromwich Albion	2-3	Blackburn Rovers	Storey Lane	10,243
27/01/1893	Woolwich Arsenal	1-2	The Wednesday	Manor Ground	15,000
FA Cup Second Round					
Date	Home	Score	Away	Venue	Gate
10/02/1894	Burton Wanderers	1-2	Notts County	Derby Turn	6,000
10/02/1894	Leicester Fosse	0-0	Derby County (AET)	Filbert Street	12,000
10/02/1894	Liverpool	3-2	Preston North End	Anfield	18,000
10/02/1894	**Newcastle United**	**1-2**	**Bolton Wanderers**	**St James's Park**	**10,000**
10/02/1894	Newton Heath	0-0	Blackburn Rovers (AET)	Bank Street	18,000
10/02/1894	Nottingham Forest	2-0	Middlesbrough Ironopolis	Town Ground	7,000
10/02/1894	Sunderland	2-2	Aston Villa (AET)	Newcastle Road	15,956
10/02/1894	The Wednesday	1-0	Stoke	Olive Grove	17,000
Second Round Replays					
17/02/1894	Blackburn Rovers	5-1	Newton Heath	Ewood Park	5,000
17/02/1894	Derby County	3-0	Leicester Fosse	County Ground	4,000
21/02/1894	Aston Villa	3-1	Sunderland	Perry Barr	25,000
FA Cup Third Round					
Date	Home	Score	Away	Venue	Gate
24/02/1894	Bolton Wanderers	3-0	Liverpool	Pike's Lane	20,000
24/02/1894	Derby County	1-4	Blackburn Rovers	County Ground	14,000
24/02/1894	Nottingham Forest	1-1	Notts County (AET)	Town Ground	15,000
24/02/1894	The Wednesday	3-2	Aston Villa (AET)	Olive Grove	2,000
Third Round Replay					
03/03/1894	Notts County	4-1	Nottingham Forest	Trent Bridge	12,000
FA Cup Semi-Final					
Date	Home	Score	Away	Venue	Gate
10/03/1894	Bolton Wanderers	2-1	The Wednesday	Fallowfield	30,000
10/03/1894	Notts County	1-0	Blackburn Rovers	Bramall Lane	20,000
FA CUP Final					
Date		Score		Venue	Gate
31/03/1894	Notts County	4-1	Bolton Wanderers	Goodison Park	37,000

Match Reports

Game: 1 ~ Saturday, September 2nd, 1893 — vs. Woolwich Arsenal

Competition: Division 2 **Venue:** Manor Field, Plumstead **Gate:** 10,000

Woolwich Arsenal 2-2 Newcastle United

Goal, Charles Williams; *backs*, Joseph Powell, John Alfred Storrs; *half-backs*, George Devine, Robert Buist, David Howat; *forwards*, Walter Shaw, Duncan Gemmell, Joseph Heath, Arthur Elliot, Charles Booth.

Scorer(s): Walter Shaw, Arthur Elliott

Referee: Mr. J. C Tillotson (Birmingham)

Goal, George Ramsay; *backs*, Harry Jeffrey, James Miller; *half-backs*, Bobby Creilly, Willie Graham, Joe McKane; *forwards*, John Bowman, Tom Crate, Willie Thompson, Jock Sorley, Joe Wallace.

Scorer(s): Tom Crate, Jock Sorley

Kick-off: 3:30 PM

First League Game in London Ends in a Draw

This was a historical game indeed, for not only did it represent Newcastle United's first-ever Football League match it also represented the first-ever Football League fixture to be played in London. Therefore, by definition, those assembled witnessed the first-ever goal to be scored in the capital too. Unfortunately, that goal did not belong to a Newcastle United player as they had to survive a real early fright, going one down in the early minutes of the first half, and falling further behind early in the second half. However, they got themselves back into the game and came away in the end with a very creditable draw.

Just like Newcastle, the Arsenal had gone through a bit of a transition during the close-season. Last season they were Royal Arsenal, this season they are now Woolwich Arsenal, last season they played at the Invicta Recreation Grounds, this season they have taken up a new home at the Manor Field in Plumstead.

Newcastle gave debuts to new men, George Ramsay the custodian, and John Bowman at outside-right. Whilst it was indeed a debut for Ramsay, he was an ex-Newcastle East End player, though he had not featured in the first-team prior to this. Bowman was a new arrival from Scotland.

Key Events	
First Half	
1 – 0	*Walter Shaw*
Second Half	
2 – 0	*Arthur Elliott*
2 – 1	**Tom Crate**
2 – 2	**Jock Sorley**

Powell, the elected captain for Arsenal, called the toss correct and opted to start the game with the light wind, and sunshine, behind them, thus giving the kick-off to Newcastle. So, the very first kick, in the very first Football League game in the Capital, went to Newcastle United and their captain, Willie Thompson.

Newcastle pressed early and they were rewarded with a corner from the efforts of Crate and Bowman. The corner was fisted away by Williams. This clearance that was followed by a fine passing run from Booth and Elliott which ultimately led to a corner for Arsenal which was unproductive as Crate and Bowman combined to relieve the pressure. Play was then said to be neutral with both teams giving as good as they got in a start that showed both teams lacked match practice.

However, that was to change in the sixth minute when Arsenal went ahead. Elliott broke away, passing to Booth who in turn played the ball to Shaw who was equal to the occasion, and with a good shot sent the ball into the net, amidst tremendous cheering, this with Ramsay failing to reach it. Subsequently Arsenal had a well-placed free-kick from Powell but it ultimately came to nothing.

Newcastle fought back and for a period it was said that they were making matters warm for Arsenal. They won two corners, but unfortunately nothing came from either. After another period of play of an even character Newcastle pressed and Sorley, after combining with Wallace, forced a save out of Williams. There then came an excellent chance for Arsenal to double their advantage when a foul by Newcastle enabled Henderson, Gemmell and Shaw to be in advanced positions and Henderson having extremely bad luck when his shot hit the left upright and went behind for a goal-kick. This rallied the Arsenal, and they had a sustained period of pressure, keeping the ball in the United half. This was ended when Wallace and Sorley transferred play to the other end. Back came Arsenal, and Henderson had hard lines with a header that went wide following a long clearance from Powell and passing between Elliott and Booth.

Approaching the latter stages of the half Newcastle pressed and had a header just over the bar and a couple of corners. Ultimately though the half ended with unfortunately them trailing by the goal from Shaw.

Shaw kicked off the second half for the Arsenal and they immediately went on the attack. Gemmell forced a save out of Ramsay. There was no respite for Newcastle either as this was soon followed by a fine solo run from Booth who single-handedly beat his opponents and passed to Elliott who delivered a stinging shot which completely nonplussed Ramsay and the Arsenal were two goals to the good.

There followed a period of even play until Newcastle forced their way forward through Wallace and Sorley only for Thompson to fall foul of an off-side. Undeterred Newcastle kept pressing but Arsenal were equal to anything they had to offer. Thompson won a corner for Newcastle when dispossessed by Powell the ball went behind. Williams made a save from the corner but a couple of minutes later a fast shot from Crate had him beaten and Newcastle were edging their way back into the match.

With Newcastle now playing prettily together they won a free-kick in front of Arsenal's goal. From this Sorley brought Newcastle level with a fine header. The last ten minutes of the game was said to be very exciting, with both teams trying their utmost to add to the score, but nothing further was added by either. So, the first of many trips to London for Newcastle United, and the first Football League game ever to be played in the capital, ended all square, a decent game, and fair result.

Pos.	Team	Plyd	W	D	L	F	A	G.Avg.	Pts.
1	Grimsby Town	1	1	0	0	7	0	7.0000	2
2	Small Heath	1	1	0	0	3	1	3.0000	2
3	Burslem Port Vale	1	1	0	0	4	2	2.0000	2
4	Liverpool	1	1	0	0	2	0	2.0000	2
5	Notts County	1	1	0	0	2	0	2.0000	2
6	Newcastle United	1	0	1	0	2	2	1.0000	1
7	Woolwich Arsenal	1	0	1	0	2	2	1.0000	1
8	Lincoln City	1	0	1	0	1	1	1.0000	1
9	Rotherham Town	1	0	1	0	1	1	1.0000	1
10	Ardwick	1	0	0	1	2	4	0.5000	0
11	Walsall Town Swifts	1	0	0	1	1	3	0.3333	0
12	Burton Swifts	0	0	0	0	0	0	0.0000	0
13	Crewe Alexandra	1	0	0	1	0	2	-2.0000	0
14	Middlesbrough Ironopolis	1	0	0	1	0	2	-2.0000	0
15	Northwich Victoria	1	0	0	1	0	7	-7.0000	0

Game: 2 ~ Monday, September 4th, 1893 — vs. Trafalgar

Competition: Friendly **Venue:** Heaton Junction, Newcastle **Gate:** *fairly large*

Trafalgar 0-2 Newcastle United

Goal, William Lowery; *backs*, Donnell, Frazer
half-backs, McCrory, Walton, Frazer
forwards, J. Patten, Neale, Smoulte, R. Patten, Atkinson.

Goal, George Ramsay; *backs*, Harry Jeffrey, James Miller
half-backs, Joe McKane, Willie Graham, John Barr
forwards, John Bowman, Tom Crate, Willie Thompson, Jock Sorley, Patterson.

Scorer(s): Patterson, Willie Thompson

Referee: Mr. G. Armstrong

Welcome Home

After their travels to the capital on Saturday it was a welcome return home for Newcastle United as they returned not only to their city, but also their old stomping ground.

This evening they faced Trafalgar, a well-respected local amateur side who had taken up residence at Heaton Junction which as we well remember was the former ground of Newcastle when they were still East End.

This was the first of a series of friendly fixtures the Newcastle United committee had arranged given that they did not have another league game until toward the month's end and that would be another away fixture against Burton Swifts. The heavy expenses incurred with the travelling to London, and those that would be incurred for the trip to the West Midlands for the Burton fixture, was a major concern to the Newcastle United committee, as was the players' wages, so the need for revenue generation was vital. The perilous financial position of the club now being well documented in the press.

As it turned out there was much interest evinced in this game, testified to by a fairly large gathering of spectators. Indeed, given that there was also a match being played at St James's Park this evening, a Northern Alliance fixture between Newcastle 'A' and Gateshead NER, the size of the crowd was pleasantly surprising.

Key Events	
First Half	
0 – 1	**Patterson**
0 – 2	**Willie Thompson**

Mr Wm. Turnbull, of the East End Hotel, set the ball in motion on behalf of Trafalgar.

With Newcastle taking possession of the ball from the kick-off Miller immediately returned it up the field where the Trafalgar flank of J. Patten and Neale combined well to work the ball back down the field again and into Newcastle territory. There was no doubt that the amateurs of Trafalgar were making an early statement as to their intent, anyone who thought that the professionals of Newcastle were going to have an easy game of this had that illusion shattered straight away.

Trafalgar applied some pressure on the Newcastle goal, but it was ultimately to no avail. Gaining possession once more Newcastle then ran the leather up the field and Lowery was forced into making an excellent save from an effort by Thompson.

This was followed by a period of some advantage to Trafalgar but again they could not make this situation count for anything substantial and the ball was soon back in their quarters.

Pressure was put on the Trafalgar goal, which Lowery defended well, and the ball was sent behind. Once more Lowery had to make a smart save and presently the ball was worked into midfield by Trafalgar to relieve the pressure. They were then given an excellent opportunity to mount an attack when 'hands' was awarded against Newcastle. Their attack was repulsed and a surge up field by Newcastle ended with Sorley sending a long shot behind. The goal kick was returned well by Miller, affording Thompson an opportunity which he unfortunately missed. Newcastle were then awarded a free-kick for a foul and Jeffrey placed it nicely but Donnell headed it away.

Another free-kick soon followed for Newcastle, this time for hands against R Patten, and Miller took this one, placing it excellently into space in the Trafalgar goal area but they managed to rush it out launching a counter-attack. This was however frustrated by the Newcastle left-back. Another Trafalgar attack was halted by him and then a third by Jeffrey. Newcastle then forced a corner which was judiciously placed by Sorley and some smart work, from both sides, ensued and entertained the gathered spectators.

A rush up from Newcastle saw Bowman send in nicely and he was unlucky to see his effort pass just outside the upright. Keeping up the pressure Newcastle returned to the attack and following some splendid play Bowman sent in a cross which was swooped upon by Patterson and with a swift shot the scoring was opened.

United rushed once more but Lowery, demonstrating great form, once again made a clever save. Trafalgar then had a little look in of their own but were met with a solid defence against which they could make no headway. In that though Ramsay did have one save to make, from a shot by J Patten. Then just before the interval was to be called a nice run up the wing was made by the Newcastle forwards resulting in Thompson scoring a second goal.

On the restart dusk was well and truly set in. Indeed, it was difficult to follow the ball unless it rose above the rooftops of the adjacent houses. Despite this Newcastle made a swift attack and Sorley missed with an effort. The subsequent goal kick relieving the pressure on Lowery and his defence.

Never giving up the Trafalgar left wing were much in evidence for a spell, but their endeavours were to no avail, Barr being evident against them. Newcastle then had a charge and Thompson made a very good attempt which only went narrowly over the bar.

A clearance from Trafalgar was returned by Sorley with a swift cross-shot and following a scrimmage a corner was won. The corner was well placed, and another scrimmage ensued resulting in another corner. Lowery made a marvellous save from this corner but at the expense of a third which proved fruitless.

Trafalgar, through some smart and hard work, managed to get the leather up the field but from their endeavours there were to make no tangible advantage. Newcastle gained ascendancy once more and Graham played a great ball to Sorley who headed it in but Lowery threw out to his left wing. Miller quickly dispossessed them to prevent any danger and sent the ball into midfield.

Darkness had now fully set in and it was with the utmost difficulty that the game could be followed. In these conditions, and having a two-goal advantage, Newcastle were quite content to allow Trafalgar the best of possession and concentrated upon keeping them out which they did without too much effort.

Supplementary notes...
Unbeknownst at the time of course but Lowery, who performed excellently for Trafalgar today, was very soon to be a Newcastle United player!

Game: 3 ~ Wednesday, September 6th, 1893 — vs. Sunderland

Competition: Friendly **Venue:** St James's Park **Gate:** 3,000

Newcastle United 1 - 3 Sunderland

Goal, George Ramsay; *backs*, Harry Jeffrey, James Miller; *half-backs*, John Barr, Willie Graham, Joe McKane; *forwards*, John Bowman, Bobby Creilly, Willie Thompson, Tom Crate, Joe Wallace.

Scorer(s): Willie Thompson

Referee: Mr. William Tiffin (Northumberland FA)

Goal, Matthew Scott; *backs*, Tom Porteous, Peter Meehan; *half-backs*, Billy Dunlop, John Auld, James Dalton; *forwards*, James Gillespie, John Harvey, Jimmy Millar, Davy Hannah, John Scott.

Scorer(s): James Gillespie, John Harvey, Davy Hannah

Kick-off: 6:00 PM

No disgrace in being beaten by the League Champions, even if it is Sunderland!

The prevailing weather, described as being *"the most miserable"*, did not deter what was large gathering for a weekday match, fully 3,000 at the smallest of estimates. The probable reason for this was Newcastle were hosting the Football League Champions at St James's Park – and they were none other than our *"nearest and dearest"* [sic] neighbours, Sunderland! Also, it was the opening of the ground for the new season, Newcastle's first as a Football Association League team, albeit they being in the second division of said league. However, none of that matters, nor does the fact that this was only a 'friendly' fixture – this was Newcastle United, this was Sunderland, this was the "Tyne-Wear Derby", even before it become known to anyone as such!

KEY EVENTS

First Half
0 – 1	James Gillespie
0 – 2	John Harvey
0 – 3	Davy Hannah

Second Half
1 – 3	**Willie Thompson**

Sunderland. won the toss and elected to play *'down the hill'* for the first half. Thompson therefore got the ball rolling for Newcastle and a corner was soon forced. From the delivery Wallace had a decent opportunity but his effort missed the target.

A good run was then made by Sunderland down their right-wing, but it was abruptly ended by a fine intervention from McKane, and he robbed them of possession. An attack was launched upon the visitor's goal but with an intervention as equally splendid as McKane's had been, Meehan for Sunderland saved magnificently. Then back at the Newcastle end Harvey sent in an effort from which he was very unlucky not to score. However, from the goal kick the ball was sent back high into the Newcastle goalmouth and Gillespie was there to head the ball home and the Wearsiders were in the lead.

Another attack was frustrated by Jeffrey, then Miller, rushing down field with the ball the ball at his feet, managed to provide Harvey with an opportunity and his effort was true and Sunderland had doubled their lead!

Newcastle tried to rally, and Scott was forced into making two saves of the utmost quality. The ball was then taken from end-to-end in quick succession until such time as the Sunderland right wing obtained possession and pressed heavily. Miller crossed the ball for Hannah to run on to and with a fine low shot he beat Ramsay, that was now three to the visitors.

The game then became rather quiet as Sunderland, like the true champions they were, held sway over possession and did not commit too much to the attack. On occasion Miller was a handful for the Sunderland right wing and a good combination attack by the Newcastle forward quintet was broken up by Auld.

On restarting Newcastle gained possession and made a great combined rush down the ground but they lost to Dalton. Play was then transferred straight up to the home goal, but the attack was short and petered out with no effect. A header forward from by Thompson launched the Newcastle vanguard into a great run and they breezed through their opponents, Creilly having the final shot which was well saved by Scott.

Working the ball down the Sunderland left wing Newcastle desperately looked for a way back into this game but ultimately were never really dangerous. Thence Wallace raced down but his shot from distance was easily fisted away by Scott. Long kicking became the 'order of the day' for the home side as they could not effectively work their way through their opponent's stout midfield and defence. From such a long kick a rushing shot from Bowman went over the bar. Graham then showed some of his customary grand form in tackling and Meehan had to send the ball out to break up his advance. The throw-in led to no real advantage for Newcastle unfortunately.

The pitch, which had always been slippery, was now so slippery that the players were having difficulty in keeping their feet. A free-kick for 'hands' let Newcastle in once again but the kick by Miller was easily returned. Ramsay was then called into action and he fulfilled his duties with a clever save and the ball was then sent behind.

In a very heavy attack by the Newcastle forwards the Sunderland custodian was forced to save really well from an excellent effort by Thompson. Newcastle shortly after that gained another free-kick, this time for a foul, and their heavy pressing resumed but it was to no avail.

Just before the game was due to finish Thompson and Creilly made a burst forward and after a brilliant run the home centre-forward scored, amid much enthusiasm from the gathered crowd. It was too little, too late, to affect the result, but never-the-less well received.

Game: 4 ~ Saturday, September 9th, 1893   vs. Middlesbrough

Competition: Friendly   **Venue:** Linthorpe Road   **Gate:** 1,400

Middlesbrough 2-2 Newcastle United

Goal, Kitson; *backs*, Walsh, Theakstone; *half-backs*, Appleton, Morren, Wynn; *forwards*, Collinson, Davidson, Mullen, Walter Frost, Godley.

Scorer(s): Godley, Walter Frost

Goal, George Ramsay; *backs*, Harry Jeffrey, James Miller; *half-backs*, Bobby Creilly, Willie Graham, Joe McKane; *forwards*, Joe Wallace, A Donaldson, Willie Thompson, Tom Crate, John Bowman.

Scorer(s): Tom Crate, Bobby Creilly

Newcastle 'Frost'-bitten in closing stages and victory is snatched away...

Newcastle should have been engaged in a League fixture against Bootle today, however, with the withdrawal of Bootle from the league had left the date vacant with little time to arrange something for today. Most of the principal clubs were already engaged in league or combination fixtures so it was against the amateurs of Middlesbrough that a fixture was arranged. Newcastle had met them no fewer than five times last season, being victorious on three of those, losing the other two. Of painful remembrance was one of those defeats being in the FA Cup [Round 1] when Middlesbrough were victorious by three goals to two at St James's Park. Revenge would have certainly been on the minds of Newcastle this afternoon.

Key Events	
First Half	
1 – 0	Godley
Second Half	
1 – 1	**Tom Crate**
1 – 2	**Bobby Creilly**
2 – 2	Frost

Middlesbrough got the game underway, but it was not long before Newcastle gained possession and began to press. However, Middlesbrough in gaining possession performed some pressing of their own during which they made on particularly desperate attack upon the Newcastle citadel which took all of their guile to resist though at length they did.

End-to-end play ensued for quite some time and at length the left wing of Newcastle was put in a very dangerous position which was only relieved by hands being awarded against Wynn. In taking the free-kick Newcastle were able to work the ball into the Middlesbrough quarters. It was not too long though before a fine kick by Mullen, the Middlesbrough centre-forward, gained them considerable ground and but for the neat intervention of Jeffrey they would have been very near the Newcastle goal.

Wynn then distinguished himself, and the rest of the home forwards, passing nicely down the left wing and getting well into goal but the Newcastle defence stayed solid and eventually repelled the danger. Any respite for said defence was short-lived however as running the ball gently down again Collinson dropped it well in, but it was headed away by Graham. Mullen then put in a very fine shot which Ramsay had to pick up pretty smartly.

A splendid bout of dribbling and kicking then followed in the midfield and once again the homesters came away with the advantage. Davison, spearheading the attack was fouled by Miller and a free-kick was awarded but Middlesbrough could not turn it to their favour. Then the right wing of Middlesbrough got away and Collinson made a very neat shot which crashed against the crossbar and fell out of play. A very lucky escape indeed!

Keeping up the pressure both Frost and Mullen had good chances but were guilty of some wild kicking. Frost later got away and dribbled smartly up but when well in range of the goal he elected to pass the ball into the centre instead of shooting and the danger was gone, albeit temporarily.

A smart and strong shot from Godley saw Ramsay get his hands to it but could not prevent from going in and the homesters were deservedly in the lead.

This seemed to liven up the visitors and for a short time they pressed but once again Middlesbrough took possession and only a mistake from the left wing relieved the pressure as they sent the ball bye. End-to-end play then followed until the whistle signalled the interval.

Immediately upon resumption of play Collinson forced a corner for the homesters but nothing came from it. Middlesbrough kept up the pressure for some time and there were only the occasional visits to their goal by the Newcastle forward quintet, with one or two corners being won and one or two shots being made, all unsuccessful. That was until a fine shot from Crate went clean through the uprights and Newcastle were level, completely against the balance of play. The ball had hardly been set down from Newcastle's equalising goal when they retook possession and neatly dribbled it down the field with Creilly ending the move with a fine shot to score and give Newcastle the lead, a very unexpected lead indeed.

There followed some fine displays of passing and moving from both sides, each goal being visited in turn. On one occasion Wallace had the goal at his mercy but somehow shot bye. Middlesbrough then took a turn and bombarded the Newcastle goal but all to no avail and before they knew it the ball was back in their quarters, but no score resulted. Each end was visited once again and in one particular attack on the home goal a shot by Donaldson was a mere inch or two over the crossbar.

Newcastle then won a free-kick in midfield which was sent well in and turned away for a corner. Bowman sent the corner beautifully in and Thompson was unlucky to see his header go over the bar. From a throw-in Crate made a splendid shot which was blocked, and another corner was won but from it nothing came.

Receiving possession, the homesters ran up the field and following a bit of play near the Newcastle goal Davison put a fine centre in and Frost banged the ball through for a Middlesbrough equaliser. Even play ruled to the finish and an exciting game ended with honours even.

Game: 5 ~ Saturday, September 23rd, 1893 vs. **Burton Swifts**

Competition: Division 2 **Venue:** Peel Croft **Gate:** *Good*

Burton Swifts	**3-1**	**Newcastle United**

Goal, Sam Jones; *backs*, Billy Furniss, Jack Berry; *half-backs*, "Ned" Lawrence, William West, Walter Perry; *forwards*, William Mason, Joseph Dewey, Alec Boggie, Jimmy Munro, George Ekins.

Scorer(s): Joseph Dewey, Jimmy Munro, Alec Boggie

Goal, Joe Ryder; *backs*, Harry Jeffrey, James Miller; *half-backs*, John Barr, Willie Graham, Joe McKane; *forwards*, Bobby Creilly, Tom Crate, Willie Thompson, Charlie Quinn, Joe Wallace.

Scorer(s): Tom Crate

Miserable Away-Day for Newcastle

After a disappointing start to the season, losing two of their opening three games, Burton were coming into this game on a bit of a high. They had entertained Ardwick in mid-week and soundly beat them by five goals to nil. Whilst for Newcastle this was only their second league game of the season, having drawn their season opener 2-2 away at Woolwich Arsenal some three-weeks prior.

Newcastle however had not been idle in those intervening weeks, they had three friendly fixtures under their belt. In the first they had made a visit to their old stomping ground in Heaton to face the new occupants, Trafalgar.

Whilst they would have been delighted to have come out of that game with a victory (2-0) it was a much harder encounter than most would have envisaged. They had also entertained the current Football League Champions at St James's Park, their *"nearest and dearest"* [sic] neighbours, Sunderland, being beaten 1-3.

They had also taken a trip to Teesside and played out a 2-2 draw with Middlesbrough.

Both teams were well represented, whilst Newcastle did make changes from the Middlesbrough game, viz: Ryder for Ramsay in goal, Barr and Quinn replacing Donaldson and Bowman, the homesters, Burton, were unchanged from the side which beat Ardwick. So, without much further ado, the game was gotten underway.

Key Events

First Half
1 – 0	Joseph Dewey
2 – 0	Jimmy Munro

Second Half
3 – 0	Alec Boggie
3 – 1	**Tom Crate**

The weather was bright, but the ground was more than a little damp and a good crowd had assembled prior to kick-off. Playing with the assistance of a stiffish wind it was not long before Burton worked their way well up into the Newcastle quarters and a promising attack saw Mason beating the Newcastle custodian, Ryder, with a grand shot, but there was great relief as Lady Luck smiled upon them and the point was disallowed for an offside decision. *Only three minutes on the clock and Newcastle knew that they were in game already!*

By no means disheartened they responded reasonably well and worked their way into the game with some neat passing and movement from the forward quintet, Burton on the other hand, quite smartened by the disallowing of the goal knew they had it within themselves to beat the Newcastle defence. Thus, the game ebbed and flowed for a while, each goal being visited, almost in turn, but all attempts at scoring ultimately failing. Two strong back lines and two very capable custodians bringing applause, and equally gasps, from the assembled crowd. However, on the ten-minute mark things were to fall apart for the visitors.

First a goal was scored with a fine strike from Dewey which gave Ryder very little opportunity to save as it arrived through a clutch of players in front of him. This led to an almost incessant period of attack following attack by the homesters. The Newcastle goal was under virtual siege and they found it difficult to relieve the pressure. After around fifteen minutes of this onslaught Ryder was again beaten as a result of a desperate scrimmage in his goalmouth and Munro forcing the ball through.

From then until the interval the Swifts had by far the better of the exchanges but were, quite unexpectedly, not as forceful in their attacks. On the other hand, this may have been a result of knowing (or thinking) they had the beating of their opponents. Possibly confirmed as Newcastle offered little in return but were at least breaking out of their own territory on occasions.

Upon resumption following the break Newcastle now had the wind in their favour and set about immediately to try to make the fullest advantage. This period of dominant possession for Newcastle lasted for a good ten minutes during which they tried desperately to lower their deficit in terms of goals but were unable to do so.

Burton then rallied and once more took control of the ball and the game. Ekins was especially prominent for the homesters, making some excellent dashing runs down the left. Indeed, it was from one of his grand sprints that Burton got their third goal as he put in a beautiful centre right in front of the Newcastle goal and in the ensuing scramble Boggie rushed the ball home.

In effect the game was now over as far as it being a contest and the Swifts naturally relaxed somewhat whilst still being in control. Fair to say Newcastle had the better of possession but could do very little with it. That was until just before the call of time when Jones made a save from an effort, but Crate was on hand to pick up the loose ball and fire it home. It was of course far too little, far too late, and Newcastle had a long journey home to contemplate the defeat.

Pos.	Team	Plyd	W	D	L	F	A	G.Avg.	Pts.
1	Burslem Port Vale	5	5	0	0	22	5	4.4000	10
2	Liverpool	4	4	0	0	10	1	10.0000	8
3	Notts County	4	4	0	0	8	2	4.0000	8
4	Small Heath	5	4	0	1	18	8	2.2500	8
5	Grimsby Town	4	3	0	1	14	6	2.3333	6
6	Burton Swifts	5	3	0	2	14	10	1.4000	6
7	Woolwich Arsenal	3	1	1	1	8	5	1.6000	3
8	Rotherham Town	4	1	1	2	8	10	0.8000	3
9	Lincoln City	4	1	1	2	6	8	0.7500	3
10	Ardwick	6	1	0	5	9	17	0.5294	2
11	Crewe Alexandra	4	1	0	3	5	12	0.4167	2
12	Walsall Town Swifts	5	1	0	4	6	17	0.3529	2
13	Middlesbrough Ironopolis	4	1	0	3	3	12	0.2500	2
14	Newcastle United	2	0	1	1	3	5	0.6000	1
15	Northwich Victoria	5	0	0	5	3	19	0.1579	0

Supplementary notes…

Some reports state the Burton goal scorers as being Downie, Ekins and Munro, whilst giving the Newcastle goal to a player called Bates.

- Burton did not field a player called Downie
- Newcastle did not field a player called Bates, *nor to the best of my knowledge*, have ever had a player called Bates.

So, it must be accepted that these are errors, compounded by the nature of 'syndicated reporting' very prevalent at the time and still widely used to this day.

It was also reported that Ekins was injured 15 minutes from the end of the game, however it has not been possible to ascertain, *with any degree of accuracy*, whether this injury resulted in him having to leave the field of play permanently or not. The 'suspicion' being yes, he did.

Match Reports

Game: 6 ~ Saturday, September 30th, 1893   **vs. Woolwich Arsenal**

Competition: Division 2   **Venue:** St James's Park   **Gate:** 2,000

| Newcastle United | 6-0 | Woolwich Arsenal |

Goal, William Lowery; *backs*, Harry Jeffrey, James Miller; *half-backs*, Bobby Creilly, Willie Graham, Joe McKane; *forwards*, Charlie Quinn, Tom Crate, Willie Thompson, Isaac Ryder, Joe Wallace.

Goal, Charles Alfred Williams; *backs*, Joseph Powell, John Alfred Storrs; *half-backs*, George Devine, Robert Buist, David Howat; *forwards*, Walter Shaw, Duncan Gemmell, Joseph Frederick Heath, Arthur Elliott, Charles Booth.

Scorer(s): Joe Wallace (3), Willie Thompson (3)

Referee: Mr. Mr. Chalmers (Middlesbrough)

United Outgun the Arsenal with Double Hat-Tricks

After the weeks of turmoil at St James's Park, the fiasco of the mass sacking (*or otherwise*), the hints and innuendoes as to who might be staying or leaving, the promises of rising stars and clever amateurs, the St James's Park faithful were to have their first glimpse of their new Football League club.

Gone was Alex Ramsay, the custodian, and forwards John Bowman and Jock Sorley who appeared at Plumstead. In came William Lowery, the admittedly very talented custodian from Trafalgar, and two local amateurs, Charlie Quinn, and Isaac Ryder both of whom were well known to the followers of Newcastle 'A' in the Northern Alliance. The former of the two taking a good part in the mauling of Southwick, by nine goals to nil, last weekend in the Northern Alliance whilst Quinn had already appeared twice for the 'A's. Incidentally Lowery replaced Ryder's younger brother Joseph, in the Newcastle goal.

So, here we are at this, the very first official Football Association League game to be played at St James's Park. Depending upon which report you read the crowd was anywhere between 2,000 and 6,000. There had been frequent rain showers prior to the match and the ground was quoted as being softened. There were also further rain showers throughout the game.

Key Events	
First Half	
1 – 0	Joe Wallace
2 – 0	Willie Thompson
Second Half	
3 – 0	Joe Wallace
4 – 0	Willie Thompson
5 – 0	Willie Thompson
	first hat-trick by a "United" player
6 – 0	Joe Wallace
	first double hat-trick in a "United" fixture

Arsenal won the toss, so it was Thompson who kicked-off for Newcastle who were set to play 'up the hill'. From the kick-off there was some loose play in midfield before Arsenal assumed the offensive and got well up, however Miller was alert and prevented any real danger and cleared with a long kick. Thompson took possession and strode towards the Arsenal citadel. A foul for 'hands' was given against Powell and Newcastle were in a dangerous position. This led to a bombardment against the defence, but they stood firm. Getting free a rush was made by Gemmell and Shaw down the wing but again Miller was there for the homesters.

Crate received the return from Miller and took the ball on before passing to Wallace. He alluded all in front of him and scored with a splendid shot, from out on the left wing, amidst great enthusiasm, and there were barely five minutes on the clock.

Play then settled after the frantic start and was mainly in midfield. However, through some clever work, the Newcastle forwards advanced once more only for a timely intervention from Storrs to stop them. Thompson led another charge, Storrs made another intervention, but this time at the expense of a corner. When it was delivered in there was some good play in front of goal, but Quinn sent it narrowly past with a smart effort. Another attack and another timely intervention, this time by Powell, another corner, and another missed effort. From this goal kick Gemmell was released and he made good progress and this time it was Arsenal who had a corner. Although some good shots were put in Lowery was equal to all, saving confidently.

Playing in fine form the Newcastle forward quintet once again advanced. Wallace sent in a grand overhead centre which was perfect for Thompson and he scored Newcastle's second goal with a beauty of a shot.

Shortly after, in a rare opportunity to attack, Arsenal had a chance and were awarded a free-kick for "hands" dangerously close, but eventually nothing came out of it as Shaw sent his effort over the bar.

Jeffrey had the crowd cheering with some excellent "feeding work", and Crate, after making a good run, almost scored a third. Arsenal's keeper, Williams, was then left limping after a collision with Quinn, who himself was winded, but recovered quickly and moments later he pulled out a great save from a snap-shot from Graham. Some of the Arsenal men now began to use their weight, of which it was said "they had superiority", but the referee was quick and alert to this and he "promptly allowed fouls". With no further score the first half ended two-nil to Newcastle.

Arsenal started the second half much better than they had played in all the first half, which caused some concerns in and around the Newcastle penalty box. It was not long however before Newcastle regained their dominance. Williams was forced to concede a free-kick in a dangerous position and when Arsenal failed to clear it the ball continued "bobbing about" close to their posts and it took Williams to do some "smart work" to eventually get it clear. At one point it looked like Williams and Thompson "showed a little desire" to deal with each other rather than the ball!

Crate only just missed scoring with great shot, and shortly after this there was controversy when Wallace scored with a shot just under the bar, but the goalkeeper threw it back out which led to a row as to whether it had crossed the line or not. The referee, Mr Chalmers, however had no doubt at all, and the goal stood.

With Lowery in the Newcastle goal being nothing more than a "passive spectator" and their backs "scarcely ever required" in their own half of the pitch there was only one team in it. Newcastle's fourth goal came after a good run by Thompson and his shot gave Williams no chance, and now both he and Wallace were looking to see who the first player would be to score a hat-trick for Newcastle 'United'.

Williams was made to make a further fair few saves, but it was not long before he was rather flummoxed by Thompson, who "screwed in" the fifth goal and wrote himself into the history books as being the first hat-trick scorer for 'Newcastle United'. The game had long been over as a 'contest' and it descended into attack after attack on the Arsenal goal and it was from one of these that "Wallace made up the half dozen". That meant he also had scored a hat-trick, so the game goes down further in history as being the first one where 'United' scored a double hat-trick. Still Newcastle attacked and numerous shots were stopped by Williams, but it was clear that his team-mates were "played out" long before the final whistle was sounded.

Pos.	Team	Plyd	W	D	L	F	A	G.Avg.	Pts.
1	Burslem Port Vale	7	7	0	0	30	7	4.2857	14
2	Small Heath	7	5	0	2	19	13	1.4615	10
3	Liverpool	5	4	1	0	11	2	5.5000	9
4	Notts County	5	4	1	0	9	3	3.0000	9
5	Grimsby Town	6	4	0	2	20	11	1.8182	8
6	Burton Swifts	6	4	0	2	18	11	1.6364	8
7	Woolwich Arsenal	5	2	1	2	11	12	0.9167	5
8	Crewe Alexandra	5	2	0	3	10	12	0.8333	4
9	Walsall Town Swifts	7	2	0	5	11	22	0.5000	4
10	Newcastle United	3	1	1	1	9	5	1.8000	3
11	Lincoln City	4	1	1	2	6	8	0.7500	3
12	Rotherham Town	6	1	1	4	9	17	0.5294	3
13	Ardwick	7	1	0	6	9	18	0.5000	2
14	Middlesbrough Ironopolis	5	1	0	4	3	17	0.1765	2
15	Northwich Victoria	6	0	0	6	5	22	0.2273	0

Game: 7 ~ Saturday, October 7th, 1893 — vs. Lincoln City

Competition: Division 2 **Venue:** John O'Gaunt's **Gate:** 2,000

Lincoln City 2-1 Newcastle United

Goal, W. Tice; *backs*, William Heath, George Bowler; *half-backs*, Edward "Ned" Mettam, Mick Richardson, Herbert Wiltshire; *forwards*, William Phipps, Albert Flewitt, Don Lees, John Irving, John Chadburn.

Scorer(s): Don Lees, Albert Flewitt

Goal, William Lowery; *backs*, Harry Jeffrey, James Miller; *half-backs*, Bobby Creilly, Willie Graham, Joe McKane; *forwards*, Charlie Quinn, Tom Crate, Willie Thompson, Toby Gillespy, Joe Wallace.

Scorer(s): Joe Wallace

Referee: Mr. Forrest (Gainsborough)

Newcastle Lose Entertaining Encounter

Newcastle went into this game having played only three league games this season, drawing the first, losing the second and emphatically winning the third by 6-0! Lincoln City had an identical start in their first three league games of the season, as far as the results went anyway. One draw, one defeat, and one victory. They drew their first game, 1-1 at home to Rotherham Town, lost their second game, 4-0 at Anfield against Liverpool, and won their third game, 4-1 at home to Northwich Victoria. They had however played an extra league game, which they lost 1-3 at home to Grimsby

Town. Perhaps more worrying for them was the fact that they had played a friendly fixture at home to Midland League outfit Gainsborough Trinity on Wednesday where they again, *and quite surprisingly*, lost. The score then being 1-3 in favour of Gainsborough. So, this game today always looked as if it would be a tough encounter, and one which could go either way.

To further add to the woes of the Lincoln City fans not only had they witnessed the two successive defeats but when the team sheets were released they found they were without Jones their custodian and Neill at the back, both according to the Lincolnshire Chronicle having put in a "miserable exhibition" on Wednesday. The 'big news' was that, against all expectations, their new forward Peter Burns was not included. It was understood that these omissions were for genuine concerns that the trio were not 100% fit and the Lincoln committee were erring on the side of caution when making their selection, knowing full well that there was a long season ahead. Nevertheless, there was a good turnout for the game with there being fully 2,000 spectators at John O'Gaunt's for the kick-off.

Key Events		
First Half		
1 – 0	Don Lees	
1 – 1	**Joe Wallace**	
Second Half		
2 – 1	Albert Flewitt	

Lincoln started the game in tremendous fashion, they totally dominated the early proceedings and rained shot after shot upon the Newcastle goal. However, they found Lowery in most excellent form, as he needed to be, and they could not turn their superiority to any advantage in terms of goals.

Following this mad flurry of intensity, the game, for the next half-hour or so became more even, Newcastle began to pass with flair and confidence and each goal was visited in turn.

With the advantage of the incline Newcastle were untiring in their efforts but just as Lincoln had found Lowery in form they found Tice equally capable. Whilst their shots weren't as numerous, they were certainly as accurate. It was then that Newcastle thought they had opened the scoring, but the point was ruled out because of an off-side decision. It was therefore Lincoln who opened the scoring, from the penalty spot. There could be no argument from the Newcastle players as to the correctness of the decision. It came during a period of sustained attacks from Lincoln and one of the Newcastle players was undoubtedly guilty of fisting the ball down, it was a deserved penalty. Lees took the spot-kick and duly dispatched it with consummate ease.

As half-time was approaching Newcastle were forcing Lincoln to defend very deep and when one of their backs, Heath, brought in from the Lincoln City Swifts in place of Neill, had an unfortunate stumble and Wallace pounced on the mistake and forced the ball through for the equaliser. Lucky for Newcastle of course, but very unlucky for Heath who had up until that point not put a foot wrong. Just before the whistle sounded for the interval Lincoln thought they had once again taken the lead as the ball was sent into the back of the Newcastle net, however they were now the ones to be disappointed as this point too was ruled out for an offside decision.

Upon resumption the game was once again very evenly contested, both elevens going for it "hammer and tongs". The defences of both were excellent, the forward quintets were at times unlucky, and the half-backs supported their forwards with gusto and were equally vehement in their support for their backs. Add to this that Tice and Lowery were both in superb form, and you have a very exciting game with nothing to separate the sides.

Truly, to all and sundry, this game appeared to be headed for a 1-1 draw, which upon reflection no one would have any cause to be unhappy about. After all each side had scored, each side had thought they had scored, only to be ruled out for offside, and each side had shown some sturdy defence and some not-so-sturdy forward play. However, football can be most unfair at times and with only five minutes left before time an effort was sent in by Lincoln, which Lowery desperately saved, but at the expense of a corner. This was expertly delivered by Chadburn and with a clever and acrobatic overhead kick Flewitt sent the ball flying into the net.

Pos.	Team	Plyd	W	D	L	F	A	G.Avg.	Pts.
1	Burslem Port Vale	8	7	0	1	31	15	2.0667	14
2	Burton Swifts	8	6	0	2	26	14	1.8571	12
3	Small Heath	8	6	0	2	24	15	1.6000	12
4	Liverpool	6	5	1	0	17	2	8.5000	11
5	Notts County	6	5	1	0	12	3	4.0000	11
6	Grimsby Town	8	4	0	4	22	19	1.1579	8
7	Woolwich Arsenal	5	2	1	2	11	12	0.9167	5
8	Lincoln City	5	2	1	2	8	9	0.8889	5
9	Ardwick	8	2	0	6	17	19	0.8947	4
10	Crewe Alexandra	6	2	0	4	11	14	0.7857	4
11	Walsall Town Swifts	8	2	0	6	11	23	0.4783	4
12	Newcastle United	4	1	1	2	10	7	1.4286	3
13	Rotherham Town	6	1	1	4	9	17	0.5294	3
14	Northwich Victoria	8	1	0	7	8	28	0.2857	2
15	Middlesbrough Ironopolis	6	1	0	5	3	23	0.1304	2

Game: 8 ~ Saturday, October 14th, 1893		vs. Notts County
Competition: Division 2	**Venue:** Trent Bridge	**Gate:** 5,000

Notts County	3-1	Newcastle United
Goal, George Toone; *backs*, Fay Harper, Jack Hendry; *half-backs*, Archie Osborne, David Calderhead, Alf Shelton; *forwards*, Arthur Watson, Jimmy McLachlan, Jimmy Logan, Sam Donnelly, Harry Daft.		*Goal*, William Lowery; *backs*, Harry Jeffrey, James Miller; *half-backs*, Willie Graham, Joe McKane, Bobby Creilly; *forwards*, Matt Keir, Tom Crate, Willie Thompson, Joe Wallace, John Inglis.
Scorer(s): Arthur Watson, Jimmy Logan, Harry Daft		Scorer(s): Joe Wallace

Referee: Mr. J. Fox (Sheffield)

The "Other" Magpies Steal All the Points

The weather was reported to be quite dull, with a southerly wind blowing and all the signs that at some point there would be rain. This however did not deter the crowd for it was a packed Trent Bridge that was to witness an afternoon of very bright football and a very exciting game!

County were without Bruce, the usual partner to Daft since the arrival of Logan and were giving a league debut to Jimmy McLachlan, late of Derby County. The team which took to the field was described as the strongest they had placed all season. Newcastle for their part were somewhat rearranged as with Charlie Quinn being injured Matt Keir was drafted in from the reserves for his first-team debut, and a debut was also given to John Inglis in the outside-right position with Wallace being moved inside.

KEY EVENTS	
First Half	
1 – 0	Arthur Watson
2 – 0	Jimmy Logan
2 – 1	**Joe Wallace**
Second Half	
3 – 1	Harry Daft

Just prior to the kick-off the County team were photographed and with pride they started the game in sterling style. Immediately on the ball being kicked towards the Bridgford End they dashed forwards and Lowery was lucky in getting to the ball to roll it away as Logan and Donnelly were bearing down upon it. This was unfortunately a taste of things to come for the Newcastle defence as for the next few minutes they were severely pressed, giving Miller and Jeffery a rare time of it.

Surviving the onslaught, the Newcastle left-flank showed their abilities in passing and moving, forcing Shelton to concede a corner as they energetically advanced. Nothing came from the corner other than giving possession to County who immediately raced up the field and won a corner of their own, with again nothing being the outcome.

Then came a very smart run by Watson. He dodged past McKane and showing superior speed to anyone opposing him cantered down and span the ball obliquely beyond Lowery. All this and there were only eight minutes on the clock!

There was worse to come for Newcastle as within two minutes of that goal County scored again, this time through Logan. He scored with a "dashing kick" that seemed as if it would drive the ball through the net itself!

Newcastle were now knocked right back on their heels. However, they did not give up despite this early shock. Gradually they fought their way back into the game. With what was 'just reward' for their gallant efforts Wallace managed to reduce the deficit with a lofted shot that dropped between Toone and Harper, each apparently leaving it for the other in a rare mix-up. So, at the half-time whistle, with Newcastle playing the superior football, the game was poised at two-one to the "other Magpies" with the second half eagerly anticipated.

The second half saw County start rather tamely and the "reds" (*we were still in East End colours at this stage*) were well encamped in the home half. The pressure was only relieved on the County goal by Daft kicking the ball into touch. The game was getting exciting and a free-kick awarded against County allowed Thompson and his colleagues to make matters warm once more for the home defence. Toone was lucky to get the ball away on one occasion as two Newcastle forwards bore down. For a good ten-minutes Newcastle were incessant with the pressure and the kicking of Miller was to be particularly admired.

In a change of fortunes Watson, assisted by Harper, broke away after Logan passed out to the right. Miller and McKane were beaten by the pace of the pair and Watson hit a rattling shot which Lowery capably held but the warning signs were there for Newcastle. Sure enough, after a few minutes of further pressure Logan had the ball in the back of the Newcastle net but in doing so had handled the ball in bundling it through and the point was disallowed.

Still the "ding-dong" battle drew on and an equalising goal for Newcastle seemed like the most expected of results however football does not work to a script and with barely five minutes left to play County put the game to bed with a third goal. On the offensive Newcastle were high up the pitch and an appeal for a foul by a County player went ignored. Before they could recover Osborne launched the ball up the field, Watson put it right into the goal and Daft breasted it through.

Supplementary notes…

In saying the "other magpies" that is a bit of a misnomer as Newcastle United had not yet acquired the "Magpies" nickname and Notts County at the time went by the more common nickname of the "Lambs".

Pos.	Team	Plyd	W	D	L	F	A	G.Avg.	Pts.
1	Burslem Port Vale	8	7	0	1	31	15	2.0667	14
2	Liverpool	7	6	1	0	21	5	4.2000	13
3	Notts County	7	6	1	0	15	4	3.7500	13
4	Burton Swifts	8	6	0	2	26	14	1.8571	12
5	Small Heath	9	6	0	3	27	19	1.4211	12
6	Grimsby Town	8	4	0	4	22	19	1.1579	8
7	Woolwich Arsenal	5	2	1	2	11	12	0.9167	5
8	Lincoln City	5	2	1	2	8	9	0.8889	5
9	Ardwick	8	2	0	6	17	19	0.8947	4
10	Crewe Alexandra	6	2	0	4	11	14	0.7857	4
11	Walsall Town Swifts	8	2	0	6	11	23	0.4783	4
12	Newcastle United	5	1	1	3	11	10	1.1000	3
13	Rotherham Town	6	1	1	4	9	17	0.5294	3
14	Northwich Victoria	8	1	0	7	8	28	0.2857	2
15	Middlesbrough Ironopolis	6	1	0	5	3	23	0.1304	2

Game: 9 ~ Saturday, October 21st, 1893   vs. Ardwick

Competition: Division 2   **Venue:** Hyde Road   **Gate:** 4,000

Ardwick	2-3	Newcastle United

Goal, William Douglas; *backs*, John McVickers, David Robson; *half-backs*, Frank Dyer, Daniel Whittle, James Caine; *forwards*, James Yates, Hugh Morris, Eric Regan, Walter Bowman, Robert Milarvie.
Scorer(s): Hugh Morris, Robert Milarvie

Goal, William Lowery; *backs*, Harry Jeffrey, James Miller; *half-backs*, Bobby Creilly, Willie Graham, Joe McKane; *forwards*, Jack Patten, Tom Crate, Willie Thompson, Joe Wallace, John Inglis.
Scorer(s): Tom Crate, OG, Joe Wallace

Excellent Fight-Back by United

A game that will go down in the annals of football history!

Ardwick's outside-right, Walter Wells Bowman, being a Canadian national, was the first non-British player to play in the English Football League.

Key Events	
First Half	
1 – 0	Hugh Morris
2 – 0	Robert Milvarie
Second Half	
2 – 1	Tom Crate
2 – 2	Own Goal
2 – 3	Joe Wallace

Thompson for Newcastle United got the game underway and forcing the play they shortly afterwards got a free kick in front of the home goal. It was well delivered and looked dangerous, but Douglas managed to fist it away. Continuing the attacking Newcastle forced Robson into making a last-ditch, though excellent, clearance. However, things were then to take a quick turnaround and play was firmly in favour of the homesters. Milvarie and Morris were causing all sorts of problems to the Newcastle defence, getting through on several occasions, and giving Lowery some work to do, of which he was equal to.

It was then the turn of the visitors to press and Thompson put in a good effort which Douglas did well to save. Then gaining a free-kick for 'hands' Newcastle were in a very promising position, but Douglas again pulled off a save of the highest order.

Immediately following this Ardwick made a speedy break through Milvarie who put the ball in front of Morris, and he dashed the leather through. Everyone, at least everyone on the side of Newcastle that is, thought that Morris was, without any doubt, well offside. However, despite the strong protestations of the Newcastle players and their followers, and much to their chagrin, the referee allowed the point to stand. He was, again without any doubt, the only person present to think that Morris was onside, but unfortunately the new association rules gave him the power to decide over the thoughts on his "umpires" or anyone else for that matter. Argue as much as they wanted, Newcastle were still a goal down!

It was not long after the game had been restarted following the contested goal when Ardwick doubled their lead. There was no doubt about this goal but let the arguments begin as to who scored it. Yates and Morris worked the ball down exceedingly well and centred it for Bowman. He sent in a decent shot and whilst it looked as if it may go into the net anyway Milarvie1 gave it a final touch to ensure that it did.

Most definitely in the ascendency now Ardwick pressed, and Yates was cheered for a fine run and centre, Miller just managing to get in a clearance. Newcastle did not at any stage give-in and tried desperately to get back into the game. Their forwards attacked vigorously, and Douglas saved his charge in splendid fashion on more than one occasion. However, try as they might, Newcastle could not reduce the deficit and when the half-time whistle sounded, they trailed by those two goals.

After the interval Regan, for Ardwick, restarted the game, and the homesters were at once on the attack, but the Newcastle defence held firm as McKane stopped Yates in his tracks and played the ball to Wallace. Having now the opportunity to attack themselves Wallace ended the dash forward with a tremendous shot which brought about an equally tremendous save from Douglas, but at the expense of a corner. Whilst the corner was well delivered it was headed over the bar. Newcastle were now having decidedly the better of the game, and following another splendid run by Wallace and Inglis the former put in a grand centre which Crate headed through for their first goal. Game on as it were!

Almost immediately from restarting Newcastle took possession and once again forced Ardwick back into their own quarters. Patten and Crate ran the ball past the Ardwick backs and when one-on-one with Douglas a wayward shot from Crate went horribly wide. Newcastle tried once again and in trying to prevent the ball from reaching the goalmouth Robson conceded a corner, but it was very badly placed, and nought came from it.

Yates then got away for Ardwick with a fast run, forcing Miller to concede a corner, but as with Newcastle's corner, nothing resulted from it. Then back up the other end another corner then fell to Newcastle, but once again the result was that nothing was gained from it. Morris and Yates then combined well and made nice run down. As the final ball was played to Morris, he sent in a great effort that was only narrowly wide of the mark.

Back came Newcastle and enjoying a period of dominancy they were let down by some very erratic shooting indeed. Then, at last, from a throw-in by McKane the ball was headed through by one of the Ardwick men, thus making the game even at two goals each. The equalising goal smartened up the game considerably. The homesters now made great efforts, and displayed some fine footballing skills, but they found Lowery in masterly form. A decent effort from Yates was sent wide and shortly after a fine centre from him was met by Milarvie but he headed it straight into the safe hands of Lowery. Not long after Whittle sent a shot over the bar.

Lowrey was again called into action and saved a splendid shot. It was an exciting end-to-end half, and looked like it would end in a draw, which on balance would probably have been a fair result, but the visitors had other ideas! With a final flourish they displayed some splendid passing and worked the ball well up. The ball was then sent into the Ardwick area and following an exciting passage of play Douglas tried to run the ball out, but Wallace took possession and scored with a hot one. With what little was left of the game each side tried in vain, for Ardwick to equalise and Newcastle to increase their lead and make the game safe. Neither of these events occurred and no further scoring was made though the play entertained the crowd. When the final whistle came the score was still in Newcastle's favour and a great fight-back was complete.

Pos.	Team	Plyd	W	D	L	F	A	G.Avg.	Pts.
1	Liverpool	8	6	2	0	22	6	3.6667	14
2	Burslem Port Vale	9	7	0	2	33	18	1.8333	14
3	Small Heath	10	7	0	3	31	20	1.5500	14
4	Notts County	8	6	1	1	17	9	1.8889	13
5	Burton Swifts	9	6	1	2	27	15	1.8000	13
6	Grimsby Town	9	5	0	4	27	21	1.2857	10
7	Lincoln City	6	2	2	2	9	10	0.9000	6
8	Walsall Town Swifts	9	3	0	6	12	23	0.5217	6
9	Newcastle United	6	2	1	3	14	12	1.1667	5
10	Crewe Alexandra	7	2	1	4	12	15	0.8000	5
11	Woolwich Arsenal	6	2	1	3	12	16	0.7500	5
12	Rotherham Town	7	2	1	4	12	19	0.6316	5
13	Ardwick	9	2	0	7	19	22	0.8636	4
14	Northwich Victoria	8	1	0	7	8	28	0.2857	2
15	Middlesbrough Ironopolis	7	1	0	6	3	24	0.1250	2

Supplementary notes...

There are references to Ardwick's second goal being scored by James Yates rather than Robert Milvarie. Local Manchester papers favour Milvarie, local Newcastle papers favour Yates. The consensus though being with the Manchester press. There are also references to Newcastle's opening goal being scored by John Patten rather than Tom Crate. However, unlike with the Ardwick goal evidence from other sources, such as overall scoring records for example clearly indicate this goal was indeed scored by Crate.

Game: 10 ~ Saturday, October 28th, 1893			**vs. Small Heath**
Competition: Division 2	**Venue:** St James's Park		**Gate:** 3,000

Newcastle United	0-2	Small Heath
Goal, William Lowery; *backs*, Harry Jeffrey, James Miller; *half-backs*, Bobby Creilly, Willie Graham, Joe McKane; *forwards*, William Simm, Tom Crate, Willie Thompson, Joe Wallace, John Inglis.		*Goal*, George Hollis; *backs*, Gilbert Smith, William Thomas Billy Reynolds; *half-backs*, William Ollis, Caesar Jenkyns, Edwin Ted Devey; *forwards*, John Jack Hallam, William Howard T. Billy Walton, Frank Mobley, Frederick Fred Wheldon, Thomas Tommy Hands. Scorer(s): Frank Mobley, Fred Wheldon

Referee: Mr. A. Cooper (Durham)   Kick-off: 2:45 PM

An Entertaining Contest Ends Unsuccessfully for Newcastle

Small Heath left Birmingham on the Friday evening, staying the night at York, before continuing their journey on the Saturday morning to arrive at Newcastle around noon. Coming into this match they had won four of their last five games. In their last match they had defeated Woolwich Arsenal quite handsomely, 4-1 at Coventry Road, and this saw them sitting third in the division. Newcastle, in only their second home game of the season, were also coming into this game on the back of a win, a hard-fought victory over Ardwick at Hyde Road by a score of 2-3, this after being 2-0 down. They were therefore ninth in the table. However, the relative positions of the two teams is a bit arbitrary as Small Heath had played ten games whilst Newcastle had only played six.

The weather was fine, but there was a strong breeze blowing across the ground which would undoubtedly militate greatly against the accuracy of any sweeping passes and crosses. However, as its direction was transversal it was not of any advantage to either side. Everything was therefore seemingly set up for good contest and as evinced by the size of the crowd it was an eagerly anticipated contest too.

KEY EVENTS		
Second Half		
0 – 1		Frank Mobley
0 – 2		Fred Wheldon

Small Heath won the toss and elected to play down the hill for the first half and it was with a hearty cheer that Thompson got the game underway for Newcastle. It was with some rapidity that Small Heath gained possession and made a concerted rush upon the home goal. Jeffrey was equal to the rush and took control of the ball, but his only outlet was to put the ball into midfield. Neither side could make much headway as play was of a loose character for a period until the home half-back trio then, through some sterling work, managed to release the forward quintet but they only found Reynolds well prepared, and he sent it back with a long kick. This then allowed the visitors to press once again and from this they gained a corner. Taken by Hallam the wind swept the ball out of play.

Undeterred Small Heath once again pressed, and Jeffrey was once more alert to any danger and relieved. The pressure from the visitors was now becoming quite sustained and they won a free-kick in a very promising position close into the home goal. It was however to avail them nothing. Their next forage forward saw Lowery having to make a clever save from a fast shot by Hallam and with the ball going to Graham he was able to clear further up the field.

The Newcastle forwards them launched an attack of their own and when a shot by Wallace was blocked an opportunity was afforded to Inglis but his effort was quite weak and easily dealt with. The homesters right-wing then exhibited fine play and worked the ball down to within a few yards of the visitor's goal. Smith however was able to clear. Once again, a period of midfield play followed.

It was Newcastle who broke this pattern and Wallace, receiving a pass from Thompson, put in a grand shot that missed by the smallest of margins, amidst much excitement from the crowd. Play was, for now, mainly within the visitor's quarters. Whilst under pressure they were never in much danger and eventually they forced the play once again. Working their way down to the home citadel they were able to get a shot away but Lowery saved magnificently and immediately from the save the ball was sent back at him and he pulled off another great save. This second save resulted in a corner for the visitors which was headed over the bar.

The game was now fast and frantic, thoroughly entertaining too. The home left-wing ran up and with some very clever working Thompson sent the ball through, only for the point to be disallowed for an offside infringement.

This seemed to serve as a jolt for Small Heath as they returned to the attack with some gusto, but Graham was able to prevent any efforts on goal, sending the ball long and back into the midfield area.

The play in midfield that followed was intense, and even, and eventually it was the visiting forwards who broke free. Jeffrey, once again, was on hand to halt their progress. Indeed, his long clearance allowed the home forwards to press, but they in turn were halted. The game was now virtually end-to-end as Small Heath made a fruitless attack, followed by a Newcastle attack which was equally fruitless. Hallam then tried a long shot which was too high.

The wind then gave assistance to the visitors, allowing them to get close in and send in an effort that was nicely saved by Lowery. The ball was quickly returned in and Lowery once again made a save. In doing so he fell but luckily Miller was able to prevent the subsequent shot. That was a close call, it appeared for a second that Small Heath would surely score!

In what was proving to be an excellent finish to the half Small Heath once again made Lowery work, and once again he demonstrated his excellence as a custodian. The Newcastle forwards forced a grand clearance from Reynolds. Both teams then had efforts which were badly affected by the wind. As the half was rapidly coming to an end Inglis had a fine effort that the wind carried just wide of the target. It was with Newcastle in the ascendancy that the half-time whistle was sounded.

If the end of the first half was exciting, the beginning of the second half was nothing short of sensational, if you a Small Heath fan that is! With a frantic rush up from the restart the ball was played to Mobley and he blasted the leather through, there had been barely half-a-minute passed since the whistle signalled the beginning of play!

A bit stunned by this Newcastle then restarted and took the ball well down looking for a quick response. Whilst they stretched the visitors defence severely, they in turn were more than equal to the task, ensuring there were no clear-cut opportunities for the home quintet. So strong were they that the next save of the match was indeed another by Lowery. From that save play was rapidly taken to the visitor's citadel. Hollis being forced into a save from an effort by Thompson.

There was then a period of very heavy pressure from Newcastle with the Small Heath defence being forced into a rather desperate display kicking out as no time was afforded to them to do anything different. Inglis had a grand effort that went agonisingly close, passing just outside, and Crate had an effort which he sent over the bar, no doubt assisted by the wind. Keeping up the attack Crate then forced Hollis into a fine save by means of which he conceded a corner. The ball was well placed in, but Jeffrey sent it behind.

The relief afforded by the goal-kick was brief as Newcastle were soon back in the Small Heath quarters and Wallace had hard lines indeed in not equalising.

In what was now a rare attack the visitors got close but the final effort from Wheldon went over. At the other end Wallace wanted too much time on the ball in preparing for his shot and Smith stole the ball away. A free-kick, for hands against Jenkins, was awarded to Newcastle but they could not play it to any great advantage. Jeffrey put in some sterling work and following Thompson took the ball well down but his final effort, from distance, was wayward. Crate was equally wayward with another long-range effort.

Small Heath then got some relief as they won a free-kick in a promising position close to the Newcastle goal but the leather was sent well over the top. Appearing now to gain the upperhand the visitors were buzzing around the home citadel and Wheldon, in clever style, scored a second goal for them.

Newcastle were now in a perilous situation indeed, two goals down and having had the best of efforts with nothing to show for them. Redoubling their efforts, they stormed the visiting defence, giving them severe work to do indeed, but ultimately there was no way through. Whenever the backs were breached Hollis was in good form. Wallace brought out a fine save from him, resulting in another corner but nothing was to come from it. Then a free-kick for hands against Ollis provided Newcastle with an excellent opportunity but the delivery from McKane was carried wide by the wind.

Play subsided for a period and the next advantage went to the visitors and Lowery was forced to throw out a keen shot. Directly after it was the visitor's goal that was the scene of some smart work until Hollis finally cleared following an effort by Simm, making his debut (*and his only appearance as it turned out*). Returning to the front Newcastle were pressing but proving weak in front of goal. Interspersed with this however was another very decent effort from Simm that went just over the bar. A corner was then won by Newcastle, but Smith headed it out for a second corner, this being easily dealt with.

From now until the final whistle it was almost exclusively Newcastle on the attack, Small Heath defending well. On more than one occasion Newcastle were unlucky not to score as shot after shot was sent in, from both close-in and from range. All however being unsuccessful.

In summing up what had been a thoroughly entertaining game the 'pick of the bunch' for Newcastle were Lowery in goal, Graham at half-back and Wallace up front. For the most part Lowery was a 'safe pair of hands' and in truthfulness he could do nothing about either of the two goals scored against him. Graham proved to be his usual solid self and Wallace played an excellent forward game. On behalf of Small Heath special praise was given to Jenkins, of whom it was said played an excellent part and was, to a large extent, responsible for the victory. Smith and Reynolds proved to be a safe pair of backs and the trio of half-backs frustrated the Newcastle forwards on many, indeed most, occasions. Hallam was the most prominent of the Small Heath forwards even though it was Mobley and Wheldon who got the goals. The latter mentioned helping his halves by falling back on numerous occasions, particularly in the second half of the game.

All-in-all, this was a hard-earned victory for Small Heath. One which on the balance of play perhaps should have been a draw but credit to Small Heath they took their chances whilst Newcastle wasted theirs.

Pos.	Team	Plyd	W	D	L	F	A	G.Avg.	Pts.
1	Liverpool	9	7	2	0	27	6	4.5000	16
2	Notts County	10	7	2	1	23	10	2.3000	16
3	Small Heath	11	8	0	3	33	20	1.6500	16
4	Burslem Port Vale	11	8	0	3	35	24	1.4583	16
5	Burton Swifts	10	6	1	3	28	17	1.6471	13
6	Grimsby Town	10	5	0	5	29	25	1.1600	10
7	Lincoln City	7	3	2	2	13	12	1.0833	8
8	Crewe Alexandra	8	3	1	4	15	15	1.0000	7
9	Walsall Town Swifts	9	3	0	6	12	23	0.5217	6
10	Newcastle United	7	2	1	4	14	14	1.0000	5
11	Ardwick	10	2	1	7	19	22	0.8636	5
12	Rotherham Town	8	2	1	5	12	20	0.6000	5
13	Woolwich Arsenal	7	2	1	4	12	21	0.5714	5
14	Middlesbrough Ironopolis	8	2	0	6	5	25	0.2000	4
15	Northwich Victoria	9	1	0	8	8	31	0.2581	2

Game: 11 ~ Saturday, November 4th, 1893   vs. Liverpool

Competition: Division 2   **Venue:** Anfield   **Gate:** 8,000

Liverpool	5-1	Newcastle United

Goal, Billy McOwen; *backs*, Andrew Hannah, Duncan McLean; *half-backs*, John McCartney, Douglas Dick, Jim McBride; *forwards*, Thomas Bradshaw, Patrick Gordon, Matt McQueen, James Stott, Hugh McQueen.

Scorer(s): Jimmy Stott, Patrick Gordon (2), Harry Bradshaw, Douglas Dick

Goal, William Lowery; *backs*, Harry Jeffrey, James Miller; *half-backs*, Bobby Creilly, Willie Graham, Joe McKane; *forwards*, Joe Wallace, Toby Gillespy, Willie Thompson, Tom Crate, Charlie Quinn.

Scorer(s): Willie Thompson

Kick-off: 3:10 PM

Anfield Table-Toppers ultimately destroy United!

Table toppers Liverpool, on goal average only, being level with three other teams, entertained Newcastle at Anfield today and added handsomely to that goal average in putting five past Newcastle and only conceding one. The positions were a bit arbitrary given that Small Heath and Burslem had played 11 games, Notts County ten games and Liverpool only nine. Of importance to Newcastle was that of those nine games they had only dropped two points, winning seven and drawing two. Of the three games they had played at home they had won all three and conceded only once. On the other hand, Newcastle had won only once in their five games away from St James's Park, and had only scored five times. As those statistics show this was going to be a very tough test for Newcastle, a very tough test indeed, and ultimately, as the scoreline suggests, it was a test they failed miserably!

KEY EVENTS	
First Half	
1 – 0	Jimmy Stott
1 – 1	**Willie Thompson**
2 – 1	Patrick Gordon
3 – 1	Harry Bradshaw
Second Half	
4 – 1	Doulas Dick
5 – 1	Patrick Gordon

For the first time in a League match this season Liverpool captain, Andrew Hannah lost the spin of the coin, and Willie Graham, the Newcastle captain, elected to defend the

Oakfield-road goal. Bradshaw took the kick-off sending to Stott, whose attempt to break through the half-back line was easily blocked by Graham. Liverpool then gave away a free-kick which allowed Newcastle to get close in, but McBride cleared in grand fashion. A run by Gordon and Dick, ably assisted by Bradshaw, saw the ball brought into the Newcastle quarters, but it was destined not to remain long, as a misunderstanding by McCartney gave possession away to Gillespy who with Wallace cleverly worked the ball into McOwen's proximity, but M. McQueen intervened.

Back then came Liverpool with Gordon, Bradshaw, and Stott combining well and when Gordon put in a centre Lowery was a tad lucky in saving from Bradshaw. Having slightly the best of the play now, the homesters kept Jeffrey and Miller extremely busy. During this period of severe pressure Jeffrey deliberately fouled a close shot by Stott. The resulting free-kick was well-placed back to Stott who, with an equally well-placed shot, opened the scoring for the homesters with nine minutes played.

The goal sparked a spell of play which was of quite brilliant order, both sides shining to great advantage. Some very neat and effective work was witnessed by Gordon, Bradshaw, and Dick, with Stott and McBride endeavouring to work their way through. However, being dispossessed by Graham the game returned to the home citadel where now it was the turn of Quinn, Crate and Thompson to show their talents. This they did admirably but it looked to have come to nothing as a final pass by Quinn seemed destined to go over the line and the Liverpool defence ignored it and it was at their peril. Thompson simply stole in and hooked the ball into the net by means of an oblique daisy-cutter. Liverpool's lead lasting just five minutes.

That unexpected, and totally preventable disaster, on the behalf of Liverpool had the effect of infusing more life into their play, and they had to be very quick to gain any advantage. However, danger to the Anfield citadel was once more threatened, and it was Thompson again who was proving to be the main threat. Only a very opportune clearance by McLean provided a temporary breather. Liverpool had great difficulty in trying to keep Newcastle at bay, and finally shake them off, but not before McKane and Gillespy both had efforts which were too close to McOwen's charge to be pleasant to watch for the Merseyside crowd.

At length the siege was raised, and the Liverpool forward quintet dashed towards their enemy's goal. Their progress was halted by Miller at the expense of a corner. When it was delivered in a foul gave Liverpool a free-kick and when this was sent in the excitement became intense as the ball bobbed about very near the goal line. With almost superhuman efforts Lowery saved, saved again, and then cleared. Undeterred back came Stott, McQueen, and McBride to put the visitors' goal under further assault. With McLean coming forward too he forced a fine save from Lowery who had no other alternative than to concede a corner in doing so. Hugh McQueen placed the corner in well and it was finely headed into the net by Gordon.

Elated by the retaking of the lead Liverpool pushed on in brilliant fashion and Lowery was put under a severe bombardment. At length some sharp play by Gordon, Dick, and Bradshaw culminated in the latter scoring the third goal from very close quarters. To their credit Newcastle attempted a rally, Thompson leading the charge, they showed some excellent combination, which was halted, only just in time, by the intervention of McBride.

Following the interval Hugh McQueen had two shots in relatively quick succession, both when excellently placed. To his undoubted eternal embarrassment, he sent both hopelessly over the bar when it looked easier to score than to miss. Creilly tried to muster the troops as he gave his wing an opening and they worked the ball nicely up only to be abruptly halted by Hannah. His clever clearance was sent to Gordon, and he dashed rather smartly along the right wing and centred beautifully. Stott made a gallant effort to reach the ball, but it fell harmlessly in favour of Newcastle.

Liverpool were becoming almost totally dominant, certainly in territorial matters they were, Newcastle trying desperately to drag themselves up the field and invariably stopped midway were said to be showing signs of roughness in their play. The game erupted into quite a fury at one point, this when the referee allowed a disputed goal by Gordon to stand, several Newcastle players were said to completely lose control of themselves, and in the ensuing melee Matt McQueen was said to be quite seriously injured. It was not a dignified end from Newcastle, a one that taints the sterling efforts they had put in beforehand.

Pos.	Team	Plyd	W	D	L	F	A	G.Avg.	Pts.
1	Liverpool	10	8	2	0	32	7	4.5714	18
2	Notts County	11	8	2	1	26	10	2.6000	18
3	Small Heath	11	8	0	3	33	20	1.6500	16
4	Burslem Port Vale	11	8	0	3	35	24	1.4583	16
5	Burton Swifts	10	6	1	3	28	17	1.6471	13
6	Grimsby Town	10	5	0	5	29	25	1.1600	10
7	Lincoln City	7	3	2	2	13	12	1.0833	8
8	Crewe Alexandra	8	3	1	4	15	15	1.0000	7
9	Walsall Town Swifts	9	3	0	6	12	23	0.5217	6
10	Ardwick	10	2	1	7	19	22	0.8636	5
11	Newcastle United	8	2	1	5	15	19	0.7895	5
12	Rotherham Town	8	2	1	5	12	20	0.6000	5
13	Woolwich Arsenal	7	2	1	4	12	21	0.5714	5
14	Middlesbrough Ironopolis	9	2	0	7	5	28	0.1786	4
15	Northwich Victoria	9	1	0	8	8	31	0.2581	2

Game: 12 ~ Saturday, November 11th, 1893			**vs. Sheffield United**
Competition: Friendly	**Venue:** St James's Park		**Gate:** 4,000
Newcastle United	**5-1**	**Sheffield United**	

Goal, William Lowery; *backs*, Harry Jeffrey, James Miller; *half-backs*, Bobby Creilly, Willie Graham, Joe McKane; *forwards*, Charlie Quinn, Tom Crate, Willie Thompson, Joe Wallace, William Milne.

Scorer(s): Tom Crate (2), William Milne, Willie Thompson (2)

Goal, Fred Wood; *backs*, Michael Whitham, William Mellor; *half-backs*, George Waller, Billy Hendry, Fred Davies; *forwards*, John Drummond, Billy Croxon, Bob Hill, Hugh Gallacher, Arthur Watson.

Scorer(s): John Drummond

Referee: Mr. Robert Campbell (Sunderland)

Five-star show from Newcastle

Smarting from their defeat to Liverpool at Anfield last weekend Newcastle won by the same scoreline that they were defeated by. A brace from both Crate and Thompson plus a goal for Milne, appearing from the reserves. The Sheffield team were short by no less than five of their first-team 'regulars'. Four being involved in the inter-association match between Sheffield and Glasgow, the fifth Cain being on their injured list. Newcastle fielded a very strong side albeit handing a "first-team debut'" to Milne, a well-known right-back in the reserves, Newcastle "A".

Key Events		
First Half		
0 – 1		John Drummond
1 – 1		Tom Crate
Second Half		
2 – 1		William Milne
3 – 1		Willie Thompson
4 – 1		Willie Thompson
5 – 1		Tom Crate

Sheffield won the toss and Thompson for Newcastle took the kick-off, but the visitors worked their way into the home territory, Miller relieving the danger with a strong clearance. This allowed the Newcastle forward quintet to take advantage, but they did not do so for long. Retaking possession Sheffield charged at a blistering pace and Drummond gave them an early lead with a very clever shot.

Barely three minutes had elapsed, and the home crowd were stunned into silence!

From the restart the Newcastle forwards got well away and forced a corner. This was well placed in, but Thompson sent his header wide. Having somewhat the better of matters now Newcastle saw Creilly and Graham putting in some excellent work. Controlling the play Newcastle slowed the pace and exercised caution in their frequent attacks as Sheffield had the occasional sally forwards to demonstrate they were still a force to be reckoned with. Graham having to make a couple of timely interventions and the goal scorer Drummond shooting past.

For Newcastle Milne made a good run up and his centre was collected by Wallace, but he also shot past. In making a saving intervention McKane put a long kick out which Quinn received and sent the ball across the goal to Milne who missed with a swift shot. Newcastle were defending well and making opportunities up front but the forwards were showing weakness in front of goal. Quinn had a fine opportunity but headed past and Milne had a shot finely saved by Wood but in any event he was offside.

However, around about the half-hour mark another dash forward by Newcastle saw Quinn put in a really fine centre which Crate sent through for the equaliser, much to the delight of the spectators.

Play was then even through to half-time but both sides had good opportunities the pick of them being a shot from Thompson which sailed narrowly over the bar and Lowery having to make a clever save from Hill.

Where there been some periods of even play in the first half the same could not be said about the second, Newcastle simply dominated proceedings. Sheffield never gave in but every time they got near the home citadel the Newcastle half-backs frustrated their movements. Rarely did they get through this line and when they did Jeffrey and Miller were in grand form and Lowery was almost like one of the spectators as opposed to being a participant.

The lead for Newcastle came when Wood was feeble in kicking away a long, fast shot from Thompson and Milne dashed onto the loose ball to send it through. The third goal came courtesy of a rush down by Milne and Wallace with the ball being fed to Thompson who scored with a stinging shot. Goal number four came after a corner was well delivered and Thompson collected to send through from close range. Number five arrived just before time was called and it was Crate putting in another fine shot.

Game: 13 ~ Saturday, November 18th, 1893		vs. Northwich Victoria
Competition: Division 2	**Venue:** Drill Field	**Gate:** 1,000

Northwich Victoria	5-3	Newcastle United
Goal, George Hornby; *backs*, William Guest, William Postles; *half-backs*, George Savage, Jack Mates, Patrick Finnerhan; *forwards*, Thomas Scanlan, William Henry "Billy" Meredith, Harry Bailey, Harry Bray, George A. Drinkwater.		*Goal*, William Lowery; *backs*, Harry Jeffrey, James Miller; *half-backs*, Bobby Creilly, Willie Graham, Joe McKane; *forwards*, Joe Wallace, Toby Gillespy, Willie Thompson, Tom Crate, Charlie Quinn.
Scorer(s): Meredith (3), Scanlan, Bailey		Scorer(s): Willie Thompson, OG [Scanlan], Tom Crate

Referee: Mr. W Roche (Liverpool)

Eight-goal Thriller goes to Victoria

From the start to the finish there was an almost gale-force wind blowing, one which was piercingly cold too. In accompaniment to this there were intermittent driving snow and sleet storms. Any delusions of playing "football" were pretty much null and void. The atrocious conditions coupled with the recent terrible form of the two teams dictated that this game was strictly for the "diehard fan".

Coming into this game Newcastle had won only two of their opening eight league games, drawn one and lost the other five, the last being a 5-1 drubbing by Liverpool at Anfield. However, they were coming into this game on the back of a 5-1 victory in a "friendly" fixture played against Division 1 opposition, Sheffield United, albeit a weakened Sheffield eleven.

The situation at Northwich was even worse than Newcastle's. They were firmly stuck at the foot of the table, as in their preceding nine games they had won just one and lost all eight of the others. Across those games they had scored only eight goals and conceded a mammoth 31.

Despite all this there was still a good compliment of spectators, no less than 1,000 people turning out to watch this league fixture.

Key Events	
First Half	
0 - 1	Willie Thompson
Second Half	
1 - 1	Billy Meredith
1 - 2	OG [Scanlan]
1 - 3	Tom Crate
2 - 3	Billy Meredith
3 - 3	Billy Meredith
4 - 3	Thomas Scanlan
5 - 3	Harry Bailey

Newcastle won the toss and very naturally choose to play with the very strong wind behind them and so the game began with them facing the slight incline. Owing to the storm anything like the scientific football oft demonstrated by the Newcastle forwards was to no avail, passing with any degree of accuracy was almost an impossibility. It took very little effort for Newcastle to keep the ball in the Victoria half of the pitch, and equally it was with great difficulty that they tried any attempts on the Newcastle goal.

Consequently, being kept on the defensive, Hornby, the Victoria custodian, *being tested time and time again*, had to be on his finest mettle to repulse the continual attacks. His defence was often deceived by the wind, and in truthfulness the Newcastle forwards were equally deceived, and it was a case of 'potluck' in most cases as to where the efforts they sent in would eventually fall.

Of the one or two sporadic attacks that Victoria were able to muster, both Finnerhan and Meredith showed to good advantage. Each were to test the Newcastle custodian, Lowery, but he was to prove quite clever in stopping them.

With all the action centred around Hornby and his defence it must be acknowledged that, in all fairness, they performed admirably. They were however ably assisted by that same strong wind that was keeping them pinned into their own half as a great many attempts by Newcastle were blown harmlessly away, going either side of the post or invariably over the bar.

Numerous corners were won as clearances from the defence were blown back over the line but most attempts to send any decent cross in from them, even those delivered low down were unsuccessful. Equally numerous throw-ins and goal kicks were the order of the day, there being no fluency to the game it was a great frustration to players and fans alike.

Then, around five minutes before half time, the breakthrough arrived and it was in favour of the visitors. A great scrimmage developed in front of the Victoria goal during which Thompson was able to force the ball home.

It was said of the Victoria men that the battle against the elements, and the "*not-to-be-despised body of Northerners*" took a lot of steel out of them, with "*a cup of hot coffee reviving them*" during the interval!

The coffee must have certainly worked as within five minutes of the restart Victoria brought about the equaliser courtesy of a fine shot by Meredith. However, for the next ten-minutes or so it was Newcastle who held the ascendancy and with a goal courtesy of a shot being deflected off Scanlan and bounding into the net, and another from a fine opportunist shot by Crate, they had given themselves a two-goal cushion. For a short time, it looked like the Victorians showed signs of breaking up and as the clock ticked down, with no success coming their way, some sections of the crowd began to whistle the "Dead March".

They were however more than a little premature as Victoria went on to score four more goals, turning a two-goal deficit into a quite remarkable two-goal victory.

The first two of the four came from Meredith, bringing up his hat-trick, Scanlan then righting the wrong of his unfortunate own goal and the final goal scored by Bailey within the last minute of the allotted time.

So ended a truly dramatic turnaround in favour of the Victoria. Very few, if any, would have anticipated such a high scoring game, nor the eventual outcome. Seven goals being scored in the second half, quite a performance under the circumstances.

Pos.	Team	Plyd	W	D	L	F	A	G.Avg.	Pts.
1	Liverpool	12	9	3	0	35	9	3.8889	21
2	Notts County	13	8	2	3	28	14	2.0000	18
3	Small Heath	12	9	0	3	38	22	1.7273	18
4	Burton Swifts	12	8	1	3	39	21	1.8571	17
5	Burslem Port Vale	11	8	0	3	35	24	1.4583	16
6	Grimsby Town	11	6	0	5	35	27	1.2963	12
7	Lincoln City	9	4	2	3	17	18	0.9444	10
8	Woolwich Arsenal	10	4	1	5	18	27	0.6667	9
9	Crewe Alexandra	8	3	1	4	15	15	1.0000	7
10	Ardwick	12	3	1	8	22	23	0.9565	7
11	Walsall Town Swifts	11	3	1	7	13	27	0.4815	7
12	Newcastle United	9	2	1	6	18	24	0.7500	5
13	Rotherham Town	10	2	1	7	14	28	0.5000	5
14	Northwich Victoria	10	2	0	8	13	34	0.3824	4
15	Middlesbrough Ironopolis	10	2	0	8	7	34	0.2059	4

Game: 14 ~ Saturday, November 25th, 1893 — vs. Liverpool

Competition: Division 2   **Venue: St James's Park**   **Gate: 2,000**

Newcastle United 0-0 Liverpool

Goal, William Lowery; *backs*, Harry Jeffrey, Tom Rodger; *half-backs*, Bobby Creilly, Willie Graham, Joe McKane; *forwards*, Charlie Quinn, Tom Crate, Willie Thompson, Toby Gillespy, Joe Wallace.

Goal, Matt McQueen; *backs*, Andrew Hannah, Duncan McLean; *half-backs*, David Henderson, Joe McQueen, Jim McBride; *forwards*, Patrick Gordon, Hugh McQueen, John McCartney, Douglas Dick, Thomas Bradshaw.

Kick-off: 2:30 PM

Surprising Stalemate in Return Encounter

This return league fixture was eagerly anticipated, perhaps more by the visitors than by the homesters given the result of the first encounter at Anfield. Liverpool were without McOwen, their trustworthy custodian, and McVean, their outside-right, due to influenza. Missing also from their front row was Stott, due to injury. Newcastle on the other hand were fielding a very strong eleven, if somewhat rearranged. Miller was missing from the back, Rodger dropped from his normal half-back position into his place and Toby Gillespy was again played up front.

Where Newcastle had started the Anfield game with forceful play but allowed themselves to 'drop off' there was no such slackening of their forcefulness this afternoon. They sustained a great earnestness and took the game to Liverpool at every opportunity. It took a very dogged stubbornness on behalf of the Liverpool defence to prevent a complete reversal of that Anfield scoreline.

With Lowery and his backs, Jeffrey and Rodger playing a very sturdy game indeed, and Graham being always to the fore in his tackling, the Liverpool forwards were made to look mediocre indeed. Their already weakened attack suffered a further blow when Gordon, around about the twenty-minute mark, saw a reappearance of an old strain in his leg, becoming quite lame and practically useless for the remainder of proceedings.

For all that Newcastle were playing a much better forward game than their opponents, they created very few clear-cut chances. Predominantly because of the sterling defence in front of them rather than any failings on their behalf.

Most of these chances came from corners conceded by what the Liverpool Mercury described as being the *"reprehensible habit of Joe McQue in frequently giving corners when at all pressed"*. Matt McQueen the Liverpool custodian, who played as frequently in an outfield position as he did in goal, was called upon repeatedly and it took his best efforts to repel a disaster. His younger brother by four years, Hugh, had a torrid time trying to play in the modified forward quintet of the Merseysiders.

As well as Matt McQueen filled McOwen's position he was ably supported by Hannah and McLean who were in splendid form and needed to be.

Newcastle sustained their constant pressure throughout the entirety of the game, and it was only down to the aforementioned that they could not get what would have been a deserved winner. However, once that has been said perhaps the defence of Liverpool were well deserved in keeping a clean sheet. The only thing that could be said with absolute certainty is that this was never going to be an Anfield scoreline, and the fact that they failed to register a goal was the correct outcome.

Thompson showed that he is a very capable centre, as well as captain. He kept his wings together, proffered numerous chances for Gillespy at outside left, and displayed some dashing play, stamp him as a first-rate man. Quinn performed well, particularly in the second half whilst his partner, Crate, was a little overenthusiastic at times. Gillespy and Wallace were the trickier and more troublesome of the two wings. All-in-all a good display from Newcastle against the league leaders who remain unbeaten, and a one that should stand them in good stead as their next league encounter is with second in the table, Notts County.

Pos.	Team	Plyd	W	D	L	F	A	G.Avg.	Pts.
1	Liverpool	13	9	4	0	35	9	3.8889	22
2	Notts County	15	9	2	4	34	16	2.1250	20
3	Small Heath	13	9	0	4	38	25	1.5200	18
4	Burslem Port Vale	12	9	0	3	36	24	1.5000	18
5	Burton Swifts	12	8	1	3	39	21	1.8571	17
6	Grimsby Town	11	6	0	5	35	27	1.2963	12
7	Lincoln City	9	4	2	3	17	18	0.9444	10
8	Woolwich Arsenal	10	4	1	5	18	27	0.6667	9
9	Crewe Alexandra	8	3	1	4	15	15	1.0000	7
10	Ardwick	12	3	1	8	22	23	0.9565	7
11	Walsall Town Swifts	11	3	1	7	13	27	0.4815	7
12	Newcastle United	10	2	2	6	18	24	0.7500	6
13	Middlesbrough Ironopolis	11	3	0	8	10	34	0.2941	6
14	Rotherham Town	10	2	1	7	14	28	0.5000	5
15	Northwich Victoria	11	2	0	9	14	40	0.3500	4

Game: 15 ~ Saturday, December 2nd, 1893 vs. Dipton Wanderers

Competition: Friendly **Venue:** Dipton **Gate:** 500

Dipton Wanderers 0-2 Newcastle United

Goal, R. Freek; *backs*, Jas. Key, T. Rowell; *half-backs*, F. Harte, E. Buck, R. Coates; *forwards*, S. Gardener, J. Gilliard, W. Coghlan, J. Hunter, T. Walker.

Scorer(s):

Goal, William Lowery; *backs*, Harry Jeffrey, Tom Rodger; *half-backs*, Bobby Creilly, Willie Graham, Joe McKane; *forwards*, Charlie Quinn, Tom Crate, Willie Thompson, Joe Wallace, A. N. Other.

Scorer(s): Willie Thompson, Charlie Quinn

Referee: Mr. Hogarth (Burnopfield)

Pleasant game ends in comfortable victory for Newcastle

Having no league engagement for today Newcastle arranged for a trip to County Durham and a friendly fixture with Northern Alliance team Dipton Wanderers. Unfortunately, there was not the interest that both teams would have hoped for, barely 500 people being present.

Key Events	
First Half	
0 – 1	Willie Thompson
0 – 2	Charlie Quinn

Newcastle won the toss and elected to play with the sun at their backs so Coghlan got the game underway for Dipton. Play at the beginning was quite even, each goal being visited in turn without being unduly threatened. Then, around about 20-minutes in, Rowell headed out a clearance which fell to Thompson who scored with a fast shot. Before many minutes had elapsed Quinn broke away on the right and beat Freek with a grand shot.

Dipton tried their best to reduce the deficit and with a beautiful run they got away ending when Coghlan brought a grand save out of Lowery. Just before the break Thompson had the ball in the back of the net once more but this third goal was disallowed for an offside.

The interval was but short and Newcastle were the team doing most of the pressing, but their shooting was of the weakest nature. Dipton made Lowery work hard on a couple of occasions but ultimately nothing further was added to the score and thus a pleasant game saw a United victory.

Game: 16 ~ Saturday, December 9th, 1893		vs. Notts County
Competition: Division 2	**Venue:** St James's Park	**Gate:** 3,000

Newcastle United	**3-0**	**Notts County**

Goal, William Lowery; ***backs***, Harry Jeffrey, Tom Rodger; ***half-backs***, Bobby Creilly, Willie Graham, Joe McKane; ***forwards***, Charlie Quinn, Tom Crate, Willie Thompson, Joe Wallace, Thomas Bartlett.

Scorer(s): Willie Thompson, Joe Wallace (2)

Goal, George Toone; ***backs***, T. Harper, Jack Hendry; ***half-backs***, Charlie Bramley, David Calderhead, A. Shelton; ***forwards***, Daniel Bruce, Sam Donnelly, Jimmy Logan, G. Kerr, Harry Daft.

Referee: Mr. J. Tomlinson (Sheffield)

Well-deserved revenge for Newcastle

Following the defeat by Notts County at Trent Bridge back in in October, by three goals to one, this return fixture was an eagerly awaited one and one which was looked upon with great interest, as evinced by the sizable crowd. This attendance being helped no doubt by fact that the weather was exceedingly fine, especially noting that we were a mere fortnight away from Christmas.

Key Events	
First Half	
1 – 0	Willie Thompson
Second Half	
2 – 0	Joe Wallace
3 – 0	Joe Wallace

Newcastle won the toss and elected to play against the hill, so Logan for Notts got the ball rolling.

The visiting forwards were immediately dispossessed, and the ball was taken well up the field, but the charge was stopped when a free-kick for 'hands' was awarded to "The Lambs". Taken by Bramley this enabled the Notts men to get dangerously near the home citadel and a short period of pressure was exerted but was ultimately fruitless as the ball was sent over the line.

Creilly headed out a long shot by Calderhead, and Rodger also saved cleverly. The Notts forwards made another rush, and Lowery saved under great difficulties, conceding a corner in doing so. The ball was excellently placed in but was got away. A long throw in by Bramley preceded a corner, which proved of no avail, and the home right wing ran the ball to the other end but Quinn, when close in, sent over the bar.

The visitors lost no time after the goal kick for, with good combination, they worked their way down the field, and pressed slightly, but the play on either side was only of a poor description. After a shot had been saved by Jeffrey, the loose ball was picked up by Wallace who made a short run up. He was stopped in his tracks by Calderhead who sent his return to the home goal, but the ball went past.

Notts soon had the upper hand again, and the home defence was called upon once more. The pressure being cleared for a while. A free kick in a good position for Notts was of no benefit to them the ball being sent wide of the goal. The "Lambs" came again with a rush, and Lowery cleverly saved at the expense of a corner, which proved abortive.

The home forwards then made a good run, but Calderhead was there again to stop further progression. He sent the ball towards the home goal, but Graham was quick and made the return. For a while the game was now played in midfield.

Notts were the ones to break this pattern and their forward line, with some clever play, travelled towards the Newcastle citadel. There they were met by a stout defence and Logan eventually sent the ball over the bar. Bartlett gained possession and made a short run, but he lost out to a challenge from Harper, his return was extremely feeble, and Newcastle easily retook possession and resumed the offensive. Getting into dangerous proximity of the Notts goal there was quite a scramble before the ball was sent behind.

Back came the Newcastle attack and Quinn sent in a marvellous cross which Harper was guilty of handling. With a free-kick in a very advantageous position Newcastle should have done better but the opportunity was wasted. Quinn once again led a charge up the wing and sent in a great shot which Toone only just managed to throw out. From the goal kick County again surged forwards but Rodger was there to frustrate them. A bit of mediocre play followed this period of excitement.

Notts made another effort and a quick fire shot from Donnelly found Lowery on the alert and he threw away. Newcastle then turned up the heat and some good play ensued, but it availed them nothing. Notts then again pressed but Graham relieved the pressure sending the ball to Quinn who made a good run, but the ball ended out of bounds. Both sides had another effort before the deadlock was finally broken.

Wallace and Thompson broke away with great speed. Playing the ball between themselves Thompson was the last in possession and eluding the defence sent the ball swiftly past Toone amidst great excitement. He soon after had another excellent shot but Toone was equal to that one. Notts tried to get back on terms but their effort was fruitless and there was no more scoring prior to the break.

The restart saw play of a very even character until, with some good work, Notts ran up and Kerr sent through what looked to be the equaliser, but he was rightly given offside. Newcastle then had a look in, playing well, but Graham sent over the line. Continuing to maintain the upper hand Newcastle were awarded a free-kick in a promising position but could not turn it to their advantage. Play was then of an uninteresting character until Newcastle were awarded another free-kick for a foul. McKane sent in and it was only narrowly over the bar.

At this juncture Creilly received an accidental kick to the head and was carried off the field of play with visible signs of blood. With a man advantage Notts forced the play and made some good attempts, Daft testing Lowery with an effort. Thompson had a good run down accompanied by Quinn but could not capitalise. Notts got another look in and whilst their attack was severe it proved useless, the ball going harmlessly behind following a loose scrimmage.

Wallace took possession following the kick in and sent well down. Thompson followed up and endeavoured to make Harper give a corner but was unsuccessful. *It was around this time that Creilly resumed play with his head heavily bandaged.* Bartlett sent in a grand shot, which Toone sent well out, and some excitement was aroused by a brisk attack on the part of the home team. Bartlett continued to do good work, and gave to Thompson, who shot, Toone throwing away. Jeffrey sent in a ball from midfield, and it went straight to the Notts goal. Toone managed to effect a save despite being charged by Thompson and Bartlett. The ball did not get travel too far out before Wallace secured it and shot through from short distance amidst loudly expressed enthusiasm.

From the kick-off the home team returned, Hendry, Bramley, and the other defenders had to do all they knew to prevent another score. Thompson just missed a grand chance, but he could not be blamed, and at the other end after a quick run, Jeffrey relieved some shots by the visiting forwards. Graham was then forced into conceding a corner, but the ball was sent behind by Kerr. Newcastle then got a corner of their own, but they were equally unsuccessful.

Undeterred the Newcastle forwards worked together splendidly, and Crate looked to have scored with a fine effort but was ruled offside.

The Notts forwards followed with a nice run but they did not long retain possession, for Rodger relieved and sent to midfield. Newcastle maintained the upper hand. Rodger put in a long kick, which was followed by a scrimmage in front of the Notts goal from which the ball was sent behind. Quinn returned the goal kick, passing it to Thompson. He in turn played the ball to Wallace who drove through a shot for Newcastle's third goal.

Within what little time there was left there was no great drama, neither goal being put under any great pressure. Newcastle were comfortable with their three goal lead, Notts seemed settled to the fact they were beaten and so revenge for Trent Bridge defeat was complete.

Pos.	Team	Plyd	W	D	L	F	A	G.Avg.	Pts.
1	Liverpool	15	11	4	0	41	9	4.5556	26
2	Small Heath	16	12	0	4	54	26	2.0769	24
3	Notts County	17	10	2	5	40	21	1.9048	22
4	Burslem Port Vale	15	10	1	4	43	30	1.4333	21
5	Burton Swifts	14	8	1	5	41	29	1.4138	17
6	Grimsby Town	14	7	0	7	41	37	1.1081	14
7	Lincoln City	10	5	2	3	25	20	1.2500	12
8	Woolwich Arsenal	11	4	2	5	20	29	0.6897	10
9	Ardwick	14	4	1	9	26	27	0.9630	9
10	Crewe Alexandra	11	3	3	5	18	23	0.7826	9
11	Newcastle United	11	3	2	6	21	24	0.8750	8
12	Middlesbrough Ironopolis	12	4	0	8	16	35	0.4571	8
13	Walsall Town Swifts	13	3	2	8	14	31	0.4516	8
14	Rotherham Town	12	2	1	9	17	42	0.4048	5
15	Northwich Victoria	13	2	1	10	16	50	0.3200	5

Supplementary notes...

Various reports are in polar opposition to each other as to how this game played out. Some say it descended into "*rough play*" others say it was "*a thoroughly gentlemanly game*". As always which is correct is ultimately up to you, just be aware that the contradictions exist.

NB: Irrespective of whether the game was rough or not the kick Creilly received to his head bears no suspicion that it was anything other than accidental.

Game: 17 ~ Saturday, December 16th, 1893		vs. Small Heath
Competition: Division 2	**Venue:** Coventry Road	**Gate:** 3,000

Small Heath	1-4	Newcastle United
Goal, George Hollis; *backs*, George Smith, William Reynolds; *half-backs*, William Ollis, Caesar Jenkyns, Edwin Devey; *forwards*, Jack Hallam, Billy Walton, Frank Mobley, Fred Wheldon, Tommy Hands.		*Goal*, William Lowery; *backs*, Harry Jeffrey, Tom Rodger; *half-backs*, Bobby Creilly, Willie Graham, Joe McKane; *forwards*, Charlie Quinn, Robert Willis, Willie Thompson, Joe Wallace, Tom Crate.
Scorer(s): Jack Hallam		Scorer(s): Robert Willis, Tom Crate, Joe Wallace, Willie Graham
	Referee: Mr. T. Armitt (Leek)	

Unexpected, but richly deserved, victory

Whilst Small Heath were in the lofty position of second in the league and Newcastle somewhat below them in eleventh position one needed to reconcile this with the fact that Small Heath had played five games more than Newcastle. However, even with five wins Newcastle could still not breach the gap, so this was universally looked upon as being a hard fixture for them. Both sides were well represented, and the weather was more akin to spring than winter.

KEY EVENTS	
First Half	
0 – 1	Robert Willis
Second Half	
0 – 2	Tom Crate
1 – 2	*Jack Hallam*
1 – 3	Joe Wallace
1 – 4	Willie Graham

From the very kick-off Newcastle took up the role of the aggressors and kept the Small Heath goal under constant pressure. For fully seven minutes a series of desperate scrimmages were played out and the Small Heath backs, try as they may, could not get the ball away. It was indeed only by ill-luck that the Newcastle forwards could not turn this superiority into goals.

At length Wheldon and Hands made some ground down the left wing, but they conceded a free-kick and from it Jeffrey sent the ball back in. Crate collected and made a great shot at goal the ball striking the post and rebounding into play. Willis was the quickest to react and smartly sent it into the net.

Maintaining their strong grip on the game Newcastle kept up the forward momentum and Wallace was unlucky with an effort that dropped onto the top of the bar. Small Heath were having the utmost difficulty in getting out of their own half and only two noteworthy efforts, one from Mobley the other from Jenkins were registered. A most one-sided half came to an end without further score.

Upon resumption following the interval there was no let up in the Newcastle pressure. Wallace made a clever run down the left wing, easily dribbled his way past Smith, then delivered in a fine cross. Hollis pushed the ball out but it went straight to Crate who easily shot it back at him and into the net.

Going further behind seemed to inject a bit of urgency into the Small Heath forwards and Wheldon and Hands make a remarkable run down their wing, centred for Hallam and he headed home to half the deficit.

From this point on the Newcastle forwards did just about anything they liked. Wallace, pulled up twice for offside, was in the thick of things in the home goal where a scrimmage was taking place as the ball rose out of it he headed home nicely.

Newcastle then had three corners in quick succession and from the last of these Graham received and smartly shot through. Four goals scored, one conceded, was not too far removed from what many expected – but for the homesters not the visitors! A remarkable, and completely deserved, victory for Newcastle.

Pos.	Team	Plyd	W	D	L	F	A	G.Avg.	Pts.
1	Liverpool	15	11	4	0	41	9	4.5556	26
2	Small Heath	17	12	0	5	55	30	1.8333	24
3	Notts County	18	10	3	5	40	21	1.9048	23
4	Burslem Port Vale	16	11	1	4	46	31	1.4839	23
5	Burton Swifts	15	8	1	6	42	32	1.3125	17
6	Grimsby Town	14	7	0	7	41	37	1.1081	14
7	Lincoln City	10	5	2	3	25	20	1.2500	12
8	Newcastle United	12	4	2	6	25	25	1.0000	10
9	Woolwich Arsenal	11	4	2	5	20	29	0.6897	10
10	Ardwick	14	4	1	9	26	27	0.9630	9
11	Crewe Alexandra	11	3	3	5	18	23	0.7826	9
12	Middlesbrough Ironopolis	13	4	1	8	16	35	0.4571	9
13	Walsall Town Swifts	13	3	2	8	14	31	0.4516	8
14	Rotherham Town	12	2	1	9	17	42	0.4048	5
15	Northwich Victoria	13	2	1	10	16	50	0.3200	5

Game: 18 ~ Saturday, December 23rd, 1893 **vs. First Royal Scots**

Competition: Friendly **Venue:** St James's Park **Gate:** *fairly large*

Newcastle United	3-0	First Royal Scots

Goal, William Lowery; *backs*, Harry Jeffrey, Tom Rodger; *half-backs*, Bobby Creilly, Willie Graham, Joe McKane; *forwards*, Charlie Quinn, Robert Willis, John Law, Tom Crate, Joe Wallace.

Goal, Cpl. Bignall; *backs*, Sgt. Houston, Pte Beveridge; *half-backs*, Sgt. Gillies, Cpl. Mitchell, Cpl. McGregor; *forwards*, Pte Robertson, Cpl. Gilmour, QM Sgt. Guthrie, Cpl. Cormack, Pte Quin.

Scorer(s): Tom Crate (2), Robert Willis

Referee: Mr. William Tiffin (Northumberland FA)

Newcastle's Festive Season begins with a Win

In the absence of a league game today Newcastle organised a friendly with the First Royal Scots who were stationed at York. The First Royal's had a reputation of being one of the finest of the Army teams and included an old friend in Corporal J. Gilmour who had been a stalwart of Newcastle West End and Blyth and a few other minor sides in the neighbourhood.

In fine weather for the time of year there was a fairly large crowd, which was especially pleasing to see, not only because Christmas was but two days away, but also because Newcastle had league fixtures on Christmas Day, Boxing Day and the day after that, which were all away from home, so the revenue generated by today's attendance was most welcome.

KEY EVENTS

First Half	
1 – 0	Tom Crate
Second Half	
2 – 0	Tom Crate
3 – 0	Robert Willis

Newcastle got the game underway, playing up the hill, and without any further ado set about the Scot's goal, arriving there with some very clever passing and movement. The assault on the visitor's defence was well sustained until the pressure was relieved by Wallace sending his shot past. From the goal-kick the soldiers worked their way up to the Newcastle goal with some solid play, but the home defence was strong and resilient, no way through for the Scots on this occasion.

A rather splendid run up from the home forward quintet saw the Scots again come under pressure. Crate sent in a shot which was kicked out by the custodian, but it was immediately returned in. Again, Bignall was called into action and made an admirable save at the expense of a corner, which proved fruitless. It was evident that the Newcastle forwards had the measure of their counterparts but were not inclined to overexert themselves, had they done so the consensus was they would have undoubtedly scored.

They however did keep up the pressure and pressed incessantly. In one such attack Wallace was very unfortunate to see his effort go past very close indeed.

Making a breakaway Robertson got down well but Lowery was quite comfortable in dealing with his resulting shot from distance and cleared with his feet. There was a return charge from the military men, but this was in turn cleared by Rodger. The home back was again called upon and acquitted himself commendably and started a move which gave Newcastle their best opportunity up to this point. Taking the ball well up he lofted the ball to Quinn but Bignall pulled off a save of some merit. Quinn proved to be the dangerman once again as he put in another fine shot which was blocked and cleared. Newcastle immediately sent the ball back in. This resulted in quite a scrimmage around the Scots' goal and from it Crate managed to put the leather through to open the scoring for the homesters.

Following the goal Newcastle continued to press, though without any great urgency. Their laxity let in the visitors and Lowery was called into action as he dealt with an effort from Gilmour, but it was from distance and he was in no real danger. Willis then tried a long shot which failed and a resulting surge up to the Newcastle goal saw Jeffrey intervening with a fine headed clearance which looked as if it would be an equalising goal, indeed if not for Jeffrey it would have been. Newcastle then had one of the finest chances as Willis sent in, but his shot went agonisingly close, but past the mark. Being the only other noteworthy action when the whistle concluded the half nothing more had been scored.

Gilmour restarted following the interval, but Newcastle quickly took possession and rushed down, the ball however being ran over the line. From the goal-kick possession once again was gained by the homesters and with a renewed sense of vigour they assailed the visitor's goal. The pressure only being relieved when Wallace sent the ball behind. From that short spurt of excitement, the game was transferred to midfield and play became exceedingly poor, neither side showing anything like the form both possessed.

A free-kick was awarded to Newcastle and Jeffrey sent the ball well in but Crate could not get on the end of it, and it sailed wide of the posts. Not long after another ball was sent in and this time Quinn was the guilty party as he failed to connect. There was now however something of a mini-revival in the exertions of the Newcastle forwards and they continued to press. Creilly sent in a cross-shot which Crate guided on its way with a fine header and the leather was put through, two to Newcastle, two to Crate.

There then followed a change of formation for Newcastle as Crate came into the centre-forward position and Law went to outside-left. This led to the Scots' defence being severely taxed indeed, though without any success on the goal front. They did however manage to win a corner which was very well placed by Wallace but Bignall managed to fist it away and thus launched a counter-attack on behalf of the visitors, this did not however get much further than deep midfield.

Newcastle won another corner, which was safely got away but the relief upon the Scots' defence was short-lived and with a shot from distance Quinn was unlucky. The ball was sent in again by Law which Bignall again fisted away and Crate headed over the bar. The pressure was intense on the visitor's defence but the numerous shots from the home forwards all went wide of the posts. The game was then said to become quite farcical.

Breaking the banality, a fine display of heading by Creilly, Jeffrey and Crate saw Newcastle advance well into the visitors' half. The ball was sent to Willis who dashed up and sent in a cross which Law collected, and he sent in a hot shot which Bignall managed, with difficulty, to push away but unfortunately for him Willis had kept up his momentum and rushing in the ex-Shankhouse man banged home the third goal for Newcastle.

Trying salvage something from the game the Scots' sallied forward and Lowery made a save from a weak shot. Regaining possession, the Scots tried again without success as the ball went wide of the posts. From then until the close of play Newcastle pressed but were unable to add to their score. So, the game ended with an easy victory when truth be told, and a Merry Christmas, morning at least, was ensured for the Newcastle following.

Game: 19 ~ Monday, December 25th, 1893   vs. **Middlesbrough Ironopolis**

Competition: Division 2   **Venue:** Paradise Ground   **Gate:** 2,000

Middlesbrough Ironopolis   **1-1**   **Newcastle United**

Goal, Roger Ord; *backs*, John Bell, John Sidney Sid Oliver; *half-backs*, Duncan McNair, Jimmy Grewer, Henry Allport; *forwards*, Fergus Hunt, John Garbutt, J. M. Mooney, Sandy Wallace, Thomas Hunter.

Scorer(s): Jimmy Grewer

Goal, William Lowery; *backs*, Harry Jeffrey, Tom Rodger; *half-backs*, Bobby Creilly, Willie Graham, Joe McKane; *forwards*, Charlie Quinn, Robert Willis, Willie Thompson, Joe Wallace, Tom Crate.

Scorer(s): Tom Crate

Referee: Mr. G. Shutt

Merry Christmas from 'Paradise'?

They might call the Middlesbrough Ironopolis home ground Paradise, but it was anything but that today! It certainly wasn't Christmas Card weather either. Yes, it was very cold, but there was not a single snowflake in sight, instead there was a wind that was extremely gusty, and the rain teemed down sporadically throughout the course of the game. Given these conditions, plus the fact it was after all Christmas day, it was very surprising to see a crowd of around 2,000 spectators gathered around the enclosure.

KEY EVENTS		
First Half		
1 – 0	*Jimmy Grewer*	
1 – 1	**Tom Crate**	

Ironopolis, sitting third from bottom of the league were only a point behind Newcastle, so a win today would have seen them leapfrog over their opponents. However, they had played two more games than Newcastle, the last being a narrow defeat to Small Heath. That same Birmingham side being that which Newcastle beat so handsomely in their last league outing.

With the wind at their backs Ironopolis got the game underway. The wind however proved to be no real advantage to them as it was so gusty, its direction changing constantly.

The game started even, there were some nice combinations from both sides, and both quickly realised that to make any advantage the ball would need to be kept along, or as near as possible to, the ground.

After these very early exchanges Ironopolis seemed to adapt to the conditions slightly quicker as it was they who showed up first. Applying a fair amount of pressing they worked their way into the Newcastle quarters and set about making life difficult for Lowery and his defence. It was not long before their pressure paid off either. Two very splendid attempts were made, with Lowery equal to both. However, when the third shot came in, though it was from a fair way out, the rapidity of the shot completely surprised him and into the net it went, much to the delight of the home crowd.

This reversal irked the Newcastle side and it brought about a change in urgency of their play. They went looking for the equaliser immediately, and it was not long before they got it. With good combination down the wing the ball was played to Crate who came inside a few yards and from around twenty-yards out he struck a beauty of a shot, that may or may not have been assisted by the wing, but in any event completely beat Ord and nestled into the net.

The second half was said to be nearly all Newcastle. However, little did their dominance count for anything as no matter how hard they pressed they couldn't break down the 'Nops defence. So, at the full-time whistle, with the scores still one-apiece, they had to settle for a draw and a point each. Both Tyneside and Teesside having an equally Merry Christmas.

Supplementary notes...

Various newspaper reports have a Newcastle United player named "Tolson" as being the scorer of their goal, however, records show that there has never been a player called Tolson at Newcastle United (*nor East End or West End either*). At first one thought that it would be fair to assume that the reporter(s) had meant Thompson (Willie). On checking other sources, it can be found that Newcastle's goal is accredited to Tom Crate.

Further analysis of the statistics clearly supports that it was indeed Crate who scored the goal. This is simply because if the goal was accredited to Thompson his total would be 48 and not 47, which everyone agrees upon, further if you do not accredit it to Crate then his total would only be 16 instead of the universally agreed 17.

It must also be noted that there exists various reports that attribute Ironopolis going into the break with a one-nil lead, meaning Newcastle's goal scored by Crate was in the second half. Equally various are the reports which indicate, *as I do in this report*, that it was scored in the first half, indeed "very soon after" Ironopolis had scored. This is probably due to the syndication of reports between the differing news outlets and so, whilst they may be many, the numbers don't necessarily equate to accuracy. However, you need to be aware of such reports so that you can make up your own mind as to which to subscribe to. I would hate to see you losing a 'pub quiz' on this one!

Pos.	Team	Plyd	W	D	L	F	A	G.Avg.	Pts.
1	Liverpool	15	11	4	0	41	9	4.5556	26
2	Small Heath	18	13	0	5	57	31	1.8387	26
3	Notts County	18	10	3	5	40	21	1.9048	23
4	Burslem Port Vale	17	11	1	5	47	35	1.3429	23
5	Burton Swifts	16	8	2	6	43	33	1.3030	18
6	Lincoln City	12	6	3	3	32	22	1.4545	15
7	Grimsby Town	14	7	0	7	41	37	1.1081	14
8	Woolwich Arsenal	12	5	2	5	24	30	0.8000	12
9	Newcastle United	13	4	3	6	26	26	1.0000	11
10	Walsall Town Swifts	14	4	2	8	17	31	0.5484	10
11	Middlesbrough Ironopolis	15	4	2	9	18	38	0.4737	10
12	Ardwick	14	4	1	9	26	27	0.9630	9
13	Crewe Alexandra	12	3	3	6	19	29	0.6552	9
14	Rotherham Town	12	2	1	9	17	42	0.4048	5
15	Northwich Victoria	14	2	1	11	16	53	0.3019	5

Game: 20 ~ Tuesday, December 26th, 1893 **vs. Walsall Town Swifts**

Competition: Division 2 **Venue:** West Bromwich Road **Gate:** 5,000

Walsall Town Swifts	1-2	Newcastle United

Goal, Jimmy Warner; *backs*, John Thomas Tom Bayley, Robert Smellie; *half-backs*, Sandy Holmes, R. Cook, Norman Forsyth; *forwards*, Joe Lofthouse, Walter McWhinnie, David Copeland, Charlie Leatherbarrow, Joe O'Brien.

Scorer(s): David Copeland

Referee: Mr. A.G. Hines (Notts)

Goal, William Lowery; *backs*, Harry Jeffrey, Tom Rodger; *half-backs*, Bobby Creilly, Willie Graham, Joe McKane; *forwards*, Tom Crate, Charlie Quinn, Willie Thompson, Joe Wallace, John Law.

Scorer(s): Joe Wallace (2)

Wallace to the Rescue

This match was played at West Bromwich Road before a sizable throng of holiday spectators, though just how many that was is open to great debate [*see note]. It is reported that the start of this match was delayed somewhat. The Glasgow Herald putting the delay at twenty-minutes, whilst the Walsall Advertiser just say that Newcastle were very late in appearing. The Advertiser goes on to add that when they did arrive *"the men bore traces of having recently had intimate acquaintance with mother earth"* with no expansion on their observations. Make of that what you will...

Key Events		
First Half		
1 – 0	David Copeland	
1 – 1	Joe Wallace	
1 – 2	Joe Wallace	

The home team started and sent the ball uphill, and immediately down came Newcastle and put Warner under pressure. This did not last for long as the Swifts raced up and forced a corner. Lowrey made three terrific saves and little relief was afforded to the Newcastle defence as Walsall played with some considerable dash. Two unsuccessful corners were won by them prior to gaining a third corner from this one Copeland took possession and shot grandly through, this after around ten minutes of play had elapsed.

From the centre kick Walsall attacked again with McWhinnie putting in an excellent effort which went just wide. For a good deal of time Newcastle had to act almost entirely on the defensive, but gradually they improved their game and began to take on the role of the aggressor and pressurised Warner and his defence. Thompson, who had been playing a dashing game at centre put the ball to Wallace who sent through a grand shot thus scoring a deserved equalising goal.

The game now became most exciting, the homesters perhaps having slightly the better of play and certainly the worst of luck as several good attempts at retaking the lead went begging. Both sides gained corners from which nothing emerged, and the visitors put Warner under some severe pressure, but he preserved his charge.

However, with half-time on the horizon, Newcastle took the lead, the opportunity resulting from a well-placed corner. The ball came to Wallace who got his and Newcastle's second goal with a fine driving shot of which Warner had no chance of reaching. The game then became very frenetic, though even in nature, so-much-so that at the half time whistle matters were unchanged.

On changing over following the interval the home team again were bright and were dangerously near scoring. Even play then ensued and nothing remarkable occurred until midway through the half when Walsall were awarded a penalty. Lofthouse, dashing through, was tripped within the twelve-yard line and the referee had no doubts about it being a penalty and Newcastle didn't really argue the case.

Lofthouse took the spot-kick but it was saved by Lowery. Unfortunately for Newcastle the ball fell straight back to Lofthouse, however with his second attempt he hit the crossbar and the ball went out of play. A very lucky escape, *double escape indeed*, for Newcastle! The game after was once again very even in nature though the homesters were perhaps the most frequently dangerous, but their forwards proved to be very weak in front of goal. Lofthouse was the exception and was noticeable for some smart centres, but he received little support from the remainder of the vanguard. Towards the end of the second half Walsall were reduced to ten men as Smellie had to retire through injury.

Pos.	Team	Plyd	W	D	L	F	A	G.Avg.	Pts.
1	Liverpool	15	11	4	0	41	9	4.5556	26
2	Small Heath	18	13	0	5	57	31	1.8387	26
3	Notts County	18	10	3	5	40	21	1.9048	23
4	Burslem Port Vale	17	11	1	5	47	35	1.3429	23
5	Burton Swifts	16	8	2	6	43	33	1.3030	18
6	Grimsby Town	15	8	0	7	44	38	1.1579	16
7	Lincoln City	13	6	3	4	34	25	1.3600	15
8	Newcastle United	14	5	3	6	28	27	1.0370	13
9	Woolwich Arsenal	13	5	2	6	25	33	0.7576	12
10	Middlesbrough Ironopolis	16	5	2	9	21	40	0.5250	12
11	Ardwick	15	5	1	9	29	29	1.0000	11
12	Walsall Town Swifts	15	4	2	9	18	33	0.5455	10
13	Crewe Alexandra	12	3	3	6	19	29	0.6552	9
14	Rotherham Town	13	2	1	10	19	45	0.4222	5
15	Northwich Victoria	14	2	1	11	16	53	0.3019	5

Supplementary notes...

The vast majority of reports quote the gate for this match being 5,000, and going with consensus so do I. However, the following needs to be brought to your attention.

According to the Walsall Town official website the capacity of the West Bromwich Road ground was just over 4,500, also, the official website intimates that the capacity was never reached. The website states *"Walsall's best attendance for a home league game at West Bromwich Road was 4,000 v Liverpool on 11th November 1893"*. So according to them all the newspaper reports are incorrect, and by default so am I.

One further thing to note, you may find reports accrediting the Newcastle goals to Thompson and Law, statistics do not appear to bear out those suppositions.

This little snippet is taken directly from the pages of the Newcastle Daily Chronicle circulated on 03/01/1894. Perhaps it should have waited until April 1st?

> *"At Walsall one of the United players ran so swiftly down the wing that his shoe laces caught fire, and the referee had to call his attention to this fact. The story may be a fact!"*

Honestly, don't blame me, that is exactly what was printed.

Game: 21 ~ Wednesday, December 27th, 1893 — vs. Crewe Alexandra

Competition: Division 2 **Venue:** Alexandra Recreation Ground **Gate:** 2,000

Crewe Alexandra 1-1 Newcastle United

Goal, Edward Hickton; *backs*, Harry Stafford, Alfred Cope; *half-backs*, Herbert Crawford, J. Rosie, Walter Cartwright; *forwards*, Robert Roberts, James Peake, Joseph Benton Sandham, Sammy Barnett, Joseph Burrows.

Scorer(s): Sammy Barnett

Goal, William Lowery; *backs*, Harry Jeffrey, Tom Rodger; *half-backs*, Bobby Creilly, Willie Graham, Joe McKane; *forwards*, Charlie Quinn, Robert Willis, Willie Thompson, Tom Crate, Joe Wallace.

Scorer(s): Willie Graham

Referee: Mr. R.E. Lythgoe (Liverpool)

Lucky Newcastle earn a point

Newcastle were extremely lucky to come away from this game with a draw. Alexandra had a goal disallowed in the second half and some desperate defending, and the woodwork, aided in *Newcastle's* rescue.

This was Newcastle's second League engagement in the Midlands during the holiday period and their first meeting with the Alexandra. The weather was fair, and there was a gate of circa 2,000 spectators assembled.

Key Events

First Half
1 – 0	Sammy Barnett
1 – 1	**Willie Graham**

Stafford, the Alexandra captain, won the toss and it was the homesters who got the game underway. They immediately forced Newcastle back into their own quarters, Lowery and his defence being subjected to great pressure. For all the strong play from the homesters, with scrimmages galore in the United goal area they could not turn that advantage into goals, no matter what they tried.

The brave defence of Newcastle managed to hold out for around fifteen minutes before the seemingly inevitable arose and they went behind when Alexandra scored "a capital goal". It was from another scrimmage in the goal area and the ball broke to Barnett who put a fine shot through.

Play after the goal settled into an even pattern each side making efforts on goal but always meeting with very good defensive play. From a concerted Newcastle attack, the whole forward quintet making a rush for the Alexandra goal, Cope was forced into conceding a corner. The ball was well placed for Graham to secure the equaliser. Nothing further of note occurred up to interval and when it was called the score remained at one goal each.

In the second half Alexandra again took up the offensive from the very beginning and it was not long before they thought they had the lead once more, but the point was disallowed. Newcastle then pressed, but found Hickton to be in quite remarkable form in the Alexandra goal. Time after time when Newcastle broke the defence he remained as the last line and foiled their utmost determined attacks.

Then back came the homesters to again take up the running, and several times had the harshest of luck. They saw their efforts striking players, they hit the bar, and the uprights were struck too. Following each, as the ball rebounded into play, it was the defence of Newcastle reacting first with desperate, but successful clearances.

Towards the finish Newcastle mounted an attack, and looked dangerous from a corner, but no more scoring was done, and the result was a draw of one goal each. On the balance of play the draw was a fair result but on the number of chances created Alexandra were well ahead and would be considering themselves unlucky in not taking both points which would have put them only one behind Newcastle with two "games in hand".

Pos.	Team	Plyd	W	D	L	F	A	G.Avg.	Pts.
1	Liverpool	15	11	4	0	41	9	4.5556	26
2	Small Heath	18	13	0	5	57	31	1.8387	26
3	Notts County	18	10	3	5	40	21	1.9048	23
4	Burslem Port Vale	17	11	1	5	47	35	1.3429	23
5	Burton Swifts	16	8	2	6	43	33	1.3030	18
6	Grimsby Town	15	8	0	7	44	38	1.1579	16
7	Lincoln City	13	6	3	4	34	25	1.3600	15
8	Newcastle United	15	5	4	6	29	28	1.0357	14
9	Woolwich Arsenal	13	5	2	6	25	33	0.7576	12
10	Middlesbrough Ironopolis	16	5	2	9	21	40	0.5250	12
11	Ardwick	15	5	1	9	29	29	1.0000	11
12	Crewe Alexandra	13	3	4	6	20	30	0.6667	10
13	Walsall Town Swifts	15	4	2	9	18	33	0.5455	10
14	Rotherham Town	13	2	1	10	19	45	0.4222	5
15	Northwich Victoria	14	2	1	11	16	53	0.3019	5

Game: 22 ~ Saturday, December 30th, 1893   vs. **Burslem Port Vale**

Competition: Division 2   **Venue:** St James's Park   **Gate:** 3,000

Newcastle United	2-1	Burslem Port Vale

Goal, William Lowery; *backs*, Harry Jeffrey, Tom Rodger; *half-backs*, Bobby Creilly, Willie Graham, Joe McKane; *forwards*, Charlie Quinn, Robert Willis, Willie Thompson, Tom Crate, John Law.

Goal, Hugh MacKay; *backs*, George Youds, Bob Ramsay; *half-backs*, Fred Farrington, Bob McCrindle, Billy Elson; *forwards*, Jimmy Scarratt, Meshach Dean, Billy Beats, Alf Wood, Lewis Campbell.

Scorer(s): Bobby Creilly, Tom Crate

Scorer(s): Billy Beats

Referee: Mr. A. Cooper (Co. Durham)   Kick-off: 2:15 PM

Excellent game, excellent result. Let the New Year festivities commence early!

The visitors today brought with them their strongest team possible whilst Newcastle made an enforced change from the team which faced Crewe in mid-week, that being Law for Wallace, who was under medical treatment for injuries he received in that game. Since Burslem Port Vale also played in red Newcastle United played in the colours of the county, kindly loaned by the Northumberland Association.

Key Events	
First Half	
0 – 1	*Billy Beats*
1 – 1	**Bobby Creilly**
Second Half	
2 – 1	**Tom Crate**

Newcastle started against the hill and play at the beginning was slow and confined mainly to the midfield area. This pattern was broken as Burslem forged their way downfield and were stopped only by a foul being made. From the free-kick Scarratt put in a hot shot but Jeffrey intercepted and sent long back out. Thompson took possession and further relieved any danger with a good run.

A return downfield was made but Burslem gave away a free-kick from which Rodger cleared back into midfield. Again, Burslem came forward only to be dispossessed by McKane who gave to Thompson. With a rush away, at great speed, he shot swiftly, and MacKay conceded a corner in making the save. Keeping up the pressure when the ball was delivered in a difficult chance fell to Quinn which whilst clever unfortunately missed. He followed this with a great centre for Thompson, but his effort went awry.

Law shot splendidly after returning with the ball, but a goal kick was the only result. An attack by Vale was frustrated by McKane then following a fine run by the home forwards Thompson shot beautifully but MacKay saved splendidly, and the ball was sent back to the centre line. Thence Scarratt ran down and tried a shot from some distance but was wide of the target. Some scrimmaging ensued in front of the Newcastle goal, but the defence was equal to the challenge. Rodger and Jeffrey kicking out smartly. Willis and Quinn made a long run up but were dispossessed by Ramsay.

Vale made a sally forward but were halted by Graham then 'hands' in favour of Newcastle allowed them to get close in. The home forwards made good progress but a miskick from Quinn saw the ball going behind. A second free-kick fell to Newcastle but they could not make any advantage. Next Burslem worked their way to the home goal and gained a free-kick close in. The ball was played to Scarratt, but his shot went over the bar.

The play which followed was of moderate description until Burslem gained an advantage from a couple of corners which were successfully defended. Newcastle then worked their way to the visitor's goal, but Law ran the ball over the line. Back again came Burslem, getting in close by virtue of a free-kick in midfield, but the home defence was equal to the attack. Creilly then saved a rush by the Vale forwards but at the expense of a corner which proved to be of no advantage.

From a free-kick in midfield Newcastle got well up into the Vale citadel where they again got another free-kick for a foul which Creilly sent over the bar. Following a goal-kick Burslem made a good advance and when the ball was delivered to Beats he managed to evade the Newcastle defence and with a powerful shot put the visitors in front. Such was the quality of his effort that Lowery had very little chance of effecting a save.

Directly afterwards Quinn, getting tight to the byline, put in a beautiful centre for Willis who saw his shot being kicked away, luckily, by Youds. Crate returned in grand fashion to Thompson who sent in a shot which first Ramsay missed and then MacKay too only for Youds to make a miraculous saving intervention virtually on the goal line!

Two free-kicks in quick succession saw Newcastle close in on the Burslem goal and from the latter Creilly sent in nicely and taking a deflection off a defender it landed in the net for a deserved, and hard fought for, equaliser.

From the centre kick Newcastle played up vigorously and Quinn sent in a magnificent shot which Ramsay frustrated with a fine intervention. A scrimmage of some severity ensued in front of the Vale goal but despite all their best efforts the ball could not be forced through the admirable defence. Another scrimmage soon followed which saw Newcastle gaining a corner but a miskick by Graham relieved the pressure. Thompson ran back and sent in a cracking shot that went very narrowly over the bar. Half-time was then signalled with the score remaining at one goal to each side.

Newcastle started the second half as they had finished the first, on the attack. Willis ran down but was stopped by a timely intervention by Elson. Rallying once more Newcastle again sallied forth and got close into the Vale citadel and applied pressure on MacKay and his defence who proved stout indeed keeping Newcastle at bay. Law then got close in but missed with his effort.

Play was fast after the kick in and Newcastle, warming once again to their task, forced a corner which was cleared out by Youds, falling to Jeffrey. His shot from distance went high over the bar. Burslem then attacked, Beats leading the charge, but when they got close Jeffrey intercepted and sent the ball well down. Willis collected and tried a shot which MacKay threw out quite easily.

Some midfield play followed prior to the Vale left wing making excellent progress but their good work was to no avail as both Creilly and Jeffrey played with a high degree of competency and prevented any real danger. Graham then, quite a distance from goal, made a speculative effort that went only narrowly wide of the target.

Willis ran down and made a grand attempt to send the ball in, it looked like MacKay had it covered as he rushed out, but disaster befell him as in his effort to make the save he stumbled. Taking full advantage of his misfortune Crate speedily made up some distance and drove the ball home.

Gaining possession immediately from the centre kick Newcastle again drove forward and Thompson was unlucky to miss with his effort. Keeping the upperhand the homesters put MacKay under severe pressure and he did well to save a header from Crate.

A corner was won by Newcastle which was beautifully placed by Quinn and a severe attack was made upon the Vale goal, but all attempts were resisted by the defence. Winning another corner, the Vale packed their goal and again there was no way through, despite some sterling efforts from the Newcastle forwards to do so. Play continued to be centred around the visitor's goal and with heroic efforts they kept it intact. In a now rare sally forward the Vale forward line worked their way right up and Lowery, who had been a mere spectator in this half, was called upon to make a save from Campbell. The ball was once again quickly transferred to the other end.

Making a now concerted effort to get themselves back on level terms Burslem made good territorial gains but there was no way through the home defence for them and before they knew it they found themselves back on the defensive and things looked quite dangerous for them. A grand effort from Willis brought out an equally grand save from MacKay however in making said save he fell and had to quickly recover before the ball rolled over the line, this he did but had to concede a corner in the process. The advantage was to prove fruitless for Newcastle.

There then followed an easing of the pressure on behalf of the homesters but perhaps they eased too much as Beats took advantage of the situation and rushed forwards. Getting close enough for a shot his attempt was a fair one, but one that was not going to overly exert Lowery who collected it easily. Throwing it clear to Law he made a mazy run through the Burslem lines and only just missed with his effort. Another lucky escape for them.

As 'time' was now within sight Burslem made another great effort to rescue a point and getting well up forced a corner but could not turn it to any further advantage. Once again they returned and applied considerable pressure, putting in some fine work but this was met by equally fine defending, from Rodger in particular and there was no way through for them.

Both goals were then attacked in turn without effect and when the final whistle sounded a great cheer was heard in appreciating both teams for their efforts, and Newcastle for their win of course.

Pos.	Team	Plyd	W	D	L	F	A	G.Avg.	Pts.
1	Liverpool	17	13	4	0	48	9	5.3333	30
2	Small Heath	19	14	0	5	63	31	2.0323	28
3	Notts County	19	11	3	5	42	21	2.0000	25
4	Burslem Port Vale	18	11	1	6	48	37	1.2973	23
5	Burton Swifts	17	8	2	7	43	35	1.2286	18
6	Grimsby Town	16	8	0	8	44	40	1.1000	16
7	Newcastle United	16	6	4	6	31	29	1.0690	16
8	Lincoln City	14	6	3	5	34	31	1.0968	15
9	Woolwich Arsenal	14	6	2	6	26	33	0.7879	14
10	Middlesbrough Ironopolis	17	5	3	9	22	41	0.5366	13
11	Ardwick	16	5	1	10	29	30	0.9667	11
12	Walsall Town Swifts	16	4	3	9	19	34	0.5588	11
13	Crewe Alexandra	14	3	4	7	20	35	0.5714	10
14	Rotherham Town	14	3	1	10	24	49	0.4898	7
15	Northwich Victoria	15	2	1	12	20	58	0.3448	5

Game: 23 ~ Monday, January 1st, 1894		vs. Lincoln City
Competition: Division 2	Venue: St James's Park	Gate: 4,000

Newcastle United	5-1	Lincoln City
Goal, William Lowery; *backs*, Bobby Creilly, Tom Rodger; *half-backs*, Tom Crate, Willie Graham, Joe McKane; *forwards*, Charlie Quinn, Robert Willis, Willie Thompson, Thomas Bartlett, John Law.		*Goal*, W Tice; *backs*, Quentin Neill, James Stothert; *half-backs*, Edward "Ned" Mettam, Mick Richardson, Herbert Wilshire; *forwards*, George Shaw, John Irving, Don Lees, Albert Flewitt, Joe Raby.
Scorer(s): Thomas Bartlett (3), Charlie Quinn, Willie Thompson		Scorer(s): Mick Richardson
Referee: Mr. Fred Hardisty (Middlesbrough)		Kick-off: 2:15 PM

Bartlett Hat-Trick leads Newcastle to a very Happy start to the New Year

There was a large gathering of spectators at St James's Park to witness this New Year's Day fixture, and the vast majority of them went home delighted. It is fair to say that Lincoln had slightly the better of play in the first half, and probably deservedly led at half time by the only goal scored. However, the second half was a complete reversal and Newcastle always had the upperhand and ultimately ran out victors very easily by five goals to one goal.

The weather was cold and damp with frequent showers breaking out, but the play was fast and bright keeping the spectators excited and entertained throughout.

KEY EVENTS		
First Half		
0 – 1		Mick Richardson
Second Half		
1 – 1		Thomas Bartlett
2 – 1		Thomas Bartlett
3 – 1		Charlie Quinn
4 – 1		Thomas Bartlett
5 – 1		Willie Thompson

Winning the toss Newcastle decided to play up the hill for the first half and without further ado Lincoln got the game underway. Right from the start both sides applied themselves vigorously and each defence was called upon in turn. The first of the attacks came when Newcastle took possession off Lincoln and forced a couple of corners in quite rapid succession, neither bearing fruit, the defence of the visitors displaying excellent form. Turning defence into attack Lincoln forged their way downfield and the leather was kept near the home citadel for several minutes. The Newcastle backs were given plenty of work to do but just as the Lincoln defence had been on top of their game so were Creilly and Rodger and they frustrated all attempts by the visiting forwards to score.

With some difficulty the Newcastle forward quintet managed to pass their way through the Lincoln defence and got very near to the goal. Law put in a good centre, but Thompson's shot smacked into one of the defenders and bounded out of play for a goal kick. Keeping up the pressure Quinn then put in a great cross and Thompson was this time very unlucky in seeing his headed effort narrowly missing.

The City forwards then made an excellent break and Flewitt, easily navigating his way through the home defence, was left with the goal at his mercy but his effort went wide. The visitors continued to have the better of things for a while, in the matter of possession, but their play was noted as being uninteresting and loose. They ultimately conceded a free kick which allowed Newcastle to clear their lines and relieve the pressure.

The relief was short lived as Newcastle could make no headway and City retook possession and made another combined rush which saw Flewitt getting dangerously near. Lowery however rushed out beating him to the ball but in doing so he conceded a corner, which proved abortive. Directly after they gained another corner which was extremely well-placed, and Richards rose to head majestically past Lowery and the visitors were in the lead.

Buoyed by their advantage City continued to give the home half-backs a pretty torrid time and when 'hands' was awarded against Crate they had an excellent opportunity which was wasted. Thompson was then hurt which saw the game halted for a few minutes and upon the ball being set in motion once more City had possession through Flewitt who put a good pass into the path of Raby who missed scoring by the narrowest of margins.

Another corner fell to City which was nicely put in but it was Law who benefitted, and he rushed up field with his comrades in support. They got the leather well up before being dispossessed by Wiltshire. It was then Newcastle won a corner of their own, but it was cleared without any drama. The leather then spent its time in midfield with neither side being able to take any advantage. During this time play was most uninteresting. Finally, Newcastle got a break as a pass from Willis allowed Law and Thompson to run up the field, but the latter's shot went well wide of the mark.

Willis returned a clearance and in doing so putting Quinn in a promising position, but he was too far up and thus missed a decent chance. Pressure was maintained on the visitor's goal, but the home forwards were feeble in their efforts. Graham having the last attempt which he sent wide, so the interval arrived with Lincoln holding onto their slender lead.

Following the interval, and the change of ends, Newcastle were now facing downhill and took the very best of advantages from it. Indeed, one could say that all the play belonged to the homesters right from this moment until time was called. Initially play followed that of the end of the first half, in that it hovered around midfield for a good few minutes. As time wore on Newcastle really began to assert themselves and played with the dash which had been evident in previous matches where they had not been beaten in nine games, a run stretching back to mid-November.

They were however very briefly pushed back into their own quarters and Lowery was called upon to make a save, which he did so with ease. Latching onto the throw from their custodian the home forwards rushed downfield, and Quinn tried a shot from distance, but Tice saved comfortably. A corner to Newcastle soon followed but once again the defence of City managed to keep their citadel intact. For a good while they kept Newcastle at bay, however, they finally succumbed to the constant bombardment and Bartlett was able to score an equaliser amidst loud cheering.

From the centre kick Lincoln forced play for a short time, but it was short indeed as their push forward was relieved by Creilly who cleared the ball long downfield. Rushing onto it Thompson took possession and when close in he slipped at the crucial moment and a very good opportunity went by. With the ball now loose some scrimmaging took place but eventually it was sent over the byline. A corner was then won by Newcastle which was headed away by the Lincoln defence but McKane took possession. He sent in a beautifully placed ball right into the danger area where Bartlett received and put the finishing touches to it by guiding it into the net.

The pace of the game quickened dramatically after this second goal for Newcastle and for a brief spell play was quite even, but it was the homesters who proved the more aggressive. Once again Thompson had a great opportunity, and bad luck, as he saw his effort go over the bar. This was followed by another shot which Neill kicked out. Bartlett then saw a headed attempt go wide whilst Quinn, directly afterwards, headed over. Another Newcastle attack brought excellent defending from Bowles and there was no let-up in the pressure until Law sent an effort, from range, high over the bar. Continuing to press their opponents Newcastle were superb in attack and following some excellent play Quinn added a third goal for Newcastle.

Directly from the restart Newcastle gained possession and took the fight to their opponents who held out admirably. So-much-so that they forced a corner of their own from which they gained nothing, and Newcastle were once again piling forward and winning themselves a corner which proved equally fruitless as Graham sent his effort wide of the target. Newcastle though took possession once more from the goal-kick and from a long pass by Quinn an opportunity was afforded to Bartlett who readily accepted and scored with a fast, low shot bring up his hat-trick and Newcastle's fourth goal.

The game was now well and truly over as a contest and when another corner was won by Newcastle it was delivered nicely in front of the goal by Law and Thompson gained the leather to power it through to record Newcastle's fifth goal. Heavy pressure was kept up on the visitor's citadel and it was of great credit to their defence and custodian that the homesters lead was not increased further.

Just before the end as Newcastle relaxed somewhat Lincoln managed to steal a march on them and Lowery had to deal with a couple of difficult shots but he did so with consummate ease. With that the game was called to a conclusion by Mr Hardisty and the New Year was heralded in with what ended up a comfortable victory for Newcastle.

Pos.	Team	Plyd	W	D	L	F	A	G.Avg.	Pts.
1	Liverpool	18	14	4	0	50	9	5.5556	32
2	Small Heath	19	14	0	5	63	31	2.0323	28
3	Notts County	19	11	3	5	42	21	2.0000	25
4	Burslem Port Vale	19	11	1	7	49	40	1.2250	23
5	Burton Swifts	17	8	2	7	43	35	1.2286	18
6	Newcastle United	17	7	4	6	36	30	1.2000	18
7	Grimsby Town	16	8	0	8	44	40	1.1000	16
8	Lincoln City	15	6	3	6	35	36	0.9722	15
9	Middlesbrough Ironopolis	18	6	3	9	25	42	0.5952	15
10	Woolwich Arsenal	15	6	2	7	26	35	0.7429	14
11	Ardwick	16	5	1	10	29	30	0.9667	11
12	Walsall Town Swifts	16	4	3	9	19	34	0.5588	11
13	Crewe Alexandra	14	3	4	7	20	35	0.5714	10
14	Rotherham Town	14	3	1	10	24	49	0.4898	7
15	Northwich Victoria	15	2	1	12	20	58	0.3448	5

Game: 24 ~ Tuesday, January 2nd, 1894 ~ vs. Middlesbrough Ironopolis

Competition: Division 2 **Venue:** St James's Park **Gate:** 3,000

Newcastle United	7-2	Middlesbrough Ironopolis

Goal, William Lowery; *backs*, Bobby Creilly, Tom Rodger; *half-backs*, Tom Crate, Willie Graham, Joe McKane; *forwards*, Charlie Quinn, Robert Willis, Willie Thompson, Thomas Bartlett, John Law.

Scorer(s): Charlie Quinn (2), Willie Thompson, Robert Willis (2), John Law, Willie Graham

Goal, Roger Ord; *backs*, Joseph Hobson, John Sidney Oliver; *half-backs*, Henry Allport, Jimmy Grewer, John Bell; *forwards*, Walter Adams, Robert Cooper, Charles Coulthard, William Knowles, Thomas Hunter.

Scorer(s): Charles Coulthard, Robert Cooper

Referee: Mr. Fitzroy T. Norris (Bolton)

Newcastle in Seven(th) Heaven

This game, brought off in wintery weather, saw Newcastle win a game which was not envisaged to produce such a score as it did today. In putting seven past Ironopolis Newcastle eclipsed their previous highest score of six which they put past Woolwich Arsenal in the first home league encounter of the season. Given such a high score it was surprising perhaps to see yesterday's hat-trick hero, Bartlett, as the only one of the Newcastle forward quintet who did not score.

KEY EVENTS

First Half		
0 – 1		*Charles Coulthard*
1 – 1		Charlie Quinn
2 – 1		Charlie Quinn
3 – 1		Willie Thompson
4 – 1		Robert Willis
Second Half		
5 – 1		John Law
6 – 1		Robert Willis
7 – 1		Willie Graham
7 – 2		*Robert Cooper*

Newcastle won the toss and elected to play with the hill in their favour for the first half, so it was Ironopolis who got the game underway. The first few minutes of the game were exceedingly cautious as both sets of players were literally trying to 'find their feet' on a St James's Park pitch which was very slippery indeed. As such play was slow, and frankly of an uninteresting nature.

As Newcastle came to the fore it was against the run of play that Ironopolis broke away and Coulthard scored with a rather soft looking effort, which in all honesty Lowery should have dealt with quite easily. Within a matter of minutes however Newcastle rallied superbly and caused an almighty scrimmage within the Ironopolis goalmouth resulting in Quinn forcing the ball home. Then, in a 'carbon-copy' of his first goal Quinn once again got the better within a melee to force the ball over the line. The Ironopolis defence and custodian were fighting hard to repel the incessant Newcastle attacks but once again they were breached as Thompson was successful in shooting through. Even though they now had a two-goal lead, and Ironopolis were offering very little in terms of attacking prowess, Newcastle kept up their ceaseless attacks and before the interval was called Willis added a fourth goal for them.

Newcastle started the second half as eager as they had finished the first and, still battling bravely, Ord, the Ironopolis custodian, stopped some excellent efforts but he could do nothing about a very smart shot from Law who now made it five for Newcastle. Nor could he do anything as Willis added a sixth to notch up his brace.

In total command, as they had been for most of the match, Newcastle were in seventh heaven as Graham got in on the goalscoring act and put through a fine shot. With a six-goal lead and time running out, Newcastle eased up somewhat. Evidently, they eased up a modicum too much as Cooper ran down and sent through a grand shot.

Pos.	Team	Plyd	W	D	L	F	A	G.Avg.	Pts.
1	Liverpool	18	14	4	0	50	9	5.5556	32
2	Small Heath	19	14	0	5	63	31	2.0323	28
3	Notts County	19	11	3	5	42	21	2.0000	25
4	Burslem Port Vale	19	11	1	7	49	40	1.2250	23
5	Newcastle United	18	8	4	6	43	32	1.3438	20
6	Burton Swifts	17	8	2	7	43	35	1.2286	18
7	Grimsby Town	16	8	0	8	44	40	1.1000	16
8	Lincoln City	15	6	3	6	35	36	0.9722	15
9	Middlesbrough Ironopolis	19	6	3	10	27	49	0.5510	15
10	Woolwich Arsenal	15	6	2	7	26	35	0.7429	14
11	Ardwick	16	5	1	10	29	30	0.9667	11
12	Walsall Town Swifts	16	4	3	9	19	34	0.5588	11
13	Crewe Alexandra	14	3	4	7	20	35	0.5714	10
14	Rotherham Town	14	3	1	10	24	49	0.4898	7
15	Northwich Victoria	15	2	1	12	20	58	0.3448	5

Game: 25 ~ Saturday, January 6th, 1894		vs. Ardwick
Competition: Division 2	Venue: St James's Park	Gate: 1,200

Newcastle United	2-1	Ardwick
Goal, William Lowery; *backs*, Bobby Creilly, Tom Rodger; *half-backs*, Tom Crate, Willie Graham, Joe McKane; *forwards*, Charlie Quinn, Robert Willis, Willie Thompson, Joe Wallace, John Law.		*Goal*, William Douglas; *backs*, Frank Dyer, David Robson; *half-backs*, Harry Middleton, Walter Bowman, Eric Regan; *forwards*, Ernie Pickford, A. Bennett, D. Robertson, Thomas William Egan, H. Saddington.
Scorer(s): Willie Thompson, Willie Graham		Scorer(s): Ernie Pickford

Referee: Mr. W.H. Stacey (Sheffield)

Fantastic start to the New Year continues...

The St James's Park pitch was a snow-covered expanse, with only the lines being cleared revealing about a three-inch depth of snow. Copious amounts of sand had been put down at each goalmouth but the protection that it afforded the custodians, in regard to their footing, was rather dubious. Added to this there was a bitterly cold wind blowing rather keenly. It was of no surprise therefore that of the many folk who would have normally been patrons stayed away. Under normal circumstances a good game would have been envisaged between these two sides, as per the excellent game between the two in their league fixture at Hyde Road, where the contest was very intense, with Newcastle coming back from being 2-0 down to winning 3-2. These however were not normal circumstances.

Nevertheless, the gate was around 1,000 at the time of kick-off and they witnessed a game that was both interesting and entertaining, even if some of that entertainment arose from the players attempting to keep to their feet. Passing was also to be somewhat of a difficulty as the snow held up the ball and at times to compensate for this many passes were dramatically overhit.

Key Events		
First Half		
0 – 1		*Ernie Pickford*
1 – 1		**Willie Thompson**
Second Half		
2 – 1		**Willie Graham**

Ardwick, winning the toss elected to play with the hill in their favour for the opening period so it was Thompson for Newcastle who got the game underway.

The visitors were the first to show but they very soon had to withstand a rush from Newcastle which got them to close quarters but ultimately halted in their tracks. Still trying to come to terms with the conditions this early flurry was followed by play of a mediocre description. Seemingly being the first to master those conditions Ardwick made the first sustained attack of the game and deservedly opened the scoring. This following a strong advance in which Lowery grandly fisted out an effort. The ball was worked to Pickford who managed to shoot the ball very smartly past Lowery from a fair distance. This was after barely five minutes had elapsed. The goal brought about an immediate response from Newcastle, and they rushed up and an almighty tussle between the Ardwick posts ensued, ending with an effort from Wallace who was unlucky to see it go past.

Ardwick returned and once again Lowery was called upon to save his charge. This served to increase the intensity on behalf of Newcastle and for the next few minutes they had the better of matters. An opportunity went begging as one of their forwards missed badly and then a corner was gained which resulted in nothing being gained. The pressure was only relieved by a good run from Bennett, initiating a spirited attack which saw several shots being sent in. The pick of which was a splendid shot from Bennett bringing about an equally splendid save by Lowery, occasioning a hearty round of applause from the crowd.

Newcastle then pressed high and from a great rush up, led by Willis, the ball was worked to Thompson who brought about the equaliser with a fine kick.

A period of even play was then witnessed, and it was the visitors who emerged from it stronger, and they were once again back in front of the home citadel. Their efforts were to prove in vain as the home defence stood firm. At length they cleared their lines and quickly feeding their forwards Newcastle were now back on the attack. Getting into close quarters Wallace was guilty of a wild kick. Twice more openings were created and twice more the ball was sent behind. Another period of play in midfield followed.

It was Newcastle who then took up the running once more and encamped themselves in the visitors' quarters. Ardwick though showed a very fine defence, Dyer and Robson being very solid and whenever they were breached Douglas proved himself to be a very safe pair of hands. They were very lucky however when Willis found himself very close in and shot well but the ball cannoned off the crossbar.

As the interval was approaching Ardwick found it increasingly difficult to have any great effect on the play as each time they cleared Newcastle brought the ball straight back. For all their dominance at this juncture Newcastle could not further the score and the interval arrived the teams, each having a goal, could not be separated.

Ardwick got the second half underway, now facing the hill and they could make little progress. Indeed, it was several minutes before they could progress past the halfway line and when they did, they were driven straight back by a determined Newcastle.

Such was the determination of the homesters that at one stage their pressing was so effective that not only did they drive Ardwick back, but they drove Douglas, the custodian, over his line and into the net! A goal only being prevented by the prompt action of Dyer who hooked away the ball from almost on the line.

Newcastle returned immediately to the attack, applying pressure of such a description that it was with the greatest wonderment that nothing resulted from it. That the ball didn't land within the confines of the posts was due as much to good fortune on behalf of the strenuous defence as it was to haphazard shooting from the home forwards.

Having looked to have survived the full fury of the onslaught Robson was guilty of making an accidental foul and a free-kick was awarded to Newcastle in a very favourable position in front of goal. From it Graham scored an easy goal to give Newcastle a lead as much deserving as Ardwick's had been in the first half.

Pressing ahead, trying to build upon their advantage, Newcastle resumed the onslaught with the same ferocity as before. For a good ten minutes they maintained a constant attack but were unable to add to their score despite some sterling attempts. The closest of these being a shot from Willis which just grazed the cross bar.

Eventually Ardwick were able to clear their lines and give their defence a little respite. Getting close in Regan made a shot for goal and it took quick work from the defence to protect the lead. Little more chance was afforded to the visitors as the ball was back once again before their citadel. Such was the display that it was questionable as to whether the rapturous applause which was heard around the enclosure was for the incessant attempts from the home forwards or the capital defence they faced.

There then came a moment in the game that almost defies description, an attempt of the most beautiful nature came from the boot of Wallace and the most astonishingly magnificent save came from Douglas. Which of the two deserved the tumultuous applause more is inconsequential compared to the event witnessed.

In continuing the offensive Douglas, aided most admirably by Robson, played up splendidly and the way they disposed of the very numerous shots sent their way was commendable. Equally the play of Graham and Wallace evoked general admiration from both the spectators and their comrades. It could quite be said that for each of the above mentioned there was deep respect from their opponents too, of that there would be little doubt.

Newcastle continued once more holding the upperhand, which they had for the vast majority of this second half and did not relinquish it. Were it not for the heroic, indeed extraordinary, play of Douglas and his left-back the score would have been heavy in favour of Newcastle. In that respect two very good efforts are worthy of note, one from Thompson the other from Wallace. Both bringing out the best in Douglas crowning a truly magnificent performance, demonstrating skill in goalkeeping that would be very hard to equal.

Just before the close of play Ardwick did make a break away but before they could effect any real challenge it was the whistle which halted them and so ended a game which encapsulated the essence of football. High drama, the combatting of difficult conditions, *it is the "winter game" after all*, two teams playing hard but fair, excellent forward play, excellent defensive play, and the occasional moments of amusement, as determined by the conditions.

It may have been one of the most poorly attended games at St James's Park this season but surely it was the best. Certainly, one that had, up to this point anyway, no equal and one that would be long remembered.

Pos.	Team	Plyd	W	D	L	F	A	G.Avg.	Pts.
1	Liverpool	19	15	4	0	54	10	5.4000	34
2	Small Heath	20	15	0	5	70	31	2.2581	30
3	Notts County	19	11	3	5	42	21	2.0000	25
4	Burslem Port Vale	20	12	1	7	51	41	1.2439	25
5	Newcastle United	19	9	4	6	45	33	1.3636	22
6	Burton Swifts	18	9	2	7	47	38	1.2368	20
7	Middlesbrough Ironopolis	20	7	3	10	29	49	0.5918	17
8	Grimsby Town	16	8	0	8	44	40	1.1000	16
9	Lincoln City	15	6	3	6	35	36	0.9722	15
10	Woolwich Arsenal	16	6	2	8	27	37	0.7297	14
11	Ardwick	17	5	1	11	30	32	0.9375	11
12	Walsall Town Swifts	17	4	3	10	22	38	0.5789	11
13	Crewe Alexandra	15	3	4	8	20	37	0.5405	10
14	Rotherham Town	15	3	1	11	25	53	0.4717	7
15	Northwich Victoria	16	2	1	13	20	65	0.3077	5

Game: 26 ~ Saturday, January 13th, 1894		**vs. Northwich Victoria**
Competition: Division 2	**Venue:** St James's Park	**Gate:** 2,000

Newcastle United	**3-0**	**Northwich Victoria**
Goal, William Lowery; *backs*, Harry Jeffrey, J Laverick; *half-backs*, Bobby Creilly, Willie Graham, Joe McKane; *forwards*, Charlie Quinn, Robert Willis, Willie Thompson, Tom Crate, Joe Wallace.		*Goal*, George Hornby; *backs*, William Guest, William Postles; *half-backs*, Stanley, T. Clark, Armstrong; *forwards*, George A. Drinkwater, Patrick Finnerhan, Thomas Scanlan, George Savage, Teddy Kettle.
Scorer(s): Tom Crate (3)		

Referee: Mr. Fred Hardisty (Middlesbrough)

Crate Hat-Trick extends unbeaten run to eleven!

Newcastle came into this game on a run of ten games unbeaten, indeed winning eight of those and drawing two. You could, should you wish, add to that run two friendly fixtures which were also victories thus extending the unbeaten to twelve coming into this game.

Northwich on the other hand were having a torrid time of things and were sitting rock bottom of the league table. Adding to their woes was the fact that they had not won an away fixture all season and had lost four of their last league five matches. A guaranteed home banker then?

Hasten yee not to your conclusion, for who was it that last beat Newcastle? Yes, you've guessed it, Northwich Victoria (on 18/11/1893), and it was a resounding victory too, as they put five goals past Newcastle at the Drill Field enclosure. In doing so they had fought back from a deficit of 3-1. This game therefore had all the hallmarks of the proverbial banana skin!

Jeffrey returned to the Newcastle line-up after having been out for a fortnight through injury and Laverick came in for Rodger who was rested. Other than that, they were constituted as during the successful run. The ground was slippery, the weather cold but fine, and there was a good gate to witness Newcastle's fifth successive home fixture.

KEY EVENTS

Second Half
1 – 0	Tom Crate
2 – 0	Tom Crate
3 – 0	Tom Crate

Northwich won the toss and elected to play with the mild wind in their favour. As such it was Thompson for Newcastle who got the game underway.

It took only a matter of seconds for Newcastle to take possession from the midfield and with an attack led by Thompson they rushed forward. Passing to Willis he centred for Quinn, but his effort went wide. From the goal kick Newcastle regained possession and once again drove forward and won a corner via a save which Hornby just managed to turn past his post. The ball was well-placed in front of the goal and a severe and prolonged scrimmage was witnessed. Both attack and defence were magnificent. Crate was unlucky in hitting the bar and the offence was only relieved when Wallace sent his effort behind.

A sally forth by the Northwich right wing then followed the kick out but they were dispossessed. In turn Willis and Quinn rushed down but were halted by a timely intervention by Postles. This gave Northwich the advantage and they progressed to close in, and Savage missed narrowly with a good attempt.

The Newcastle left then worked their way down and a good centre by Willis saw Crate firing over the bar. Maintaining the pressure Hornby had to concede a corner when saving from Thompson nut nought came from it.

In end-to-end play now Northwich attacked again but the Newcastle defence kept them out. Back at the other end Crate had an effort saved by Hornby. Then from a long-range shot by Willis Hornby errored but was saved by Guest getting the ball away. A fruitless visit was then made by the Northwich forwards. Crate then when well-placed shot feebly and Guest got the ball away with ease. Laverick then intervened to prevent a rush by Northwich.

Newcastle then thought they had opened the scoring as Thompson ran down, crossed to Quinn who put the ball through, however the point was disallowed as he was adjudged to be offside.

Willis then had an effort go too high, followed by another shot from Thompson which was only narrowly wide. Laverick again prevented an attack from Northwich but his intervention was ruled as being unfair and a free-kick was awarded. Taken by Stanley it went harmlessly behind. Once again, the home forwards ran down and this time Quinn's shot went behind but in doing so it took a deflection. The corner however proved fruitless. Back came Newcastle and only grand work from Hornby saved the day for the visitors.

A fine display of tackling by Graham allowed Newcastle to get near but the defence stood firm once again to the attack. Then gaining an opening Northwich advanced and forced Lowery into a save, conceding a corner in the process but they could not take any advantage from it. Thompson forced another save from Hornby who was displaying capital form. Another corner was won by Northwich, but the ball was carried behind by the wind when delivered in. From then until the whistle Newcastle had much the better of matters, gaining a free-kick in a very favourable position close in which was wasted, an abortive corner, and another close shot from Thompson.

Scanlan got the second half underway but was immediately dispossessed and the ball was sent out wide to the right-wing. Wallace drove forward before sending the ball inside to Crate who shot through very smartly, giving Hornsby little chance of making any save. Not even a minute had elapsed!

Things almost got even better for Newcastle as within a couple of minutes they were again to the fore and were awarded a free-kick. The delivery from Jeffrey was superb and Thompson was extremely unlucky to see his effort go narrowly past. It was not long however before they did get their second, and again Crate was the scorer. This time with a swift shot following a sustained attack.

At this stage the Northwich forwards could make no headway against the Newcastle half-back line and all the pressing was being done by the Newcastle forwards. Crate had another attempt at goal and was unlucky to see his effort go narrowly over the bar. This he repeated very shortly after.

Hornby was being given a quite torrid time, but he was admirable in his performance. He did concede a corner from a fine header by Thompson, but Newcastle could take no further advantage. A brief respite was afforded the Northwich defence as Scanlan carried the ball swiftly into the home territory, but he was soon stopped and back came the pressure on Hornby and his defence.

Making another good save Hornby conceded another corner which was also abortive and then he was called upon to make yet another save from a splendid effort by Crate. Winning a free-kick in midfield a rare sally forward was made by Northwich and whilst they got close in they could not muster an effort on target and Newcastle once more came into their quarters. Quinn making excellent progress but upon putting in a fine centre Creilly sent the ball over the line.

With a show of great determination, the Newcastle forwards, led by Quinn, were back in front of the Northwich citadel. The first opportunity, by Creilly was sent by, then from a splendid effort by Willis the ball could only be fisted out by Hornby, rather weakly, and Crate duly put the ball through off his chest and the hat-trick was his!

In an attempt to salvage something from the game Scanlan and Savage made a run forward but, in their haste, ran the ball over the line. A return was made which presented Wallace with an opportunity, albeit from distance, but he sent it over the bar. Another Newcastle attack was halted unfairly and when the free-kick was delivered in they won a corner, but nothing resulted.

Northwich then had a look-in, but their attempts were both feeble and futile. Another corner was then won by Newcastle with Hornby once again making an admirable save, and once again conceding a further corner from it. From this one a good shot was sent in and Hornby saved in a grand manner.

From then, right up until the final whistle, the pressure from Newcastle was constant, equally constant was the form of Hornby.

It should probably be mentioned that Hornby, in every report I read, came out of this game with high acclaim despite conceding three times. On each of those occasions he was mentioned as being blameless.

Supplementary notes...

There are reports which state that Willis scored the final goal for Newcastle and it was not therefore a hat-trick by Crate which took the honours. However, a review of officially reported goal tallies for both Willis and Crate do not bear this supposition out and Crate should be, deservedly, accredited with his hat-trick.

Also please note that dependent upon which report you subscribe to the gate for this fixture can be anywhere from 2,000 to 3,000 spectators. In the cases where there is not a number quoted for the gate it is described as a "large one". In quoting the 2,000 for this report I am merely going with what appears to be the consensus.

Pos.	Team	Plyd	W	D	L	F	A	G.Avg.	Pts.
1	Liverpool	20	16	4	0	59	11	5.3636	36
2	Small Heath	21	16	0	5	75	34	2.2059	32
3	Notts County	20	12	3	5	46	23	2.0000	27
4	Burslem Port Vale	21	12	1	8	54	46	1.1739	25
5	Newcastle United	20	10	4	6	48	33	1.4545	24
6	Burton Swifts	19	10	2	7	52	41	1.2683	22
7	Grimsby Town	17	9	0	8	49	40	1.2250	18
8	Middlesbrough Ironopolis	21	7	4	10	29	49	0.5918	18
9	Lincoln City	16	6	4	6	35	36	0.9722	16
10	Woolwich Arsenal	16	6	2	8	27	37	0.7297	14
11	Ardwick	18	5	1	12	30	37	0.8108	11
12	Walsall Town Swifts	17	4	3	10	22	38	0.5789	11
13	Crewe Alexandra	16	3	4	9	23	42	0.5476	10
14	Rotherham Town	17	3	1	13	28	62	0.4516	7
15	Northwich Victoria	17	2	1	14	20	68	0.2941	5

Game: 27 ~ Saturday, January 20th, 1894 — vs. Rotherham Town

Competition: Division 2 **Venue:** Clifton Grove **Gate:** 1,500

Rotherham Town 2-1 Newcastle United

Goal, Arthur Wharton; *backs*, Fred Turner (Snr), Walter Hobson; *half-backs*, John Barr, Albert Rodgers, Walter Broadhead; *forwards*, Fred Turner (Jnr), Billy Longden, Peter Rae, Johnny McCormick, Arthur Fairburn.

Scorer(s): Johnny McCormick, Arthur Fairbairn

Referee: Mr. L. W. Furniss (Manchester)

Goal, William Lowery; *backs*, Harry Jeffrey, J Laverick; *half-backs*, Bobby Creilly, Willie Graham, Joe McKane; *forwards*, Tom Crate, Robert Willis, Willie Thompson, Joe Wallace, Charlie Quinn.

Scorer(s): Joe Wallace

Kick-off: 2:50 PM

All good things must come to an end...

Newcastle's run of eleven unbeaten games, thirteen if you count the two friendlies, came to an end today as did their run of five consecutive home game, with this visit to Clifton Grove. It was quite a surprise defeat too as they were flying high in fifth place whilst only Northwich Victoria, whom Newcastle beat handsomely last week, kept Rotherham off the bottom of the table. Newcastle having more than three times the number of points held by their hosts today.

Frequent showers had fallen during the morning, ending around noon, but the ground was quoted as being in excellent condition. Newcastle were fielding the same team that defeated Northwich whilst Rotherham were forced into fielding a couple of men considered to be reservists in Hobson and Broadhead.

Key Events		
First Half		
0 – 1		Joe Wallace
Second Half		
1 – 1		Johnny McCormick
2 – 1		Arthur Fairbairn

Winning the toss Newcastle set the homesters to face the park end with both the sun and a strong breeze to their faces. So, without further ado Rotherham got the game underway and at once their left wing dashed down to the Newcastle goal but Fairbairn carried the leather too far and it went by. They at once came again but with the same disappointing result.

From the goal kick Newcastle were able to get well into the home territory and there they remained for quite some time, despite the valiant efforts of the home backs. A good centre from Creilly put the home goal in some jeopardy and Wharton rushed out. When out of position he was lucky to see the ball headed into touch.

Rotherham then tried a run down with their right wing and succeeded in getting close in and surrounding Lowery they were unlucky to see him bravely clear under the bar. To many it seemed he had done so from behind his line and that a goal had been scored but credit to Rotherham they did not make any great appeal for one.

Newcastle then had a couple of fruitless corners and subsequent to these Wallace sent a shot in that struck the post before bouncing over the line and into the net. This was after some twenty minutes or so of play.

Rotherham attacked from the centre kick and Fairbairn was brought down as he looked dangerous. Play was halted briefly for him to receive attention. Nothing came from the resulting free-kick. The following play was mainly a struggle between the back divisions before Rotherham gained another free-kick due to Quinn being ruled offside. This got them right in front of the Newcastle goal, but they could not turn this to their advantage. At this juncture Fairbairn had to retire from proceedings.

Going a man down Rotherham did very well to keep play even and indeed approaching the interval were the more dangerous. In a concerted attack they swarmed over the Newcastle goal, but Rodger sent the final effort just wide of the upright.

On resuming after the break numerical equality was restored as Fairbairn re-entered the affray. Newcastle then were reduced to ten men, albeit briefly, as Wallace, who had made some good runs, was struck by the ball in the stomach *"rather too forcibly to be comfortable"*. Upon his return he and Creilly combined to force another fruitless corner.

A return by Barr saw the leather being placed under the Newcastle bar and the home inside rank, along with Rae, crowded around so much so that they got in each other's way and a golden opportunity went begging. Soon after another scrimmage in the Newcastle goal ended equally unsuccessful for the Rotherham forwards. Turner (Jnr) shooting a little too high. Going up the other end Newcastle had yet another corner which they could not turn to any advantage.

This turned out to be much to their regret as following the corner the Townsmen neatly cleared the ball and raced away at such a pace as to leave the Newcastle forwards stranded up-top. They blazed past the midfield too and now, fully exposed, the full-backs and Lowery could do nothing to stop McCormick getting the equaliser. A swifter counter-attack would rarely be seen one believes.

There now followed very vigorous play from both sides, each thinking they had the better of their opponents, but it was the homesters who were to be proved true. With a strong advance down the wing the ball was given to Fairbairn who sent in a tremendous shot and with McCormick and Rae said to be *"keeping the opening clear for the ball to go into the net"*. Delighted at taking the lead Rotherham played with some dash and were soon knocking on the Newcastle door again giving the defence a torrid time and it took more than a little while before Newcastle could break the stranglehold.

This they eventually did and set about trying to redress the deficit. Time and again they visited the Rotherham quarters and time and again they were repulsed. The same descriptor could be applied to the Rotherham men as they took their turns in pressing the Newcastle defence. Play was thus brisk and entertaining but without any major challenges to either custodian. The game therefore ended with the somewhat surprising result of a win to the home team, on balance though a deserved win.

Pos.	Team	Plyd	W	D	L	F	A	G.Avg.	Pts.
1	Liverpool	20	16	4	0	59	11	5.3636	36
2	Small Heath	21	16	0	5	75	34	2.2059	32
3	Notts County	21	13	3	5	48	23	2.0870	29
4	Burslem Port Vale	21	12	1	8	54	46	1.1739	25
5	Newcastle United	21	10	4	7	49	35	1.4000	24
6	Burton Swifts	19	10	2	7	52	41	1.2683	22
7	Grimsby Town	18	9	1	8	52	43	1.2093	19
8	Lincoln City	17	7	4	6	38	36	1.0556	18
9	Middlesbrough Ironopolis	21	7	4	10	29	49	0.5918	18
10	Woolwich Arsenal	16	6	2	8	27	37	0.7297	14
11	Ardwick	18	5	1	12	30	37	0.8108	11
12	Crewe Alexandra	17	3	5	9	26	45	0.5778	11
13	Walsall Town Swifts	18	4	3	11	22	40	0.5500	11
14	Rotherham Town	18	4	1	13	30	63	0.4762	9
15	Northwich Victoria	18	2	1	15	20	71	0.2817	5

Game: 28 ~ Saturday, January 27th, 1894 — vs. Sheffield United

Competition: FA Cup [1st Round] **Venue:** St James's Park **Gate:** 7,000

Newcastle United	2-0	Sheffield United

Goal, William Lowery; *backs*, Harry Jeffrey, Tom Rodger; *half-backs*, Bobby Creilly, Willie Graham, Joe McKane; *forwards*, Charlie Quinn, Tom Crate, Willie Thompson, John Law, Joe Wallace.

Scorer(s): Joe Wallace (2)

Goal, Charlie Howlett; *backs*, Bob Cain, Harry Lilley; *half-backs*, Rab Howell, Billy Hendry, Ernest Needham; *forwards*, Jack Drummond, Harry Hammond, Bob Hill, Billy Fleming, Hugh Gallacher.

Referee: Mr Jack T. Howcroft (Bolton)

Record crowd sees Newcastle win through...

One local Newcastle paper reported that *"never in the annals of Northumbrian football has an interest so keen and widespread been evinced in any match as there was in (this) tie"*. A heady claim indeed, but the record crowd of *"fully 7,000"* bore out this claim. This was even more impressive when one considers the inclemency of the weather. There had been periodic during the morning and around 2 o'clock it fell heavily, even at that time there were already a couple of thousand in the St James's Park and the crowd just kept growing.

Owing to the huge slope in the ground the bottom half of the pitch, the Gallowgate end, was looking already like a quagmire and a strong wind prevailed. Not ideal conditions at all, but seemingly the Newcastle public were oblivious and kept pouring in to make up that record, being entertained by the Gateshead Borough Brass Band prior to the eagerly awaited kick off.

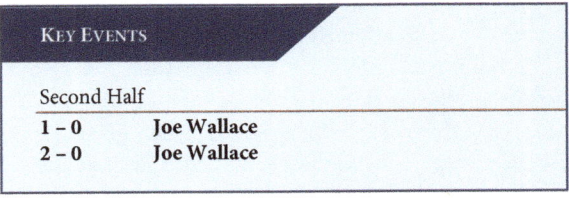

KEY EVENTS

Second Half
1 – 0   Joe Wallace
2 – 0   Joe Wallace

Newcastle won the toss, deciding to play with the wind, and the hill, in their favour so it was Hill who got the game started for Sheffield. Making a short run down they were dispossessed by Graham. This allowed Newcastle to advance to well into the visitors quarters but a free-kick for 'hands' stopped them. From the kick Sheffield ran quickly up once more, and their attack was nullified by a free-kick too. In a return rush they were halted by Jeffrey with a fine intervention, back they came and this time Creilly was there making a similar intervention. There followed a period where play was concentrated around the home goal, but Lowery the custodian was not unduly stressed.

Eventually Thompson led his confreres away and managing to break through a stout resistant put up by Lilley the ball was given to Graham who sent in a grand shot which narrowly missed the target.

From the goal kick the Sheffielders, through some good work, particularly from Hendry, were once again well into Newcastle territory. They were however to give up possession rather easily and Thompson raced towards the other end but before any real pressure could be exerted Law was guilty of a foul. Next up Wallace, when presented with a chance of getting away dallied and he lost possession, much to the chagrin of the crowd and his teammates! Thompson retrieved possession and play was in midfield once more for a goodly period of time.

Breaking this pattern Drummond ran up and shot but a save was affected by Lowery but at the expense of a corner which proved fruitless. Making a break from the resulting goal kick Thompson made a fine shot which Howlett was equal to and he threw out. A free-kick for a foul then gave Newcastle a chance and though it was well placed by Rodger it was eventually sent behind by Wallace.

The weather was *"miserable in the extreme"* and the quagmire which had been the bottom half was now a literal 'mud bath' and anywhere there was grass left was awfully slippery. Fouls, no doubt accidental, were numerous, and another one awarded to Newcastle gave them a grand chance but Howlett kicked it away, long up the field.

The home territory was visited but briefly as Jeffrey made a huge clearance which found its way to Quinn who only just missed with a terrific shot. The left wing of Sheffield then surged forward but Rodger got the ball away, Hammond sending in close with his return. Though play was going from end to end it was of a poor nature, more a 'kick and rush' rather than the flowing football Newcastle had in the past weeks provided. However, given the aforementioned conditions this was of little surprise.

Hammond missed with a fast shot when well placed. Then from a throw-in to Newcastle Thompson headed in and Cain intervened with a strong kick. Back came Newcastle, now having the best of matters, and Crate shot in but a scrimmage in front of the goal saw the ball come back out. Graham took possession but sent the ball behind. Briefly attacking the other end Jeffrey made another fine intervention. Newcastle renewed their offensive but a ball from Wallace to McKane was intercepted allowing Hammond to advance dangerously but nought came from his move. A fast run was then made by Thompson, Law and Wallace but Cain relieved with a kick out of bounds.

A long-range effort was saved again by Cain this time giving away a corner, Howell heading away the kick. McKane retrieved but sent it over the bar. Another corner befell Newcastle which Wallace placed in grandly. Hendry kicked out and a beautiful return by Jeffrey saw Wallace heading through to open the scoring.

From the centre kick Sheffield attacked with vigour but Jeffrey was in excellent form and halted the advance feeding his forwards expertly. They, rushing away, then won another corner which advantaged them nothing further. Fleming, for Sheffield, then made a rush and shot in well but Lowery caught in grand style. The visitors then won a corner from which a scrimmage ensued, but Graham kicked out finely seeing Law and Thompson advancing once more. The latter just missing with an effort. From yet another corner Wallace just missed too. It was then the turn of the Newcastle half-backs to show their mettle as they frustrated numerous advances.

Wallace got possession and passed to Law who put in a fine centre which Cain kicked out. The ball however came back to Wallace who shot through in beautiful style giving himself and Newcastle a second goal.

No headway was made by Sheffield from the centre kick and indeed nor was there any made from them for the remainder of the half. From another corner to Newcastle an opportunity fell to Crate and he just missed with a grand effort and soon after the whistle sounded.

Thompson restarted for Newcastle after the interval and each end was visited in turn, but the state of the pitch was appalling and the nature of the play, though exciting at times, was generally poor. Both sets of players were showing distinct signs of tiredness due to the heavy ground, indeed often going to the touchline to relieve themselves of copious amounts of mud, and no doubt have a quicker breather!

Hill went closest for Sheffield when he brought about a magnificent save from Lowery with a long-range shot, and Rodger almost put the ball through his own net due to its slippery nature but thankfully only conceded a corner which Wallace cleared. There was a period where Sheffield were dominant but Lowery and his backs played superbly. Whenever they got forward Newcastle looked dangerous but Howlett and his backs were in no mood to concede further. Thus, an exciting game, in atrocious conditions, saw the record crowd, or most of them, going home very happy.

Supplementary notes...

In an effort to get this game changed from St James's Park to Bramall Lane it was reported the Sheffield committee offered the Newcastle committee a series of financial inducements, their latest inducement being of £125, plus half the gate receipts. The directors of Newcastle however were adamant in their refusal of this, as they had been of all previous offers. The receipts taken at the gates of St James's Park were £175. As this does not include, *or we are led to believe doesn't include*, any ticket sales, advance or season, it would seem the decision was validated.

Game: 29 ~ Saturday, February 3rd, 1894 vs. Burslem Port Vale

Competition: Division 2   **Venue:** Cobridge Athletic Ground   **Gate:** 2,000

Burslem Port Vale	**1 - 1**	**Newcastle United**

Goal, Hugh McKay; *backs*, Samuel Eccles, George Youds; *half-backs*, Joseph Boughey, Bob McCrindle, Billy Elson; *forwards*, Jimmy Scarrett, Meshach Dean, Billy Beats, Alf Wood, Lewis Campbell.

Scorer(s): Alf Wood

Goal, William Lowery; *backs*, Harry Jeffrey, Tom Rodger; *half-backs*, Bobby Creilly, Willie Graham, Joe McKane; *forwards*, Charlie Quinn, Tom Crate, Robert Willis, Joe Wallace, John Law.

Scorer(s): Joe Wallace

Referee: Mr Tillotson (Birmingham)

Late goals in either half, for either side, ensures a draw.

Newcastle returned to league duties this afternoon after their victorious FA Cup excursion last week. This was the return fixture between these two sides, Newcastle having won the rather exciting corresponding home fixture at St James's Park back in December by the odd goal in three. The weather was fine, but cold, and Newcastle fielded their strongest eleven whilst Burslem where without Ramsay who was suffering from a knee injury.

In that first fixture Newcastle played in the colours of the county (Northumberland), as both they and Burslem Port Vale having a red uniform shirt. It was quite bizarre therefore to see both teams emerging wearing said red shirts. The only difference between the two being the colour of their knickers (*or 'shorts' as we call them today*). Burslem sporting black knickers and Newcastle sporting dark blue ones, most bizarre indeed.

Key Events

First Half
| 0 - 1 | Joe Wallace |

Second Half
| 1 - 1 | Alf Wood |

Newcastle won the toss and set Burslem to face a stiff breeze and having the sun in their faces. Without further ado the game was gotten underway. It was Newcastle who at first pressed but Elson intervened to send Campbell away, he in turn was halted by Rodger with a fine intervention. The attire of both teams being almost identical there was some confusion when long passes were made, not helped, or used as an excuse perhaps, when the wind made the error of such passes even more pronounced and more frequent.

Winning a free-kick in midfield Vale attacked strongly and the final shot by Campbell went just outside the post. A quick retaliation by Newcastle saw Quinn forcing a corner off Elson but the resulting flag-kick was put behind. Campbell and Wood then showed up well and within sight of Lowery and his charge they were dispossessed by Rodger.

It was then Willis and Law darting up the other end who looked threatening. Two corners were won by Newcastle, in rapid succession, but on each the ball was carried over the line by the wind.

The game was being played at a tremendous pace, with both sides trying their utmost to gain the upperhand. Indeed, there was very little between them, as their respective league positions evinced. An attack from the Vale right flank saw Jeffrey conceding a free-kick in fouling Scarrett, but from it the ball was sent harmlessly behind. Newcastle then had the most sustained amount of pressure the game had seen so far but the defence that opposed them proved excellent.

McKay, the Vale custodian, being so well protected by said defence faced his first real test on the half-hour mark when Willis sent in a very clever shot, but he was equal to it, kicking away nicely. There then followed a very dangerous time for him as Vale conceded a free-kick right in front of goal and it took the most strenuous of efforts to clear amidst the melee that ensued, ending with a lightning shot from Crate which struck the legs of Elson. At the other end Wood had the ball at his feet and almost under the crossbar collided with Lowery. An almighty scrimmage then took place from which Vale gained a corner. From this a long, low shot from Wood was turned around the post by Lowery when making his save and ultimately this advantage was fruitless too.

Quinn and Crate got nicely away for Newcastle down the right but a timely intervention from Youds put a halt to the attack. Returning to the offensive the Newcastle forwards and Vale defence were involved in some excellent exchanges in front of the Vale goal ultimately though the ball was sent behind for a goal kick.

The interval was on the horizon and Newcastle were piling on the pressure, wave after wave of advances were made on the Vale goal but that strong defence was proving to be impenetrable. Even with the wind in their favour, and sometimes as a fault of that same wind, the Newcastle forwards were finding it impossible to gain the goal that their efforts perhaps deserved. Law looked set to get through but Boughey and Youds did enough to make him send his effort behind. For all their efforts Newcastle could not even get through to McKay never mind trouble him.

On the one occasion they did, he being forced to come off his line to save from Crate, the return was sent over the line. However, from the goal kick the ball was immediately sent back in and seconds before the whistle Wallace got the leather through to give Newcastle the lead.

When the second half was gotten underway it was Vale who were the first to show and they were able to keep up the pressure on the Newcastle defence for some minutes. Whilst they gave Rodger and Jeffrey plenty to do, they did not unduly stress Lowery. Gaining a corner, they could not take further advantage and in their next attack Beats was very unlucky to see his effort go narrowly wide of the upright.

Play was kept concentrated near the Newcastle citadel but as their forwards had met with an impenetrable defence in the first half so did Vale during this period. Lowery was untroubled and there was simply no way through for the homesters. The Newcastle backs and half-backs displaying the most excellent form.

At length Law managed to relieve the pressure as he raced away only to be penalised for being offside. The respite this gave to Newcastle was short-lived as the Vale were back once more. Campbell saw a terrific effort go narrowly wide and moments later Scarrett saw his effort go a matter of inches over the bar. This was followed by two successive corners which were defended wondrously by Newcastle. Whilst it is not meant to be harsh on his confreres Graham was performing outstandingly.

Newcastle were twice in such a situation as to have to kick the ball directly out of play in order to relieve the pressure. It was then noted that a player was cautioned by the referee for rough play.

Still there was no let up on the Newcastle goal, attack after attack being made by Vale but their defence protected Lowery so well that rarely were they given any shooting opportunities. Any that they did have were made from distance and these were headed and kicked away.

Eventually they did work their way in close and an almighty tussle took place right in front of the Newcastle goal with the ball eventually being gotten away by Graham. Then a great ball through from Dean to Campbell afforded him an excellent opportunity which he sent harmlessly, and quite hopelessly, wide. Wood then also missed hopelessly when he had a good opportunity, indeed the Vale forwards were displaying some miserably weak shooting.

Newcastle were making no headway against the wind and were rarely able to venture outside their own half, McKay being a mere spectator to events. Yet another corner fell to Vale and again it was fruitless though at least this time their efforts were more accurate, and the Newcastle goal was to have the narrowest of escapes.

Just when it looked like Newcastle would survive the continuous onslaught disaster would occur. With barely five minutes left to play Lowery was beaten. He made a dashing save from an effort by Elson, but as the return was lofted in he could do nothing against a fine header from Wood. Buoyed by the equaliser there was no let-up in the pressure by Vale, but they could not improve their score.

In game that exemplified the saying that *"football is a game of two halves"* a draw was called. Newcastle dominating the first, and scoring, Vale dominating the second, and scoring, the draw was a fair result.

Supplementary notes…

Some reports put the gate for this game as 1,400 whilst others indicate it was nearer the 2,000 mark. The consensus appears to be with the latter, 2,000, which is what I've quoted here.

This note is just to inform that there are discrepancies, and you will, *as always*, need to make up your own mind as to which report you subscribe.

It should perhaps be also noted some believe Newcastle were sporting white knickers rather than the dark blue ones. This could of course be true, and indeed be, *to me at least*, the more likely and the numerous mentions of there being "confusion" being caused may be a result of the white soon becoming indistinguishable from the black due to mud and grass stains. However, given there is early mention of the confusion, *i.e. within reports on the first half*, it is difficult to see why there would be confusion enough to warrant there being a mention; the different coloured shorts should have avoided 'early' confusions at a minimum.

Confused? I certainly am!

Pos.	Team	Plyd	W	D	L	F	A	G.Avg.	Pts.
1	Liverpool	21	17	4	0	63	11	5.7273	38
2	Small Heath	22	16	0	6	76	37	2.0541	32
3	Notts County	22	14	3	5	51	24	2.1250	31
4	Burslem Port Vale	22	12	2	8	55	47	1.1702	26
5	Newcastle United	22	10	5	7	50	36	1.3889	25
6	Burton Swifts	19	10	2	7	52	41	1.2683	22
7	Grimsby Town	19	10	1	8	54	44	1.2273	21
8	Lincoln City	18	8	4	6	41	36	1.1389	20
9	Middlesbrough Ironopolis	22	7	4	11	30	51	0.5882	18
10	Woolwich Arsenal	17	6	2	9	27	40	0.6750	14
11	Ardwick	19	6	1	12	34	39	0.8718	13
12	Crewe Alexandra	18	4	5	9	28	45	0.6222	13
13	Walsall Town Swifts	19	4	3	12	24	43	0.5581	11
14	Rotherham Town	20	5	1	14	33	67	0.4925	11
15	Northwich Victoria	20	2	1	17	22	79	0.2785	5

Game: 30 ~ Saturday, February 10th, 1894		vs. Bolton Wanderers
Competition: FA Cup [2nd Round]	Venue: St James's Park	Gate: 10,000

Newcastle United	1-2	Bolton Wanderers
Goal, William Lowery; *backs*, Harry Jeffrey, Tom Rodger; *half-backs*, Bobby Creilly, Willie Graham, Joe McKane; *forwards*, Charlie Quinn, Tom Crate, Willie Thompson, John Law, Joe Wallace.		*Goal*, John William Sutcliffe; *backs*, John Somerville, David "Di" Jones; *half-backs*, Alex Paton, Archibald "Archie" Hughes, James "Jimmy" Turner; *forwards*, Robert Tannahill, Jim Wilson, James Cassidy, David Weir, Handel Bentley.
Scorer(s): Tom Crate		Scorer(s): Archie Hughes, OG [Rodger]
Referee: Mr J. Howcroft (Redcar)		Kick-off: 3:00 PM

New record crowd, alas they witness narrow defeat.

Smashing the previous record of 7,000 set in the First-Round tie against Sheffield United there were fully 10,000 spectators crammed around the St James's Park enclosure today. The gates had been opened at 2o'clock and from thence they poured in continuously. Detachments of police and infantrymen from the barracks had previously been requisitioned by the Newcastle committee, which at the time had been viewed as excessive, but perhaps proved to be justified. Not that they had much to do as the throngs of spectators were orderly in the extreme. The noise which greeted the red-shirted homesters was deafening and the visitors, in their spotless white shirts were given at hearty welcome too. The excitement was almost tangible.

Key Events		
First Half		
0 – 1		Archie Hughes
0 – 2		OG [Rodger]
Second Half		
1 – 2		**Tom Crate**

Bolton won the toss, electing to play with the westerly wind in their favour and without further ado Thompson set the ball in motion. The centre kick was soon returned and both sides played pretty football within the confines of midfield for some minutes. The first real attack came from the visitors, but this was quickly repelled by the home defence who headed the ball away.

A long throw-in from Turner was headed away by Creilly at the expense of a corner which was fruitless. Continuing to pressure Bolton had another fruitless corner giving rise to a breakaway by Quinn, this halted by Turner. Giving to Bentley he sent his effort behind. End-to-end exchanges followed as Wallace was stopped by Cassidy and Creilly did well to prevent an effort from Wilson, then from Weir, thus allowing Newcastle to get a look in. Thompson sent in a a clever kick and Quinn crossed to Law, rushing in, and he shot grandly but narrowly wide. Newcastle returned the goal kick and neutral play followed.

Weir got Bolton away again but when close in he shot wide. From the goal kick Newcastle pressed their opponents defence, Hughes heading away. With a slight upperhand Thompson played the ball through to Crate, he in turn gave to Quinn who sent the ball through, but the goal was disallowed for offside.

Rain then started falling and the ground became slippery. Bolton pressed and winning a throw-in it was again launched long by Turner, but Graham took possession and sent to Quinn. His race up the left wing was marvellous and was unlucky to see his grand shot go inches wide. A run up the right wing by Bolton was halted by Rodger and from this the "Trotters" quarters were occupied. The Newcastle left making matters uncomfortable for the defence. It looked as if the goal had fell once more, but again hopes were dashed, as a magnificent save from Sutcliffe tipped the ball out. Whilst all Newcastle supporters thought he did this behind his line the referee was not in agreement.

A free-kick to Newcastle sent them back in again and Sutcliffe and Somerville were tested severely. Wallace and Law playing up grandly during this period. Eventually Bolton broke away and following a terrific run Hughes had a good opportunity but, *much to the delight of the partisan crowd*, missed quite badly. For some minutes the ball was kept in and around the Newcastle citadel.

Numerous attempts were made, all repelled by Jeffrey and Rodger, covering Lowery splendidly. Bolton got a free-kick, in a favourable area, but could not turn it to any advantage, Newcastle finally got the ball away. Somerville stopped their advance and sent long back down, this was returned by Graham, cleverly feeding the left wing whose attack was swift, once again Somerville intervened.

An advance from Newcastle, brought about by some neat passing between their forwards, was met with equally good tackling by Hughes and once again they were stopped. This gave rise to a rush up from Bolton and when well placed to shoot Tannahill was given offside. Sustaining the pressure Jeffrey was called upon to make some great interventions and when he was breached Bentley shot harmlessly over the bar.

This was quickly followed up by an equally unsuccessful attempt on behalf of Weir.

Thompson led a sally, getting Newcastle right up, Jones making a saving intervention. That was brief respite for the home defence, the pressure being once more applied, their response though was heroic. Packing their goal, they made sure there was no way through for the Bolton forwards.

From a free-kick the Newcastle left advanced and they won a corner. Nothing came from it but on returning they got another free-kick for a foul in front of the posts. When this was sent in Jones headed away beautifully. Both sides were now passing in grand fashion and each citadel was visited in turn. Lowery, Creilly and Graham had to be on the highest alert and Rodger cleared magnificently from Cassidy. Long kicks between the half-backs followed.

Then came the strangest of goals. Hughes sent in a shot from range which looked to be passing wide. As such Jeffrey made no attempt to stay its progress and it was far too late for Lowery to reacted as it passed into the net.

Bolton now ahead, pressed ahead, with all the dash of a team that were winning, and it was not long before they got another stroke of luck. Awarded a free-kick this was lofted in by Turner and it passed between the heads of the Newcastle players crammed around the goalmouth. Eventually headed clear a little play outside saw it sent back in and, off the legs of Rodger, the ball landed in the net.

More than a little disheartened by two such "soft" goals Newcastle remained pinned in their own half for some minutes. Their left wing got away but could not make any inroads until a shot by Law went narrowly wide. Somerville was called upon and put in a saving tackle allowing Bolton to come again at great speed. Lowery made a save and great applause met a saving tackle by Creilly. Pretty passing from both sides, minor calls upon each defence, led us to half time.

Cassidy for Bolton got the second half underway, but it was Newcastle who played up first, and with great determination! Now aided by the wind they took better advantage of it than Bolton had in the first half and were very soon encamped around the opposition citadel. Sutcliffe was forced into a good save from Thompson. Gaining a corner another save was brought out of the custodian. This led to the leather being worked away by the Bolton wing, the respite however was brief. Crate gave Sutcliffe a 'warm' save to make and in doing so he knocked it up into the air, the wind then carried it towards his goal, and he was lucky to be able to retrieve the situation, saving in marvellous fashion.

A corner was gotten and was very well placed in but 'hands' was given against Creilly. Newcastle came back and from a free-kick Thompson headed narrowly outside the post. The excitement in St James's Park was enormous, and rising by the minute, as Newcastle kept up their momentum.

Graham played the ball to Thompson and his fantastic screw-shot smashed into the post and span out.

Following the goal kick possession was once more gained by Newcastle and a grand shot from Quinn was saved by Sutcliffe at the expense of a corner. Whilst it was fruitless Newcastle kept up the offensive. The wind was strong now and hampered attempts by Bolton to clear their lines.

Another free-kick to Newcastle availed them nothing as the ball was sent behind by Law. Soon after a great scrimmage was witnessed in the Bolton goal but was forced wide and from this position the ball arrived at Wallace but perhaps too quickly. A now rare sally forth by Bolton saw Wilson playing the ball to Cassidy who when excellently placed made a wretched effort that went way beyond the post. A little loose play then followed before the home forwards once again asserted themselves.

Wallace and Quinn made great advantages and the ball was sent to Quinn who shot through with a grand effort, once more the point was disallowed for offside.

Thompson made another run and Law missed with a good shot. A shot from range was made by Crate but this was dealt with by Jones but at the expense of a corner. Delivered nicely it was sent past by Quinn. An effort by Law then went narrowly past.

Newcastle now dominating proceeding sent in shot after shot, all being kicked out by Bolton. The pressure though paid off as when a hard low shot was sent in by Crate neither the defence nor the custodian could prevent it nestling into the back of the net, amidst the loudest of cheering and applause.

The crowd urged Newcastle on to gain an equalising goal, or even a winning one! The pressing play of Newcastle up to the goal had been impressive, what was to follow was even more so. Time after time Sutcliffe had to demonstrate his international class as he fisted, kicked, and even headed out the plethora of shots that came his way. His defence too, Jones in particular, had to make a series of interventions. It was only by their performance, and slices of luck, that Newcastle did not score. Fortune and Lady Luck were however not with them today and Bolton eventually cleared their quarters to midfield.

As the final whistle was approaching Sutcliffe again made a save, kicking out wonderfully. Back came the return and Newcastle got another free-kick in a favourable position, which ended up being tossed over the bar. As the whistle arrived Newcastle were still pressing the Bolton defence hard.

Supplementary notes...

Bolton wanted this tie changed to their ground of Burden Park; this was refused by the Newcastle committee. Bolton then lodged a complaint with the Football Association regarding the fitness of St James's Park as a venue for this tie, given the nature of the pitch. An "emergency committee" of the FA made a pitch inspection, (Wednesday 8th) at St James's Park and following it they dismissed the objection.

Game: 31 ~ Saturday, February 17th, 1894 vs. Rotherham Town

Competition: Division 2   **Venue:** St James's Park   **Gate:** *very low*

Newcastle United	**4-0**	**Rotherham Town**

Goal, William Lowery; *backs*, Harry Jeffrey, Tom Rodger; *half-backs*, Bobby Creilly, Willie Graham, Joe McKane; *forwards*, Charlie Quinn, Tom Crate, Robert Willis, Joe Wallace, John Law.

Goal, Arthur Wharton; *backs*, Walter Hobson, James Nisbet; *half-backs*, Joe Barr, F. Dawson, Walter Broadhead; *forwards*, Fred Turner (Jnr), J. McCrindle, Peter Rae, Walter Sylvester, Arthur Fairbairn.

Scorer(s): Joe Wallace, Tom Crate, Willie Graham, Charlie Quinn

Referee: Mr. W. Stacey (Sheffield)   Kick-off: 3:00 PM

Newcastle win in mud bath!

After there had been three days of almost non-stop rain it was not expected that this game would survive a 2o'clock pitch inspection. The lower end, *the Gallowgate end*, was literally a pool of standing water, and the rest of the pitch was in a simply 'deplorable state'. Another inspection took place just before the scheduled kick-off and with mountains of sawdust placed at the Gallowgate goal the referee decided the game could go ahead.

Key Events		
First Half		
1 – 0	Joe Wallace	
2 – 0	Tom Crate	
Second Half		
3 – 0	Willie Graham	
4 – 0	Charlie Quinn	

Rotherham won the toss and elected to play down the hill and therefore Newcastle got the ball rolling. They had the better of the earliest exchanges, keeping Rotherham penned in, other than for a brief break away from their right wing. Willis gave Newcastle the first serious shot of the game, missing narrowly. Broadhead and Barr made a run for Rotherham, but Rae ended up shooting wide. Play was then mediocre, confined mainly to the midfield area.

Wallace, Law and Willis broke the monotony, the latter unlucky in seeing Nisbet making a grand intervention. Pressing still, shots were made by Crate and Wallace then another from Crate. Though the ground was slippery the pace of the two forward lines was impressive. Quinn forced the first corner of the game which was well placed, causing a bit of a scrimmage from which Crate sent over the bar.

Returning the goal kick both Hobson and his custodian, Wharton, made good saves. On one occasion Wharton fisting away when he was lying on the ground! A brief sally down by Rotherham was halted and a good passing move between the Newcastle forwards got them up once more, drawing appreciative applause from the crowd. The attack being ended when Willis played in Law who very narrowly missed the target.

From another return Graham shot behind and midfield play followed. Rodger sent the ball long up-field, Willis took possession getting very close and in the ensuing scrimmage Newcastle got another corner off Nisbet but it was fruitless. The goal kick was returned by McKane and Nisbet conceded a further corner. This was splendidly placed, and Hobson headed away from under the crossbar.

Back came Newcastle and just when it looked like the ball was through Broadhead, with another goal-line clearance, relieved. The Newcastle left wing regained possession and with pretty play Wallace sent in a low shot with Wharton just failing to catch hold of it.

From the centre kick possession was soon gained by Newcastle and the pressure on the Rotherham goal was resumed, in relentless fashion. The left wing got very close in and Hobson make a fine intervention. Willis sent the ball straight back at the goal, but the ball went wide.

Keeping up the pressure Newcastle continued to surround the Rotherham citadel. Graham sent in a fine effort which Wharton could only punch away. The ball however fell nicely for Crate who scored with his effort before Wharton could recover himself from his previous save.

Trying to retrieve the situation Rotherham played up well, had it not been for an intervention from Jeffrey on Fairbairn they may have even scored. However, the respite was short for the visiting defence as the homesters once again stormed their citadel. A centre was put in from the left for Crate and he shot through marvellously, only for the point to be disallowed for offside.

A series of exchanges then followed which favoured the visitors and with some clever passing their forwards got well down, but Rodger dispossessed them. Rotherham then had a short spell of dominancy but eventually Barr shot wide.

Wallace then released Law to run up the wing and he tried an effort from distance which went wide. Another sally forth led by Wallace advantaged Newcastle nothing and the returning Quinn tried a shot from distance, his too going wide. No doubt having by far the better of matters the home forward quintet were keeping the visiting defence busy indeed. Rae managed to briefly break the siege, getting to the centre line but Jeffrey stopped him and sent the ball long back in.

Another break-away saw Rae sending in a good shot from distance that had Lowery flat out in the mire to save. Before his area could be cleared Broadhead got possession but sent his effort over the bar.

Willis then ran clean up the middle, nicely evading the centre-half and passed to Quinn. In the most favourable of positions, he shot hopelessly, the ball going yards wide! Hobson then intervened to save a long shot from Crate.

The falling rain had now ceased and the siege on the Rotherham goal ceased too as they began to force play into midfield and then into Newcastle quarters. McCrindle when close in was penalised for offside. Once again, the respite was short-lived for the visitor's defence.

Newcastle won a corner and Nisbet intervened to save an effort from Willis. Another effort from Willis was well saved by Wharton. With Newcastle encamped in the Rotherham goal area half time was called.

When the second half was gotten away it was noted that the St James's Park pitch was akin to a "ploughed field" and had "pools of water in many places"! It was therefore with no surprise that attempts to play the ball along the ground, *with any degree of accuracy*, were to prove difficult in the extreme. Also noted was that "the spectators all gathered at the lower end", a clear indication of the meagreness of the attendance. Giving both sets of players the utmost credit they gave of their best in the face of these most adverse conditions.

It was Newcastle who showed up first as Law was presented with an opportunity but shot wide. Rotherham then had a brief look-in but Jeffrey relieved. McKane and Graham worked their way up to no avail and Rotherham again played up well to reach the Newcastle citadel but were not overly taxing on the defence. Creilly and Quinn making a good intervention between themselves and breaking away once more. Racing away at a speed defying the conditions the ball was gave to Wallace, but he was ruled offside.

In defending another attack Hobson and Nisbet were strong, denying numerous shots from even reaching their custodian. Their efforts being applauded warmly. From a free-kick Broadhead made a sterling intervention and when Rotherham won a free-kick Graham intervened smartly.

Hobson conceded a corner and Graham almost got through with a header, but Wharton saved well. When given the opportunity some erratic shooting ensured Rotherham could not improve their position. Crate brought out another save from Wharton. It was clear that should another goal come it would be surely to the homesters and so it ultimately proved to be the case.

With the crowd shouting, perhaps more intent on keeping themselves warm as anything else, it still inspired Newcastle to keep up the press. Willis sent in an effort which Wharton kicked out and from a throw-in by Creilly possession was given to Graham who scored with a very smart shot indeed.

From a period of play where Rotherham were having the better of the exchanges Newcastle took possession and with a quick combined rush the forward quintet put Wharton and his defence under pressure resulting in Quinn getting the leather through.

Play from this point was end-to-end without being overly exciting. Both sides were showing the strains of having to play on a field of mud, tiredness was evident in sloppy passes and mistimed tackles. Newcastle kept the upperhand and never really looked like surrendering a goal.

Supplementary notes...

Scorers: There are widely different accounts as to who scored Newcastle's goals. Several reports accredit Wallace's goal to Quinn, giving him two for the game, others give Crate's goal to Law. Consensus, and statistics, however, indicate that these are perhaps incorrect. I've opted to agree with the reports which ensure each player's goal scoring efforts tally with those officially produced by Newcastle, though even then, who's to say they cannot be incorrect?

Gate: It is truly anyone's guess as to what the gate today was. Some, i.e., the Rotherham Independent, put the attendance as low as 600, others indicate up to 6,000. The only thing that is in no doubt was that the gate was far, far, below that of the record set last week, whether it was as low as 600 is greatly debatable. As the gate receipts for today weren't published knowing the truth is more guesswork than scientific.

Pos.	Team	Plyd	W	D	L	F	A	G.Avg.	Pts.
1	Liverpool	21	17	4	0	63	11	5.7273	38
2	Notts County	23	15	3	5	60	25	2.4000	33
3	Small Heath	22	16	0	6	76	37	2.0541	32
4	Newcastle United	23	11	5	7	54	36	1.5000	27
5	Burslem Port Vale	23	12	2	9	56	49	1.1429	26
6	Grimsby Town	21	12	1	8	62	45	1.3778	25
7	Burton Swifts	20	10	2	8	53	44	1.2045	22
8	Lincoln City	20	9	4	7	44	41	1.0732	22
9	Woolwich Arsenal	21	9	3	9	37	44	0.8409	21
10	Middlesbrough Ironopolis	22	7	4	11	30	51	0.5882	18
11	Ardwick	20	7	1	12	38	40	0.9500	15
12	Walsall Town Swifts	21	5	3	13	27	46	0.5870	13
13	Crewe Alexandra	20	4	5	11	31	57	0.5439	13
14	Rotherham Town	23	5	2	16	35	79	0.4430	12
15	Northwich Victoria	22	2	1	19	23	84	0.2738	5

Game: 32 ~ Saturday, February 24th, 1894		vs. Grimsby Town
Competition: Division 2	**Venue:** St James's Park	**Gate:** 4,000

Newcastle United	4-1	Grimsby Town

Goal, William Lowery; *backs*, Harry Jeffrey, Tom Rodger; *half-backs*, Bobby Creilly, Willie Graham, Joe McKane; *forwards*, Charlie Quinn, Robert Willis, Willie Thompson, Tom Crate, Joe Wallace.

Scorer(s): Tom Crate, Charlie Quinn, Harry Jeffrey, Willie Thompson

Referee: Mr. Fitzroy Norris (Bolton)

Goal, James Whitehouse; *backs*, Thomas Frith, James Lundie; *half-backs*, Sandy Higgins, James Graham, James Russell; *forwards*, John Ackroyd, Joseph Rogers, Harry Fletcher, Thomas Rose, David Riddoch.

Scorer(s): Harry Rose

Kick-off: 3:00 PM

Terrific second half sees the Mariners all at sea!

Key Events		
First Half		
0 – 1		Harry Rose
Second Half		
1 – 1		Tom Crate
2 – 1		Charlie Quinn
3 – 1		Harry Jeffrey
4 – 1		Willie Thompson

Grimsby won the toss and elected to play with the stiff breeze in their favour and so Thompson for Newcastle got the game underway. The home forwards were immediately checked. Grimsby showed up first with a couple of shots being sent at Lowery but on each Jeffrey prevented them getting through. Rodger sent the right wing away and Lundie stopped a shot from Thompson reaching his custodian. With neat passing Grimsby worked their way to the centre but Thompson disposed J. Graham and sent in a long shot which missed. Crate and Wallace combined well and from a throw-in Thompson forced a good save from Whitehouse with a fine header.

Russell cleared well but Crate and Wallace brought the ball speedily back down with Crate giving Whitehouse a hot shot to save. Next up was J. Graham who looked dangerous but was stopped by Rodger. A free-kick for 'hands' put Newcastle favourably close in but they could not take further advantage. From it Grimsby got down and won a free-kick of their own but it proved equally fruitless as Jeffrey intervened. A counter, led by Wallace, brought about a little sustained pressure on the Grimsby defence. Higgins eventually cleared with a run but was quickly checked by Quinn leading to neutral play in midfield. The mediocrity broken by a dash and shot from Thompson which went wide.

A minute later and Thompson sent in again and Whitehouse needed all his skill to save and send the ball out. Wallace was quick on the return but lost out to Frith. The pressure was soon reapplied by Newcastle and Whitehouse had to save from Crate, fisting out smartly. Still pressing Newcastle got a free-kick for 'hands' close in. McKane put it in beautifully but Wallace sent over the bar. With some tricky play Wallace then won a corner off Frith but this was easily cleared. Jeffrey returned with a long shot and this when sent out was received by Quinn who shot behind.

Grimsby worked their down and withstanding the grand tactics of the home half-backs got close in but could not penetrate the backs though they made several attempts to do so. Rodger broke the pressure and sent long to Thompson who raced away but was halted by Lundie. Quinn then put a fine centre in, but Crate sent it over the bar. From the goal kick Grimsby raced away and Lowery had to fist away an effort. This led again to neutral play in midfield.

Fletcher emerged from this and playing superbly between himself and Rogers got close and sent the ball through, the point being disallowed for offside.

Coming as a 'wakeup call' to Newcastle they set off grandly and Whitehouse performed heroics in fisting away a shot from Thompson. Back came Newcastle giving the Grimsby defence some work to do, which they did admirably. Numerous attempts were made, the pick of them being from Wallace which forced another flying, fisting save from Whitehouse. The pressure was only relieved when Grimsby were able to clear their lines courtesy of a free-kick.

It was also a free-kick, for 'hands', following more midfield mediocrity, that got Newcastle close in but Frith made an excellent intervention. Grimsby then caused concern to Creilly and Graham, but they stood firm. Creilly, by clever play, eluded Russell and got the Newcastle right away once more but Whitehouse was equal to the efforts and eventually Crate shot wide.

From the goal kick Grimsby got well in and Rodger made a couple of saving interventions before a most bizarre incident indeed. Rose banged the ball at Lowery, and he caught it with ease, *or so all thought*, as he allowed the ball to fall, and it rolled away into his net!

Grimsby now played up strongly and just when it looked like Fletcher would double their advantage his shot went inches wide. Newcastle then got a look in but Lundie proved to clever. Crate and Wallace came racing down again and this time it was Frith who halted any further progress. Further neutral play followed from which Grimsby emerged stronger and an assault on the home goal began. They forced a corner off Graham which was fruitless, and Jeffrey put a sound kick well into midfield. Here Higgins and Willis had a marvellous tussle, the Newcastle man winning out and play was before the visiting citadel. Unfortunately, the shooting of the Newcastle forwards was erratic to say the least and Whitehouse was never in any real danger.

A dash was then made at each end, first Grimsby wasted an excellent opportunity then Crate and Thompson were well in, Whitehouse having to rush out to save from Thompson. Then Lowery had to save from Riddoch and just before the break Whitehouse again had to save a hot shot from Thompson which ended the half.

Getting the second half started Grimsby made a rush to the home citadel but a clever tackle from Graham prevented their travel from posing any threat. Feeding his forwards an assault was then made on the visitor's goal. Lundie frustrating a swift Crate effort. The venue was changed to the home goal, but Thompson broke away and for a time play was in midfield. The play witnessed was loose as the ball was knocked into touch on several occasions.

With the crowd urging Newcastle to 'play up' they encamped themselves around the Grimsby citadel. They could not however break the stout defence and in turn resisted their efforts to relieve the pressure. A corner fell to Newcastle, which proved fruitless. Crate then saw an effort from range go wide. Directly after he had another effort which was only inches wide. Grimsby were now in a situation where their only means of defence was to kick the ball out as far as they could, playing out was not an option.

A long shot from Wallace brought a smart save from Whitehouse. Trying again with a long overhead shot Lundie was forced into heading out for a corner. Some nice play was witnessed by its good delivery, but J. Graham sent it away. Creilly was unlucky when his shot grazed the crossbar and Jeffrey returned the goal kick sending it narrowly wide.

Maintaining the pressure Crate sent in a grand effort which went through the legs of Whitehouse and into the net. Newcastle having a thoroughly deserved equaliser.

From the centre kick Rose led a charge giving his defence some respite. Willis made a run but was brought up by Frith and a period of further loose midfield play followed. With a combined rush this was broken by the home forwards, led by Willis, and the ball was played to Quinn who sent through a glorious shot and now Newcastle had the lead.

On forcing play once more Frith conceded a throw-in and from it being well placed Wallace shot over. He very soon had another effort, this time from a difficult angle, which he sent wide. A series of corners came Newcastle's way, but all proved to no avail. There was no let-up in their pressure and Whitehouse and his defence were kept busy.

On the very odd occasion that Grimsby were able to get out of their own half they found the Newcastle defence, and Rodger in particular, impassable.

At 2-1 the next goal was going to be of the utmost importance. Both teams were trying, Newcastle by far the better, and as it was to show it was they who secured that vital goal, but it came with more than a little luck.

A long ball sent in by Jeffrey struck Lundie and went into the net. It was not recorded as an "own goal" but accredited to Jeffrey. Either way it gave Newcastle an increased lead.

Grimsby tried desperately to reduce the deficit from the centre kick but were stopped by clever play from Jeffrey, earning warm applause. They came back once more and occupied home territory for a short period before the home forwards raced away and receiving the ball Thompson, with a beautiful shot gave Newcastle a fourth goal. This was met by rapturous applause and loud cheering, fully deserved too.

For the remainder of the game Lowery in the Newcastle goal was a mere spectator whilst Whitehouse was subjected to the most intense pressure. All the Newcastle forward quintet tried shots, from varying angles and distances, but all were repelled. Frith, on two occasions intervening superbly when Newcastle were awarded free-kicks for hands.

Pos.	Team	Plyd	W	D	L	F	A	G.Avg.	Pts.
1	Liverpool	21	17	4	0	63	11	5.7273	38
2	Notts County	23	15	3	5	60	25	2.4000	33
3	Small Heath	22	16	0	6	76	37	2.0541	32
4	Newcastle United	24	12	5	7	58	37	1.5676	29
5	Burslem Port Vale	24	12	3	9	58	51	1.1373	27
6	Grimsby Town	22	12	1	9	63	49	1.2857	25
7	Burton Swifts	21	11	2	8	61	49	1.2449	24
8	Lincoln City	21	9	5	7	46	43	1.0698	23
9	Woolwich Arsenal	22	10	3	9	43	47	0.9149	23
10	Middlesbrough Ironopolis	23	7	4	12	33	57	0.5789	18
11	Ardwick	21	7	2	12	39	41	0.9512	16
12	Crewe Alexandra	21	4	6	11	32	58	0.5517	14
13	Walsall Town Swifts	22	5	3	14	32	54	0.5926	13
14	Rotherham Town	23	5	2	16	35	79	0.4430	12
15	Northwich Victoria	22	2	1	19	23	84	0.2738	5

Game: 33 ~ Saturday, March 10th, 1894		vs. Walsall Town Swifts
Competition: Division 2	**Venue:** St James's Park	**Gate:** 1,000

Newcastle United	**2-0**	**Walsall Town Swifts**

Goal, William Lowery; *backs*, Harry Jeffrey, Tom Rodger; *half-backs*, Bobby Creilly, Willie Graham, Joe McKane; *forwards*, Charlie Quinn, Robert Willis, Willie Thompson, Joe Wallace, Tom Crate.

Goal, Tom Hawkins; *backs*, John Thomas Tom Bayley, Pinches; *half-backs*, Sammy Holmes, R. Cook, Norman Forsyth; *forwards*, Joe Lofthouse, Walter McWhinnie, David Copeland, Joe O'Brien, Charlie Leatherbarrow.

Scorer(s): Tom Crate, Harry Jeffrey

Referee: Mr. J. Beckton (Ironopolis) Kick-off: 3:00 PM

Two goals, two points, not too bad at all…

Key Events

First Half	
1 – 0	Harry Jeffrey [pen]
Second Half	
2 – 0	Tom Crate

Playing up the incline Newcastle had an uphill struggle in the very early exchanges, Swifts pressing hard and Lowery was called into action and made two very good saves. Soon Wallace and Crate sped away, evading all in front of them, Crate's effort was a good one, but Hawkins made an equally good save and sent the ball into midfield. There Rodger dispossessed Lofthouse and played to Quinn and a corner was won. Quinn sent in the flag-kick, placing it well, but the defence marshalled it away.

In trying to get up Leatherbarrow was stopped by Jeffrey who gave to Thompson and his effort just grazed the crossbar. Wallace then had hardlines and Willis just grazed the crossbar too.

O'Brien and Leatherbarrow made some advance with grand passing but Jeffrey intervened and sent Quinn and Willis on their way. Putting the ball across the goal it arrived at Crate who, from an awkward position, shot past. The Swifts got down again and Lowery was tested but not too severely as was Hawkins, holding a great shot from Crate. This end-to-end play continued then came the decisive moment of the half.

Thompson, Quinn, and Willis raced down, but it looked as if the ball would go over the byline. Quinn backheeled it and in following it was tripped by Forsyth and a penalty was awarded. Jeffrey took the spot-kick and scored easily. The remaining five-minutes of the half being spent in midfield neither side having an advantage.

Now playing downhill Newcastle started the second half with great dash. They were oft able to evade the half-back line of the Swifts, but the backs and custodian were demonstrating great steel. Shot after shot was saved by Hawkins, and Pinches and Bayley tackled well and kicked strongly. Holmes; Cook; and Forsyth, those same half-backs would always come back in support of their colleagues with dogged determination. Even the forward quintet found themselves called upon to help defend.

No matter what Newcastle tried, and they tried shots from just about every conceivable angle, some from range, some from close in, nothing was getting through. Hawkins was magnificent in fisting, kicking, and heading away, his performance akin to that of the great one put in by Sutcliffe of Bolton. An appreciative crowd applauding his efforts as much as the shots sent in.

During this extended period there was no way out for the Swifts but as long as they kept the deficit to a single goal they were always in with a chance. For the Newcastle forwards their inability to score from open play, *the goal having come from the spot*, saw frustration enter their game and some of their shooting was erratic.

Finally, Crate got the ball on the left and put in a screw shot that went across the face of the goal and passed into the net at the right-hand post.

Newcastle continued to have the best of matters up until the end and whenever the Swifts got past the halfway line they found no way through a solid defence.

Pos.	Team	Plyd	W	D	L	F	A	G.Avg.	Pts.
1	Liverpool	22	18	4	0	66	12	5.5000	40
2	Notts County	23	15	3	5	60	25	2.4000	33
3	Small Heath	23	16	0	7	77	39	1.9744	32
4	Newcastle United	25	13	5	7	60	37	1.6216	31
5	Grimsby Town	24	14	1	9	68	52	1.3077	29
6	Burslem Port Vale	25	13	3	9	63	54	1.1667	29
7	Woolwich Arsenal	24	11	4	9	44	47	0.9362	26
8	Burton Swifts	23	11	3	9	63	53	1.1887	25
9	Lincoln City	22	9	5	8	49	48	1.0208	23
10	Middlesbrough Ironopolis	25	8	4	13	35	59	0.5932	20
11	Ardwick	21	7	2	12	39	41	0.9512	16
12	Crewe Alexandra	23	4	7	12	34	61	0.5574	15
13	Walsall Town Swifts	23	5	3	15	32	56	0.5714	13
14	Rotherham Town	23	5	2	16	35	79	0.4430	12
15	Northwich Victoria	24	2	2	20	25	87	0.2874	6

Game: 34 ~ Saturday, March 17th, 1894		vs. Burslem Port Vale
Competition: Friendly	**Venue:** St James's Park	**Gate:** 2,000

Newcastle United	6-1	Burslem Port Vale
Goal, William Lowery; *backs*, Harry Jeffrey, Tom Rodger; *half-backs*, Bobby Creilly, Tom Crate, Joe McKane; *forwards*, Charlie Quinn, Robert Willis, Willie Thompson, Joe Wallace, John Law.		*Goal*, Hugh MacKay; *backs*, Bob Ramsay, George Samuel Eccles; *half-backs*, Joseph Boughey, Bob McCrindle, Billy Elson; *forwards*, Jimmy Scarratt, Meshach Dean, John Edwards, Alf Wood, Lewis Campbell.
Scorer(s): Robert Willis (3), Willie Thompson, Joe Wallace, Charlie Quinn		Scorer(s): Bob Ramsay
Referee: Mr. William Tiffin (Northumberland FA)		Kick-off: 3:00 PM

'Six of the best' is best surprise!

In the two league encounters between these sides Newcastle won the first by the odd goal in three and the second was a draw at one goal each, this scoreline was therefore a huge surprise. Graham was rested for Newcastle. The sun was shing very brightly and would make any high balls difficult to follow and it was exceedingly warm for March. The slight breeze did little other than move the warm air around, it had little if any cooling effect. Burslem were resplendent in red and slate whilst Newcastle bore the county colours.

KEY EVENTS

First Half
1 – 0		Robert Willis
2 – 0		Willie Thompson
3 – 0		Joe Wallace
4 – 0		Charlie Quinn

Second Half
5 – 0		Robert Willis
5 – 1		*Bob Ramsay*
6 – 1		Robert Willis

Newcastle won the toss and elected to play up the incline for the first half and Edwards for Burslem set the ball in motion. No headway was made by Burslem and McKane took possession and sent Wallace on his way, he played to Law and a corner was won off Ramsay. The ball was sent behind and the goal kick saw Crate return and Law brought out a save from McKay at the expense of a second corner. Nothing resulted but the return made by Newcastle saw a third corner being won. Again, nothing was won from it.

The goal kick was received by Creilly who returned, and Thompson gave to Willis and the first goal was scored.

Keeping up the pressure McKay had to deal with some hot shots. Willis, Wallace, and Law severely taxed the Burslem defence, but they held out for a short period. At length Wallace passed to Law and he sent in a shot which McKay was uncharacteristic in the feeble manner in which he scooped it away and Thompson rushed in to easily put on the second goal for Newcastle.

From the centre kick Burslem tried an advance which was repelled by Jeffrey sending long into midfield. There followed a period of slow and uninteresting play from both sides. Crate injected some good work into the mediocrity, but Wallace spoilt the move with long shot which missed. Scarrett then made a run up the wing, played to Wood and his snapshot cannoned off a post. The rebound was shot back in by Edwards and Jeffrey had to concede a corner which was fruitless. Burslem had another look in which was abortive then Wallace led Willis and Law on a charge. A grand shot was made by Wallace which went just wide. Cue the mediocrity once more.

Quinn broke this with an effort that went inches wide, and play settled in Burslem quarters without anything of note happening. McKay had a couple of saves to make and Eccles made a fine intervention but ultimately Wallace, with a very clever shot, sent through for Newcastle's third goal.

Thompson missed with a shot and when the return from the goal kick came in Quinn got possession from the play and sent in a shot which McKay had no chance of saving. With a four-goal advantage Newcastle maintained territorial supremacy without overly exerting themselves.

The second half followed the pattern of the first, Newcastle dominance, Burslem breakaways, and long periods of mediocrity. However, it did produce another three goals. Through their left-wing Newcastle got the ball well up and sent it into the centre before the backs could react Willis neatly sent it through the posts.

Both ends were then visited without success, but Newcastle relaxed too much and a scrimmage in front of their goal saw Ramsay, *normally a goalkeeper, but playing at centre-half*, got the ball through. There was an anxious moment for Newcastle when Lowery fell in making a save but Rodger was alert and cleared the danger.

Just as time was to be called Newcastle made a final push and Wallace centred from which Willis put through for his hat-trick, and so an affair that was more one-sided than anyone could have imagined.

Game: 35 ~ Friday, March 23rd, 1894		vs. Crewe Alexandra
Competition: Division 2	Venue: St James's Park	Gate: 10,000

Newcastle United	2-1	**Crewe Alexandra**
Goal, William Lowery; *backs*, Harry Jeffrey, Tom Rodger; *half-backs*, Bobby Creilly, Willie Graham, Joe McKane; *forwards*, Charlie Quinn, Robert Willis, Willie Thompson, Joe Wallace, Tom Crate.		*Goal*, Edward Hickton; *backs*, Harry Stafford, Walter Cartwright; *half-backs*, Herbert Crawford, Albert Bayman, J. B. Sproston; *forwards*, A. J. Hall, Jack Woolfe, Joseph Benton Sandham, John Jones, Sammy Barnett.
Scorer(s): OG[*unconfirmed*], Harry Jeffrey		Scorer(s): J. B. Sandham

Kick-off: 3:30 PM

Bumper Holiday Crowd makes this a real Good Friday

The advertised start for the game was three-o'clock, as per the posters dotted around the city streets and Crewe Alexandra duly took to the field at that time. Newcastle however did not enter the field until half-past three. It is anybody's guess therefore as to why there was a delay, but a quick review of the morning's Newcastle Journal shows them stating that kick off would indeed be "3.30 precisely". If that wasn't strange enough when Newcastle turned out it was not in their normal red jerseys, but in "county colours", with no official explanation as to why. It most certainly was not due any clash of colours with those of Crewe Alexandra as they were reported to have entered the field "clothed in white jerseys".

Key Events	
First Half	
0 – 1	J.B. Sandham
Second Half	
1 – 1	OG [*unconfirmed*]
2 – 1	**Harry Jeffrey**

Newcastle won the toss and elected to play uphill in the first half so Sandham got the game underway for Crewe. They were quickly dispossessed by Thompson who led his confreres well up. Several attempts were made at goal, each being turned away and eventually Graham sent past. Crewe then worked their way down via their right wing and showed some good football in and around the Newcastle goal without being overly dangerous and eventually Graham kicked long away into midfield.

Wallace took possession and moved play to the Crewe citadel for a period, again there was no overly dangerous play. Each side was playing an interesting game, the defence against the attack now becoming exciting. All of the Newcastle forward quintet tried their hand at shooting, but all were repelled then the pressure was relieved with a long kick out by Cartwright, the return by Jeffrey being sent over the line. Further pressure was applied, and it too was broken with a long kick out.

Barnett made progression with a good dribbling run but was stopped by Rodger who rushed out to dispossess him and send the ball back up the field. Play was now fast and exciting from both sides the exchanges being well appreciated by the crowd. In making an intervention Creilly mistimed it and the ball went past him allowing Hall to take possession. He passed to Jones who hit a tremendous shot which looked a certain goal but Lowery popped up with an equally excellent catch. This he threw to Rodger who launched it back up with great alacrity.

That narrow escape put some urgency into the homesters who vigorously set about the visiting citadel. Some great scrimmaging took place and Crate, in a difficult position, sent narrowly over the bar. Willis then caught one of the opposition unawares and dispossessing him made a run, unfortunately he too was dispossessed. The Crewe right wing again ran through, and again they were met by Rodger. He sent to Wallace who crossed to Quinn, but he sent behind.

Play then slackened somewhat but after a short period the excitement rose once more as Woolfe rushed past the home backs but once again Rodger was there to make a saving intervention. His long clearance again led to scrimmaging in front of the Crewe goal and their defence had to be commended. The ball was eventually sent into midfield where Newcastle won a free-kick. This was sent back in and a free-kick for 'hands' given to Crewe allowed them to clear their lines once more.

Another free-kick befell Newcastle in a favourable position but Graham sent over the crossbar. On the return from the goal kick Quinn had the same result. Crewe then had hard lines as a great rush looked set to get through, but Jones accidentally handled and the attacked was halted for the free-kick. This allowed Newcastle to rush up and gain a corner. Well placed this led to a scrimmage and a further corner and again a scrimmage ensued in front of the Crewe goal. Crate sent in a grand shot and Stafford headed it well away for some midfield play to take place.

A good bit of pressure saw Sandham get away and though bothered by Jeffrey and Rodger he bested them but kicked past in doing so. Stafford sent a long kick back in and Woolfe's excellent centre forced Jeffrey into conceding a corner. The ball was placed right in front of goal but Sandham headed wide. Hall returned with a swift run and Jeffrey, coming to the aid of Lowery, cleared. As half time was approaching both the pace of the game, *and the intense heat*, had the players flagging somewhat but Crewe kept pegging away. Sandham gained possession in a dangerous position not too far out and sent in a fast shot that beat the attempt of Lowery to reach it. and the scoring was opened.

Newcastle tried to respond, winning first a free-kick, then gaining a corner off Barnett. In the scrimmage another corner was won but was fruitless, a quick break saw an equally fruitless corner for Crewe and on the stroke of half time the Newcastle forwards bungled a grand chance.

The start of the second half saw brisk play from both sides and Newcastle were the first to show up as Willis sent a shot across the goal. Creilly then had an effort which he sent behind. A further attempt was saved by Hickton. Maintaining their pressure Newcastle were unlucky to see Stafford make an intervention when a goal looked certain. They then won a free-kick for 'hands' and Jeffrey was desperately unlucky to see his effort hit the right-hand post. He was even unluckier moments later when Thompson was fouled, and a penalty was awarded. Jeffrey saw his kick being cleared by a rush. The same tactics saving Crewe a minute later when they gave away another free-kick.

Newcastle then gained a couple of unsuccessful corners. Bad luck and stout defending were frustrating a concerted effort from Newcastle and the feeling that the Crewe goal would succumb was tangible and poetically it came from the boot of Jeffrey, though not directly. With one of those long shots for which he is quite famed, he put the ball in the Crewe goalmouth and the forward quintet rushed in an instant and amidst great excitement the leather, *and half the Crewe defence*, was fairly carried over the line.

There was almost a repeat of this very soon after before Crewe managed to clear their lines. There then came a brief halt to play as Quinn was injured in some midfield play. When play was restarted both Wallace and Crate made excellent shots but Hickton was equal on each occasion.

Playing against the hill towards Leazes Park the visitors were making very heavy work of it, Lowery was a spectator, enjoying the sunshine no doubt, though always keeping a vigilant eye on proceedings.

Crate made a dashing run into the Crewe quarters, but they rallied well and play of a neutral nature followed in midfield. This lasted a full five minutes but was indeed the "calm before the storm".

Newcastle, seemingly now to have the full measure of their opponents made an irresistible advance on their citadel. At once a corner was won. On the ball coming out Jeffrey caught it beautifully on his toe and directed it between the posts, accompanied by one loud drawn-out shout of delight from the assembled masses, *well the vast majority of them anyway*. A thoroughly deserved goal topping his excellent performance and making up for his previous bad luck.

Now in the lead for the first time in this hard-fought game Newcastle were in no mood to relinquish it and indeed pressed ahead to try to increase it. The Crewe defence was performing exceptionally and held the enthusiastic attacks at bay. Another short lull in the intensity of the Newcastle press was met by an attempt at an advance by Crewe but it was to no avail. The hill, the heat, the stiff defence, and a very partisan crowd, whilst appreciative of their efforts, were all against them.

There was not to be another change in the score, and it was with a sense of relief Newcastle won, fully justifiably.

Supplementary notes…

Change of colours: One possibility to explain this may, *and I emphasise may*, be that Newcastle Postmen held a match today, kick-off 3.15, against Sunderland Postmen, the teams were to play in the colours of Newcastle United and Sunderland respectively, the jerseys being lent to them by the clubs. Perhaps this is just a coincidence, or a stretch of the imagination, but there it is, could that be the explanation?

Change of time: Why the change of time from that advertised on the posters? One explanation could be that Newcastle United 'A' had an Alliance match against Dipton Wanderers at St James's Park this morning, which kicked off at 11-o'clock. Then why did Crewe take to the field at 3-o'clock? Perhaps whilst Sir Alec Ferguson may have been the master at mind-games he was not the initiator.

Pos.	Team	Plyd	W	D	L	F	A	G.Avg.	Pts
1	Liverpool	23	18	5	0	67	13	5.1538	41
2	Notts County	26	17	3	6	68	27	2.5185	37
3	Small Heath	25	18	0	7	90	43	2.0930	36
4	Newcastle United	26	14	5	7	62	38	1.6316	33
5	Grimsby Town	24	14	1	9	68	52	1.3077	29
6	Burslem Port Vale	25	13	3	9	63	54	1.1667	29
7	Woolwich Arsenal	25	12	4	9	50	47	1.0638	28
8	Burton Swifts	24	12	3	9	70	53	1.3208	27
9	Lincoln City	24	9	6	9	50	51	0.9804	24
10	Middlesbrough Ironopolis	26	8	4	14	35	66	0.5303	20
11	Ardwick	23	7	2	14	41	56	0.7321	16
12	Walsall Town Swifts	24	6	3	15	34	57	0.5965	15
13	Crewe Alexandra	24	4	7	13	35	63	0.5556	15
14	Rotherham Town	24	5	2	17	37	82	0.4512	12
15	Northwich Victoria	25	2	2	21	25	93	0.2688	6

Game: 36 ~ Saturday, March 24th, 1894 — vs. Burton Swifts

Competition: Division 2 **Venue:** St James's Park **Gate:** 3,000

| Newcastle United | 4-1 | Burton Swifts |

Goal, William Lowery; *backs*, Harry Jeffrey, Tom Rodger; *half-backs*, Bobby Creilly, Willie Graham, Joe McKane; *forwards*, Tom Crate, Robert Willis, Willie Thompson, Joe Wallace, John Law.

Scorer(s): Robert Willis (2), Joe Wallace, John Law

Referee: Mr. Mr. Tomlinson (Sheffield)

Goal, Samuel Jones; *backs*, William "Billy" Furniss, Jack Berry; *half-backs*, Walter Perry, Ollie Hackett, Thomas J. Walker; *forwards*, Joseph Dewey, Alexander "Sandy" Rowan, Alex Boggie, James "Jimmy" Munro, Frederick George Ekins.

Scorer(s): Alex Boggie

Kick-off: 3.00 PM

Excellent revenge for earlier defeat.

This return fixture against Burton saw Newcastle avenge the defeat they suffered in only their second League fixture way back in September. Newcastle were a much-improved side and had won their last four league games. Burton on the other hand were displaying mediocre form having won two, lost two and drawn one in their last five games. A good match was anticipated and whilst the Good Friday attendance could not be matched a goodly crowd assembled around the St James's Park enclosure.

Key Events	
First Half	
1 – 0	**Robert Willis**
1 – 1	*Alex Boggie*
2 – 1	**Robert Willis**
Second Half	
3 – 1	**Joe Wallace**
4 – 1	**John Law**

Newcastle won the toss and elected to play downhill in the first half, mainly to put the strong sun in the faces of their opponents. Rowan therefore got the game underway for the Swifts. Loose play followed the start, but it was to soon explode into action.

Newcastle pressed and gave the defence a severe testing, several shots being sent in but all were repelled. Then with a smart combination the Newcastle quintet got Law away and from out on the wing he centred beautifully for Willis who shot through in grand style. There were barely four minutes on the clock.

From elation to deflation within a matter of minutes was to follow for Newcastle.

The Swifts left wing ran smartly down and when a shot was sent in it was sent straight back out by Jeffrey. Unfortunately, it fell to the feet of Boggie who equalised with a very clever shot, a total of three minutes having elapsed since the Newcastle goal.

Despite this stunning start the game lapsed into the most desultory of play. Burton made a weak effort on the Newcastle goal, easily foiled by Graham. He fed Crate who got well down, but his centre was so feeble that Perry had no difficulty in transferring the ball to the Newcastle quarters.

Wallace and Law tried a run down but were easily dispossessed and then Walker and Davey made a rush resulting in a corner when Walker centred and Creilly tried to clear. This was well delivered but in the ensuing scrimmage Creilly got badly winded and the game was halted for some moments.

The first to show from this were the visitors and a series of throw-ins ensued on the Leazes side, the ball eventually being sent by. Wallace made a poor pass and Perry once again took advantage sending the ball down and Jeffrey returned with a long kick. Thompson played in Law who sent an overhead shot narrowly over the bar.

A free-kick for 'hands' against Berry saw Jeffrey put a great ball into the danger area but Willis headed over. Crate then made a run down and Berry was forced to concede a corner, but Crate sent that one by too. There soon followed another Newcastle corner but this was gotten away by Ekins who took it well down. A miskick by Graham looked likely to be an own goal but Rodger saved the day, and his blushes. Walker then missed when well placed.

This all seemed to shake Newcastle up more than a little as they began a charge in earnest. Jones was forced to save from Law and following a little relief Newcastle were back through Willis who shot through whilst Thompson occupied Jones.

Taking possession directly from the restart Willis sent in another fine shot which Jones was feeble in his clearing. Thompson immediately rushed in and put the ball into the net, but the point was disallowed for offside.

Maintaining their momentum Newcastle came again and won a corner. This was well sent in and smart play was seen by both defence and attack in the ensuing scrimmage. Numerous shots were sent in, numerous repulsions were made, an exciting passage of play indeed. Newcastle then got a free-kick close in but nothing came from it. Another corner came Newcastle's way and a severe bombardment took place upon the Burton goal, eventually Law sending behind. Then another corner and Crate this time was guilty of sending behind. Two quick corners were then won by Burton, one off Crate the other off Jeffrey, both were abortive, and the game slowed considerably up until the break.

The interval was very short, barely five minutes, and when the second half was started at ten-minutes to four the sun had lost none of its strength. Now of course it was in the faces of the Newcastle men, and they were facing the hill too.

It was perhaps not unsurprising then that Burton took the early aggression and forced Newcastle back immediately. The home defence were thankfully alert, and the ball was quickly returned to neutral territory. Play was in midfield for quite some minutes before Burton resumed their press and won a corner. This was fruitless as was another soon after which Crate helped on its way with a huge kick out. This initiated an attack of their own.

Graham sent in a shot which hit one of the backs and rebounded. Wallace took possession from this and sent it into the goal area. Thompson nipped in and was unlucky to see his header go across the front of the goal, the slightest of touches by anyone would have seen it go in. Interesting play followed in and around the visitor's citadel, Law distinguishing himself and it was mainly through his efforts that a corner was gained. This was cleared out.

A scrimmage took place out on the wing and from it the ball was directed towards the Swifts posts where Wallace was standing. With an unbelievable swift [*pun*] screw-shot he turned the ball into the net.

From the centre kick Burton tried an assault but they were quickly repelled by Jeffrey with a grand intervention. This launched another onslaught upon the Burton citadel. For quite a period of time the Newcastle forwards and half-backs continually harassed the visitors, but they held firm.

Newcastle were temporarily reduced to ten men as Crate retired with an injury but returned without Burton having been able to take advantage of their numerical supremacy. Once parity was restored it served as a new lease of life to Newcastle who pressed strenuously once more. It was Crate himself who made the next notable effort, but he sent it just over the bar.

Burton then had a look in and Lowery made a save which Jeffrey cleared long up the field. The right wing took up possession and gained further ground before sending to Crate. He put in a grand centre to Law who with a fine shot from range sent through to record a fourth goal for Newcastle amidst hearty applause and cheering.

The excitement was maintained as further attacks from the homesters kept the visitors pinned into their citadel. They did have a brief respite when they tried a very spirited counter-attack but it was a short lived one as Newcastle were soon back in their territory.

Both sides now looked to gear themselves for a final spurt. During this period Burton looked very dangerous on occasions which brought out the best in Jeffrey as he knocked out several efforts, one particularly dangerous shot being gotten away under thunderous applause.

Burton were enjoying their best spell of the second half and Newcastle were in the strange position of they being the ones penned in. The spell was quite a sustained one two but within it Lowery was never in any real danger, Jeffrey and Rodger protecting him very well.

Newcastle had a quick look in without any success and Burton upon clearing their lines were straight back with their pressing. Camped in and around the home citadel Burton were territorially superior but again were not troubling Lowery, there was simply no way through to him for them. A decent effort from Davey was the best they could muster, again this causing no real danger.

It looked as if that was how the game would end, with Burton on the ascendancy, but they were to be rocked back by a determined Newcastle. Working their way nicely up they entertained the crowd with two very decent efforts indeed, one from Law the other from Wallace, whilst spectacular they were far from being close enough to alter the score. Within seconds the whistle then sounded to end the game and Newcastle's revenge was complete.

Pos.	Team	Plyd	W	D	L	F	A	G.Avg.	Pts.
1	Liverpool	24	19	5	0	69	13	5.3077	43
2	Notts County	27	18	3	6	70	28	2.5000	39
3	Small Heath	26	19	0	7	96	43	2.2326	38
4	Newcastle United	27	15	5	7	66	39	1.6923	35
5	Grimsby Town	25	14	1	10	68	57	1.1930	29
6	Burslem Port Vale	26	13	3	10	63	60	1.0500	29
7	Woolwich Arsenal	26	12	4	10	51	49	1.0408	28
8	Burton Swifts	25	12	3	10	71	57	1.2456	27
9	Lincoln City	25	10	6	9	56	51	1.0980	26
10	Middlesbrough Ironopolis	26	8	4	14	35	66	0.5303	20
11	Walsall Town Swifts	25	7	3	15	39	57	0.6842	17
12	Ardwick	24	7	2	15	41	62	0.6613	16
13	Crewe Alexandra	25	4	7	14	35	65	0.5385	15
14	Rotherham Town	24	5	2	17	37	82	0.4512	12
15	Northwich Victoria	25	2	2	21	25	93	0.2688	6

Game: 37 ~ Monday, March 26th, 1894		vs. Leicester Fosse
Competition: Friendly	**Venue:** Walnut Street Ground	**Gate:** 10,000

Leicester Fosse	2-0	**Newcastle United**
Goal, James Thraves; *backs*, Harry Bailey, George Smith; *half-backs*, Jack Lord, W. Henrys, Thomas Seymour; *forwards*, William Dorrell, William Thomas Miller, James Brown, Henry Ross Harry Edwards, John Hill.		*Goal*, William Lowery; *backs*, Harry Jeffrey, Tom Rodger; *half-backs*, Bobby Creilly, Willie Graham, Joe McKane; *forwards*, Tom Crate, Robert Willis, Willie Thompson, Joe Wallace, John Law.
Scorer(s): John Hill, William Thomas Miller		
Referee: Mr. A. Bates (Nottingham)		Kick-off: 3:35 PM

Bumper Holiday Crowd, but Blues for United...

There was a bumper Easter Monday crowd at the Walnut Street Ground today and the vast majority would be going home to continue the celebrations whilst a hardy band had a tough travel back to Tyneside as their favourites six game unbeaten run came to an end. The consolation being that this was only a friendly fixture, so no league points were lost. Fosse, with the return of Edwards, were at full strength as were Newcastle. The weather was glorious.

KEY EVENTS	
Second Half	
1 – 0	John Hill
2 – 0	William Thomas Miller

Newcastle won the toss and set the homesters to face a brilliant sun and they kicked off towards the gas works goal. From the centre kick they at once set about the Newcastle quarters but Dorrell overran the ball when a shot was open opportune. From the goal kick Newcastle got down quickly and Willis sent in a hot shot which Thraves saved sharply.

Throwing out well he set his forwards away once more. Enjoying a spell of dominancy, the appreciation from the crowd was warm and Edwards, in particular, receiving a good share of that. On one or two occasions Newcastle tried to 'spoil the party' and Crate was unlucky with an effort, sending it wide. A well-played combination brought the homesters back in front of the Newcastle citadel ending with Miller shooting over the bar. This being the same result from attempts by Brown then Dorrell. Maintaining their pressure Miller then grazed the bar with a shot.

At the other end McKane and Willis made good efforts. Play settled into a very even exhibition of fine passing, stiff defending, hard lines, and at times pretty poor shooting. Nothing was scored up to the break.

Following the interval, the early exchanges were confined to the midfield, each set of backs being tested only mildly. Newcastle were the first to break this cycle and a good, combined rush saw them in front of the home citadel but Law, just at the point of shooting was ruled offside.

Following this Hill tried a shot from almost on halfway, which was fruitless and only gave Newcastle the possession to return once more. Lord conceded a free-kick for a foul close in but Newcastle could not capitalise.

There followed some warm exchanges in front of the Fosse goal and Newcastle were having by far the better of matters but could not break the very resilient Fosse defence, though many attempts were made. These missed opportunities were to be rued as with two 'break away' rushes Fosse scored twice in quick succession.

The first Fosse goal came as Dorrell raced away down the wing and Hill put in a tremendous of work, greatly amusing the crowd as he took up every position along the forward line. Finally, he manoeuvred himself into a grand position right in front of goal and with a very clever shot he drove the leather past a crowd of players and into the corner of the net.

The second goal came within a minute or two of the first. Hill was once again causing major issues for the Newcastle defence with his movement across the forward lines and he and Brown were playing in around the Newcastle goal in central positions. This allowed Miller to be in space and upon getting possession he just squeezed the ball past Lowery.

Newcastle tried desperately to get back into the game. Crate had a golden opportunity to reduce the deficit when the ball came to him when in front of the goal. He somehow completely missed the ball when he went to kick it!

Fosse edged back into the game and Miller, Hill, Brown and Seymour each had numerous efforts at goal but none of them worried Lowery unduly, most going wide or over. Equally Thraves was untroubled by a couple of opportunities afforded to Newcastle by Fosse giving away free-kicks for fouls in favourable positions. As the game was nearing its conclusion Newcastle were on the offensive but due to some horrendous mistakes on behalf of their forwards they could get nothing out of their dominance. The game thus ended in favour of the homesters.

Game: 38 ~ Saturday, March 31st, 1894		vs. Middlesbrough Ironopolis
Competition: Friendly	Venue: St James's Park	Gate: 1,000

Newcastle United	3-0	Middlesbrough Ironopolis

Goal, William Lowery; *backs*, Harry Jeffrey, Tom Rodger; *half-backs*, Bobby Creilly, Willie Graham, Joe McKane; *forwards*, Willie Thompson, Robert Willis, Tom Crate, Joe Wallace, John Law.

Goal, Roger Ord; *backs*, John Oliver, George Nokes; *half-backs*, Donald McNair, Jimmy Grewer, Henry Allport; *forwards*, Walter Adams, A.N. Other, Charles Coulthard, J. M. Moonie, Thomas Hunter.

Scorer(s): Tom Crate, Joe Wallace, John Law

Dominant second half earns Newcastle the victory...

With both Newcastle and Ironopolis having a vacant date in their respective calendars this friendly encounter was arranged between the two sides. This was the third meeting between the teams this season, having already played out their league fixtures. The points at the Paradise Ground, on Christmas Day, had been shared, resulting as it did in a one-one draw, but the return match at St James's Park, on January 2nd, had seen Newcastle run out easy victors by a score of seven goals to two goals. Though in fairness to Ironopolis they were greatly understrength that day.

Even though this was just a friendly there was a good degree of interest shown in the game, testified to by a crowd of circa 1,000 spectators. Whilst that was lower than had been seen at St James's Park this season one has to remember that this was a Bank Holiday weekend and there were numerous competing attractions in town. So, in glorious weather the keen, but friendly, rivalry between Newcastle and Ironopolis was engaged.

KEY EVENTS

Second Half
1 – 0	Tom Crate	
2 – 0	Joe Wallace	
3 – 0	John Law	

Ironopolis won the toss and elected to play downhill in the first half thus Crate set the ball in motion for Newcastle. Though they tried the home forwards could make little headway up the hill and were soon dispossessed, the ball being sent well down, but Jeffrey received and kicked it long back up. This afforded the home forwards the opportunity to camp around the visiting citadel for some moments but ultimately Law sent behind with his effort. The goal kick signalling some loose play in midfield.

Working their way slowly but gradually up the hill Newcastle got close and Ironopolis could only clear by kicking the ball out. From a long kick by Graham Newcastle won a corner which was beautifully placed, and a scrimmage ensued in front of the goal but between themselves Oliver and "A.N. Other" relieved the danger.

Regaining the upperhand Ord was forced into fisting away a fine header by Crate. When the ball was returned from midfield by Rodger it was received by Wallace who sent in a swift shot from range which caught the defence by surprise, but Ord was alert. Untroubled, as there was no one around him, he threw it well away. Thompson subsequently also tried a long shot, but he sent wide.

Newcastle got a free-kick for 'hands' but could not capitalise and from the clearance Ironopolis broke with speed and a corner was gained off Jeffrey. When the ball came in it was Jeffrey who cleared it. Willis raced away and being fouled Newcastle had a free-kick which Creilly sent behind. Another Newcastle attack saw Willis sending in a long shot which Ord saved with difficulty. Upon the return Willis had another effort, this one going over the bar. Back came Newcastle, winning two corners in quick succession. Crate missed with a decent chance as did Wallace soon after.

With no let-up Newcastle kept pressing and from a scrimmage in front of goal another corner was won. Thompson lofted it in and Graham headed it on to Law who in turn headed it back to Graham and then he headed it into the goal. Ord however prevented it crossing the line and threw it out where it fell to Law who sent it narrowly over the bar. Still Newcastle pressed but they could not break the stubborn defence, despite their numerous attempts.

In a rare foray out of their quarters Oliver, with a long shot tested Lowery but he saved easily and, in another Adams, sent an effort behind. McKane took the ball back into the visitors' citadel and a veritable bombardment took place. It was only 'hands' being given against Crate that the pressure was released. The respite was short as upon returning Thompson won a corner off Oliver but Crate, when the ball was well delivered, sent it over the bar. When the whistle blew for half time Ironopolis were very lucky in not having conceded.

As soon as the interval was over Newcastle went straight back on the offensive. Oliver showed great alertness and made a fine intervention to halt a move by Newcastle and gain possession for his side, though they did not hold it long as they were dispossessed by Graham.

He sent the ball long down the field but in trying to further advance it McKane sent it out. Gaining the ball once more Creilly was afforded an opportunity but sent his effort over the bar. The goal kick was returned without much ado and this time the opportunity fell to Crate and his swift shot went agonisingly wide, a matter of inches in it.

Ironopolis then had a break away but their advanced was nullified by 'hands' on the behalf of "*A.N.Other*". The game then lapsed into a period of quite sedate averageness, almost as if it was just a 'breather' for Newcastle so that another assault could be raised as Ironopolis offered little, and Newcastle stopped pressing. As such the 'action', *for want of a better word*, took place in midfield.

Eventually a bit of excitement was put into proceedings as Willis took possession and ruched away. Getting well into the Ironopolis quarters he ensured that the visitors' goal was once again put in danger. Oliver did well to make an intervention and cleared with a long kick.

Another rush was led by Willis and he drew a save from Ord, which was made with his feet, kicking away. However, it only came back to Willis who this time sent his shot over. Some scrimmaging play ensued and from it Creilly gave to Law who put a great header into the goal but once again Ord prevented it going over the line and managed to throw it out. A brief sally forwards by Ironopolis was stopped by Jeffrey. Oliver was alert when a shot came in from Graham, but he had to concede a corner which proved fruitless. A run up by the Ironopolis forwards from the goal kick led to nothing. At once Newcastle came back through Willis making a rush.

Ord made a clearance up the field which Graham returned. Law took possession and put in a grand centre for Crate who caught the ball beautifully on his toe and crashed the leather through.

The game had barely been restarted when Newcastle gained possession and the forward quintet advanced on the Ironopolis citadel. Upon receiving the ball, and still some distance out, Wallace sent in a shot which fizzed past Ord at such speed he had no chance of getting to it.

Ironopolis tried to retrieve the situation with a speedy run up but were soon forced back and as time was on the horizon a third goal fell to Newcastle. Receiving a cross from Thompson a swift shot from Law completely beat Ord.

Supplementary notes...

In the Newcastle Daily Chronicle, the Ironopolis team is listed with "A.N. Other" but within the text of the article an unlisted player called "Hughes" is mentioned. However, in the text of the article in the Newcastle Daily Journal there is reference made to a player called "Wright". To further complicate issues there is a reference to a player called "Costella". One can only assume that A.N. Other is therefore either Hughes, Wright or Costella, *whoever they may be*. As to which of these it is, one cannot say with any degree of certainty at all.

Game: 39 ~ Thursday, April 5th, 1894　　　　　　　　　　　　　　　　　　　　　　　　　　　　　　　**vs. Sunderland**

Competition: Friendly　　　　　　　　**Venue: St James's Park**　　　　　　　　**Gate: 5,000**

Newcastle United	1-2	Sunderland

Goal, William Lowery; *backs*, Harry Jeffrey, Tom Rodger; *half-backs*, Tom Crate, Willie Graham, Joe McKane; *forwards*, Charlie Quinn, Robert Willis, Willie Thompson, Joe Wallace, John Law.

Scorer(s): Willie Graham

Referee: Mr. W. Chard (Gateshead)

Goal, Ned Doig; *backs*, Peter Meehan, Donald Gow; *half-backs*, Jimmy Dale, Will Gibson, Hughie Wilson; *forwards*, Jimmy Hannah, John Harvey, Jimmy Millar, Davy Hannah, John Scott.

Scorer(s): Davy Hannah, Jimmy Hannah

Kick-off: 5:15 PM

A Bizarre Encounter Indeed...

In honour of his Royal Highness the Duke of York making a visit to Newcastle to perform the opening ceremony of the new Rutherford College in Bath Lane various festivities were arranged throughout the day, one of which was a fixture between Newcastle United and their nearest and dearest footballing neighbours, Sunderland. This was a fixture that was fast becoming the most eagerly awaited games of the season for both sets of fans. This despite the fact that this, and none of the preceding games had been a competitive fixture. Sunderland were by far the more illustrious of the two sides, being Football League champions for the last two seasons and being second to Aston Villa this season. Newcastle of course only just starting out in the league existence. So even though there was nothing more than bragging rights at stake these so-called friendlies were fiercely competed affairs. In testament to this there was a large gathering of circa 5,000 spectators in the St James's Park enclosure. Creilly was absent for Newcastle, whilst Sunderland were without prolific goal scorer Johnny Campbell but presented a very strong team indeed.

Key Events	
First Half	
0 – 1	*Davy Hannah*
0 – 2	*Jimmy Hannah*
Second Half	
1 – 2	**Willie Graham [pen]**

Winning the toss Newcastle decided to play downhill for the first half so without further ado Sunderland got the game underway.

The home forwards pressed from the beginning, but it was not long before the visitors took the ascendancy and forcing his way up D. Hannah forced a corner off Jeffrey. This was got away by Willis who launched a splendid counter-attack which was halted by a timely intervention by Wilson who sent the ball well back up the field with a long kick. Sunderland then applied considerable pressure which was eventually relieved by Graham.

Willis and Quinn, in good combination, worked their way into a dangerous position near the Sunderland goal and Gow did marvellously with his intervention to prevent any further danger. Play was fast and exciting but the quality of the Wearsiders was beginning to tell and they were soon to force Newcastle into a period of defence. Not out of it by any means though Graham tried a long effort from midfield which missed and from the goal-kick Thompson made a thunderous return which Doig only just saved at the expense of a corner from which a most bizarre goals was scored.

J. Hannah rushed up the wing and crossed inside to D. Hannah. Thinking he was offside Lowery made no attempt to make the save and Hannah therefore put the ball into the goal uncontested. To Lowery's, and Newcastle's, dismay the referee overruled their protests and the goal stood. On the reflection of play perhaps Sunderland deserved of their lead, but it was most curious indeed.

This decision by Mr Chard irked Newcastle, understandably, and they exerted themselves most strenuously in an effort to get an equaliser. McKane had an excellent opportunity from a free-kick, but Doig was equally excellent in his saving of it. Sunderland once again pressed, and it was only the awarding of hands against Scott that the danger to the Newcastle citadel was relieved.

The game then became quite even in nature, but Sunderland eventually progressed down the right and Scott sent in a decent cross but Lowery was able to throw it out. This started a good move from the homesters, and Willis was unlucky to see his long-range effort go close by. Sunderland then won a free-kick about thirty yards out and with a tremendous effort Dale sent the ball through. However, in doing so the ball had not touched anyone else so the point was not allowed. Newcastle then forced a corner which was beautifully placed, and Thompson shot well, but once again Doig was on top form and threw out. Protestations from Newcastle followed as they claimed the ball had been over the line when Doig threw it and in another quite bizarre decision the referee award not the goal to Newcastle but another corner for hands against one of the visitors! This corner proved fruitless as was a subsequent one. Perhaps adding insult to injury Sunderland then broke away and forced their way through the Newcastle defence resulting in J. Hannah scoring a second for the visitors. This signalled a sustained, if ineffectual, Sunderland press up until the interval was called.

Upon the restart Newcastle played up well and Dale conceded a free-kick in an advantageous position for them. Crate sent the ball in well and heavy pressure was put upon the Sunderland defence, but Wallace eventually shot past. The visitors reacted well and Gow sent in a shot from range. This was headed out by Jeffrey but only to Wilson who sent his effort by.

Graham then beat the Sunderland forwards to a ball, but his clearance only went to Dale who sent his effort by too. From the resulting goal-kick Newcastle forged forwards but their attack was futile and upon returning Sunderland were frustrated by Rodger and McKane. In a dangerous position close to his own goal Crate was guilty of hands but nothing could be made of this advantage by the visitors.

Newcastle rallied and Law and Wallace in combination forced a corner which proved fruitless. Returning on another attack Thompson sent in a speedy effort which Doig saved at the expense of a corner, this he saved and sent the ball well up-field with a long kick. Wallace took possession and ran speedily up the wing and was unlucky to see his cross-shot land on the roof of the net. Sunderland then had an opportunity which Miller sent high over the bar. Back up the other end and Doig once again was equal to the efforts of Willis. The home defence then survived a prolonged attack from the visitors, but they stood up well and turning defence into attack released their forwards who ran up, but Thompson sent behind.

As the game was coming to a close Newcastle won a corner, then from it a penalty and yet another bizarre incident occurred. There was some disputing taking place resulting in Sunderland completely declining to defend the penalty kick, consequently Graham rolled the ball into an empty and unguarded net.

Supplementary notes...

It came to light that one potential reason the Newcastle penalty was undisputed is that as Wallace was about to take the penalty kick Wilson, the Sunderland captain, barged him in the back and the ball went over the bar. The referee spotted this and ordered the penalty to be retaken. It was then noted that Graham was to take this second penalty kick and as he stepped up to do so Wilson, in either a fit of gentlemanly conduct, or perhaps repentance, ordered Doig to stand aside and Graham had an empty net to roll the ball into.

Game: 40 ~ Saturday, April 7th, 1894		**vs. Dundee FC**
Competition: Friendly	**Venue:** Carolina Port	**Gate:** 2,000

Dundee FC	8-2	Newcastle United
Goal, Frank Barrett; *backs*, Bill Ferrier, George Campbell; *half-backs*, George McNaughton, William Longair, Harry Matthew; *forwards*, Bill Thomson, David McInroy, James Dundas, Alexander "Sandy" Gilligan, Alexander "Sandy" Keillor.		*Goal*, William Lowery; *backs*, Harry Jeffrey, Tom Rodger; *half-backs*, Bobby Creilly, Willie Graham, Joe McKane; *forwards*, Charlie Quinn, David Willis, Willie Thompson, Joe Wallace, George McFarlane.
Scorer(s): Bill Thomson, James Dundas (3), David McInroy, William Longair (2), Sandy Gilligan		Scorer(s): George McFarlane, Robert Willis

Referee: Mr. Black (Forfar)

Disaster over the border...

The attendance at today's game, whilst quite healthy, was perhaps not as healthy as the organisers had hoped for. It had to be taken into account however that many of those who would have been expected to attend would have been at Parkhead, Glasgow for the international match between England and Scotland. Dundee fielded a full-strength eleven whilst Newcastle were without Crate, his place being filled by McFarlane. The ground was said to be in excellent condition. The game was actually far more even than the scoreline suggests and at 2-2 at half time no one expected the collapse of the Newcastle defence that occurred. Even then their forwards had ample opportunities to redress the balance, but their shooting was abysmal.

KEY EVENTS	
First Half	
1 – 0	Bill Thompson
2 – 0	James Dundas
2 – 1	**George McFarlane**
2 – 2	**Robert Willis**
Second Half	
3 – 2	James Dundas
4 – 2	James Dundas
5 – 2	David McInroy
6 – 2	William Longair
7 – 2	William Longair
8 – 2	Sandy Gilligan

Newcastle won the toss and elected to have the wind in their favour and thus defended the east goal. It was they who were the first to show from the kick-off and quickly forced a save out of Barrett. A little after he was called upon to save again, which he did, fisting the ball away.

The Dundee forwards then made a charge, but they were repelled and when the ball was transferred to their territory McKane sent in an effort, but he sent the ball out. From the throw in Thomson secured and passed to Keillor he was fouled by Jeffrey and Dundee had a free-kick in a good position. Thomson took the kick and sent it unerringly past Lowery to register the first goal of the game.

From the centre kick Dundee gained possession and attacked again immediately and perhaps taken aback by the swiftness of it all Dundas was able to put on a second goal very easily for the homesters.

Following a period of midfield play Newcastle forced matters into the Dundee citadel. Barrett made several saves then was beaten by a long, swift shot from McFarlane. Shortly after this they forced a second and equalising goal from Willis. From then until the break Newcastle had by far the better of matters but could not augment their score and therefore at half time all was level.

Following the interval Dundee, now with the wind in their favour scored almost immediately when Thomson sent through Dundas and they were back in the lead. Dundas soon after scored with a header from a fine centre from the right. Newcastle tried to counter-attack but a swift shot from the left was sent behind.

Dundee attacked again and a scrimmage ensued in front of the Newcastle goal and McInroy succeeded in forcing the ball through for their fifth goal.

A period of midfield play followed and in truthfulness Dundee were so much in command that they could do as they pleased. A little time elapsed before Lowery was called upon to make a save, the ball being cleared back into midfield. Dundee were the ones to break out of the midfield cycle and in a rush forward Longair scored their sixth goal. Newcastle gave away a free-kick for a foul in proximity of the posts and from this Longair secured a seventh goal for Dundee.

The rout was completed as the game was concluding. Even though they had relaxed their efforts somewhat in the preceding minutes Dundee made one last push and Gilligan scored an eight goal for them. It was a long way home for a very sorry looking Newcastle United.

Game: 41 ~ Saturday, April 14th, 1894		vs. Grimsby Town
Competition: Division 2	**Venue:** Abbey Park	**Gate:** 2,000

Grimsby Town 0-0 Newcastle United

Goal, Jimmy Whitehouse; *backs*, Jimmy Lundie, Tom Frith; *half-backs*, Sandy Higgins, Charlie Frith, James Russell; *forwards*, Harry Rose, John Ackroyd, Tommy McCairns, Harry Fletcher, Jack Jones.

Goal, William Lowery; *backs*, Harry Jeffrey, J Laverick; *half-backs*, Bobby Creilly, Willie Graham, Joe McKane; *forwards*, Charlie Quinn, Robert Willis, Willie Thompson, Joe Wallace, Tom Crate.

Referee: Mr. J. Jeffries

League Season Ends with a Draw

This was the concluding league fixture for both teams. Coming into the game Newcastle were fourth in the table with Grimsby fifth. With the points difference being four, no matter what the result today Grimsby could not overtake Newcastle, similarly Newcastle could not match the tally of third placed Notts County, who had already finished their league engagements. It would seem therefore that this game was a '*dead rubber*', but far from it. Grimsby could have their fifth place taken by either Burslem Port Vale or Burton Swifts. The former were only one point behind Grimsby but faced the dominant, and unbeaten, champions-elect Liverpool at Anfield, where they would have to win as their goal average was inferior to that of Grimsby. The latter also needed both a win and Grimsby to lose as they were two points behind them but had a superior goal average, they having a tough, but winnable, game at Woolwich Arsenal. So, for the homesters this was an important game indeed.

Newcastle got the game underway with a very strong wind blowing across the field, because it was a cross-wind it held no advantage to either team but made control of the ball very difficult. No doubt due to the conditions the game was slow and stop-start in nature as the number of throw-ins was numerous indeed, as was the number of corners, all proving fruitless. Both custodians had to be on top of their game as the shots were rained upon both goals and the flight of the ball was very difficult to predict. Not surprisingly therefore most attempts that were made on goal were low in nature and were frequently blocked by the defences or saved by the feet of Whitehouse and Lowery.

The visitors adapted to the conditions quicker than the homesters, whose play was at times careless, using high ball crosses which invariably missed their target and often led to a throw-in. Newcastle were a bit cleverer on the ball and tried to keep it low, but even then it was prone to be blown into touch. On balance Newcastle had the best of the first half but either side could have scored with some fast shot being sent in, perhaps faster than usual due to being wind assisted. Credit was to the defences and custodians who performed admirably under the prevailing conditions. Upon resumption following the interval it was again Newcastle who had the better of the play however Grimsby began to apply themselves significantly better than they had done so in the first half. Indeed, they forced some rather marvellous saves from Lowery and bothered the defence more than a little. This all made the game a lot more interesting but then again it was the wind which dominated the game. The team who could get a handle on that would indeed be the team who would prove victorious.

Once again, the corners were numerous, and once again they all proved fruitless. As the half progressed Newcastle were banging the ball in at Whitehouse at every available opportunity, no doubt hoping to capitalise on the unpredictability of the ball's flight. At times they were perhaps too eager to shoot, too eager to take advantage of the wind, when closer controlled play may have been a better option. Ultimately neither side could score, Whitehouse and Lowery deserved the greater credit, and an interesting, very much wind affected, match ended all-square, which upon reflection was probably the fairest result.

Pos.	Team	Plyd	W	D	L	F	A	G.Avg.	Pts.
1	Liverpool	24	19	5	0	69	13	5.3077	43
2	Notts County	27	18	3	6	70	28	2.5000	39
3	Small Heath	26	19	0	7	96	43	2.2326	38
4	Newcastle United	27	15	5	7	66	39	1.6923	35
5	Grimsby Town	25	14	1	10	68	57	1.1930	29
6	Burslem Port Vale	26	13	3	10	63	60	1.0500	29
7	Woolwich Arsenal	26	12	4	10	51	49	1.0408	28
8	Burton Swifts	25	12	3	10	71	57	1.2456	27
9	Lincoln City	25	10	6	9	56	51	1.0980	26
10	Middlesbrough Ironopolis	26	8	4	14	35	66	0.5303	20
11	Walsall Town Swifts	25	7	3	15	39	57	0.6842	17
12	Ardwick	24	7	2	15	41	62	0.6613	16
13	Crewe Alexandra	25	4	7	14	35	65	0.5385	15
14	Rotherham Town	24	5	2	17	37	82	0.4512	12
15	Northwich Victoria	25	2	2	21	25	93	0.2688	6

Game: 42 ~ Saturday, April 21st, 1894		vs. Sunderland
Competition: Friendly	**Venue:** St James's Park	**Gate:** 7,500

Newcastle United	**4-1**	**Sunderland**

Goal, Joe Ryder; *backs*, Harry Jeffrey, Tom Rodger; *half-backs*, Bobby Creilly, Willie Graham, Joe McKane; *forwards*, Tom Campbell, Charlie Quinn, Robert Willis, Tom Crate, John Law.	*Goal*, Ned Doig; *backs*, Peter Meehan, Hughie Wilson; *half-backs*, Davy Hannah, John Auld, Jimmy Dale; *forwards*, James Gillespie, John Harvey, Jimmy Millar, Tommy Hyslop, John Scott.
Scorer(s): Charlie Quinn, Robert Willis, Tom Campbell, Tom Crate	Scorer(s): Jimmy Millar
Referee: Mr. Fred Hardisty (Middlesbrough)	Kick-off: 3:30 PM

Third Time Lucky for Newcastle!

This was the third meeting this season between Newcastle and Sunderland. The first two had went the way of the Wearsiders, as they won 3-1 on September 6th and 2-1 on April 5th, the Royal Visit. Both games held, as this was at St James's Park. Sunderland had strong support in the enclosure, many of their supporters having made the short journey from Wearside to Tyneside. Taking to the field at just after 3 o'clock in crisp white jerseys they had a long wait before Newcastle came out in contrasting red costumes.

KEY EVENTS		
First Half		
1 – 0		Charlie Quinn
1 – 1		Jimmy Millar
Second Half		
2 – 1		Robert Willis
3 – 1		Tom Campbell
4 – 1		Tom Crate

Sunderland won the toss and elected to play uphill in the first half, normally a wise choice but seemed quite surprising today as it gave Newcastle the benefit of having the strong sun at their backs and having the slope to their advantage.

Willis got the game underway for Newcastle and with great alacrity the ball was got down the left with Crate and Law getting almost to the byline. A centre was put in and Quinn took it at his toe and with the greatest of ease the ball was through for a goal. There was not even a minute registered on the clock! Miller restarted for Sunderland and tried a press but were restricted to a shot from distance by Scott which went wide. The goal kick saw Newcastle advance into midfield where Law gave Dale a deal of trouble with clever footwork. Making one trick too many Law ended up putting the ball out of play. The throw-in gave Sunderland good possession and they got well up to the home citadel, but their attack was feeble, and Gillespie sent behind.

Newcastle were then the aggressors and Doig was forced into making a clearance, as was Meehan, twice, conceding a corner on the last. Nothing came from the flag-kick other than to give the visitors possession and they then came away and Gillespie won them a corner, which again was fruitless to the takers.

Some pretty, and even, play then followed, at times centred around Ryder but equally around Doig. Just when it looked like Newcastle would take their lead into the interval a quick break, against the run of play at that time, saw Sunderland making a dash. Millar, who made a grand run up took advantage of some dilatoriness by Jeffery, who tried to shoulder him away, and very cleverly equalised by spinning the ball past Ryder. Jeffrey should have took the ball, instead of trying to take the man!

The break was but a short one and Millar got the second half underway, and as far as the rapidity of Newcastle scoring was in the first it was almost repeated in the second.

Getting possession Willis dashed up and played the ball to Campbell and in an attempt to dispossess him Dale was adjudged to have handled the ball. The free-kick was beautifully placed by Jeffrey and Willis headed through in magnificent style. One Sunderland newspaper reported that "*the enthusiasm with which the point was greeted was simply deafening*"! As within the first half play settled into an even affair, both ends being visited in turn but the better of the opportunities befalling the homesters whilst the Sunderland forwards were displaying uncharacteristically poor form in front of goal. As it was Newcastle were to prove their dominance on that front with another two goals. McKane sent in a long cross-shot towards goal. Willis headed it in but Doig managed to get a fist to it, but not with enough purchase, and the ball fell free which saw Campbell react quickest and he rushed in and powered the ball over the line. Law made a beautiful centre and Crate, rushing in, got hold of the ball and sent through with a splendid shot, which was unstoppable to Doig, and the accompanying applause, it was said, was even more thunderous than that which was heard before. Sunderland did make an objection to the goal, but the referee was having none of it and the point stood.

Game: 43 ~ Monday, April 23rd, 1894 vs. Willington Athletic

Competition: Benefit Match   **Venue:** Wallsend   **Gate:** *large*

Willington Athletic	0-2	Newcastle United

Goal, Potts; *backs,* Bell, Delaney; *half-backs,* McLean, Kirk, Redpath; *forwards,* Comings, Rice, Millar, McFarlane, McLucas.

Goal, Joe Ryder; *backs,* Harry Jeffrey, J Laverick; *half-backs,* Bobby Creilly, Willie Graham, Isaac Ryder; *forwards,* Charlie Quinn, Tom Crate, John Law, Joe Wallace, Tom Campbell.

Scorer(s): John Law, unconfirmed

Referee: Mr. J. McPhail   Kick-off: 6:00 PM

This game was played at the ground of Wallsend Celtic, adjoining the cricket field at Wallsend. The match was arranged for the benefit of Mr. Wm. Steele, an assistant foreman at the Tyne shipbuilding yard of Messrs. C.S. Swan and Hunter and an ardent supporter of Willington. Unfortunately, as a result of accident, Mr Steele had been unable to follow his employment for several months now, hence the agreement between the two clubs to hold this friendly for his benefit.

Apart from the fact that it was for a very good cause this encounter gave rise to a considerable amount of interest, especially in the mid-Tyne district. Adding to the interest was the fact that Newcastle had just beaten their nearest and dearest neighbours, Sunderland on Saturday past. Willington Athletic themselves were also a team of great note all across Tyneside, enough to ensure that this encounter would not be a foregone conclusion and raised many a debate as to which of the two sides would emerge victorious.

Though the weather was cloudy and dull there was still, rather fittingly, a large assemblance as the allotted time grew near. So, on a pitch which was slightly greasy from some rain earlier in the day Dr Henry H. Aitchison, MB., CC. set the game in motion on behalf of Willington.

KEY EVENTS

First Half
0 – 1	John Law
0 – 2	*Unconfirmed*

Taking immediate possession Graham returned the ball with a will, and at once play became very fast, the Willington team playing with great dash. However, despite their best endeavours it was Newcastle who opened the scoring very early in the game, after only five minutes in actuality. The United forwards had carried the ball into very dangerous proximity of the Willington goal and following a couple of efforts, and returns by the home defence, Law got his head to one of those returns and sent the ball flying between the posts. This was accompanied by very loud cheering from the Newcastle contingent in the crowd.

Willington were certainly not prepared to let this early upset dishearten them too much and returned with interest. Some very fine play was witnessed, from both sides. Rice and McLucas were playing notably grandly for Willington, whilst for Newcastle their left-wing formation of Wallace and Campbell were very prominent. End-to-end play ensued, much to the delight of those present and the performance of Willington, against the prowess of a team of the standing of the Newcastle United, was the subject of much favourable comment.

McFarlane at one stage succeeded in taking the ball deep into Newcastle territory, but their defence was so playing so excellently that nothing resulted, and the danger was halted. More give and take play followed, with some fine displays of dribbling, and very dexterous passing, being witnessed on behalf of both sides. A series of fast rushes followed by the Newcastle forwards, in very rapid succession, and from one such rush they managed to get the ball over the line and double their lead.

Despite the continued efforts of each side there was no more scoring leading up to the interval and a very enjoyable first half ended.

Upon the resumption both teams once again showed flair and passion. Each side created chances for themselves but for each chance created the defences of both were magnificent. Try as they might Willington could not get themselves on the scoresheet, and equally Newcastle could not increase their lead. When the final whistle came, ending a very fine game, Newcastle were victorious. Perhaps however the real victors were the crowd who had been keen throughout with their enthusiasm and had been rewarded with some splendid entertainment.

Supplementary notes...

The Newcastle players, to a man, gave their services free of charge, as it was believed did the officials. Their collective would-be renumerations being added to the monies raised.

Game: 44 ~ Wednesday, April 25th, 1894 vs. Shankhouse

Competition: Friendly **Venue:** Shankhouse **Gate:** *large*

Shankhouse 1-1 Newcastle United

Goal, Hicks; **backs**, Robson, Patten; *half-backs*, Endean, Rendell, Ritson; *forwards*, Willis, Johnstone, Hume, White, Gibson.

Goal, William Lowery; **backs**, Harry Jeffrey, Tom Rodger; *half-backs*, Bobby Creilly, Willie Graham, Joe McKane; *forwards*, Charlie Quinn, Robert Willis, Tom Crate, Joe Wallace, John Law.

Scorer(s): Johnstone

Scorer(s): Tom Crate

Referee: Mr. R. Glass (Newcastle)

Kick-off: 6:00 PM

This match was arranged for the benefit of the widow of the late George Matthews. It was said that no one worked harder, or did more, to enable Shankhouse to gain their current position and status in the footballing world. In lament the Newcastle Daily Chronicle said: *"His clever football and good generalship will not readily be forgotten"*.

Apart from it being for a very good cause there was considerable interest shown as Shankhouse, holders of the Northumberland Cup and Charity Shield, were said to be in grand trim and they and their supporters were relishing the opportunity to overcome league opponents. Newcastle having had a successful first season in the Football League had just beaten Sunderland on Saturday past and Willington Athletic two days ago in another benefit meeting. Yes, the result of this game was by no means a foregone conclusion and many a debate was raised as to which of the two sides would emerge victorious.

Key Events		
First Half		
0 – 1	Tom Crate	
1 – 1	Johnstone	

Shankhouse won the toss, electing to play with the slight breeze at their backs. Newcastle though were the first to play up and forced Hicks into fisting away a couple of difficult shots. It was however not long, circa ten-minutes before Crate sent through a clinking shot which beat had Hicks beaten all the way.

Shankhouse reacted marvellously. Gibson banged in a beauty following a centre by Endean. Lowery was then forced into handling a difficult shot from Johnstone and immediately following this the ball fell back to Johnstone and, *from the corner of the field at an acute angle*, he guided his second attempt through for the equaliser. There was no further scoring up to the interval.

After the break Newcastle had decidedly the best of matters. Willis saw a swift shot go past. Three corners were won in quick succession, from the last Graham hit the bar. Try as they might Newcastle could not further lower the colours of the villagers, they maintaining a stiff defence.

Supplementary notes…
The Newcastle players, to a man, gave their services free of charge, as it was believed did the officials. Their collective would-be renumerations being added to the monies raised.

Game: 45 ~ Saturday, April 28th, 1894 vs. Middlesbrough Ironopolis

Competition: Friendly **Venue:** Paradise Ground **Gate:** 2,000

Middlesbrough Ironopolis 0-0 Newcastle United

Goal, Gordon; **backs**, McQuade, John Sidney Sid Oliver; *half-backs*, J. Carlin, Jimmy Grewer, E. Hughes; *forwards*, George Millar, T. Kelly, William Hughes, O'Brien, Thomas Dixon.

Goal, William Lowery; **backs**, Harry Jeffrey, Tom Rodger; *half-backs*, Bobby Creilly, Willie Graham, Joe McKane; *forwards*, Tom Crate, Charlie Quinn, Robert Willis, Joe Wallace, John Law.

This was an interesting, if not overly exciting, match between two old friends, and as time was to tell it was the last meeting between the two. Ironopolis had no fewer than six new players on show, four from Broxburn Shamrock; Gordon, McQuade, and both the Hughes. From Paisley Abercorn they had Carlin and O'Brien. Newcastle were at full strength.

It was Newcastle who started with a strong sun in their faces. Other than a corner and a couple of saves made by Gordon the first half was even. Lowery being pressed but not exerted. The second half followed a very similar pattern. Play being mainly in midfield, with clever and interweaving passes, however Ironopolis did hit the crossbar twice.

Game: 46 ~ Monday, April 30th, 1894		vs. Sunderland
Competition: Friendly	**Venue:** St James's Park	**Gate:** 6,000

Newcastle United	1-3	Sunderland
Goal, William Lowery; *backs*, Harry Jeffrey, Tom Rodger; *half-backs*, Joe McKane, Willie Graham, Bobby Creilly; *forwards*, Charlie Quinn, Tom Crate, Robert Willis, Joe Wallace, John Law.		*Goal*, Ned Doig; *backs*, Donald Gow, Tommy Hyslop; *half-backs*, H. Dowe, John Auld, Hughie Wilson; *forwards*, James Gillespie, John Harvey, Jimmy Millar, Davy Hannah, John Scott.
Scorer(s): Tom Crate		Scorer(s): Unconfirmed, John Scott (2)

Referee: Mr. R. Glass (Newcastle)

Season ends in defeat...

An unexpected end to the season as Sunderland were supposed to be playing Preston North End today but the Prestonians cancelled the fixture at the last moment. Looking to find a substitute they asked "their old friends" their "*nearest and dearest*" neighbours, Newcastle, and they agreed to play at St James's Park with the gate receipts shared equally between the two.

Key Events		
First Half		
0 – 1	Unconfirmed	
0 – 2	John Scott	
Second Half		
1 – 2	Tom Crate	
1 – 3	John Scott	

Sunderland won the toss and played downhill in the first half. Willis started for Newcastle and passed to Law who was dispossessed by Dowe who sent down. Rodger returned with a kick into midfield and erratic play followed. Then after some pressing Sunderland won a corner off Graham. This was excellently placed in by Gillespie and during the ensuing commotion in front of the Newcastle goal the ball was rushed through by the Sunderland forwards, it being uncertain as to who got the final touch. About five minutes having elapsed.

For a little while Newcastle battled to keep play in midfield, Rodger doing well to return one or two rushes. Gradually though Sunderland worked their back to the home citadel. A shot was sent in and Lowery moved to get to it first and push it away, however there was no great distance on his save and before he could get back in position Scott stole in and drove the ball home.

Sunderland remained the dominant side until the break, but they could not further defeat the sterling defence of Newcastle. McKane, Graham and Creilly putting in some grand work and when they were breached Rodger and Jeffrey protected Lowery with some very clever work.

Following the interval, even though they now faced the hill, Sunderland picked up from where they left off and pressed immediately. Millar and Hannah had attempts but both shot wide.

It was then the turn of the homesters to press and Doig had to concede a corner when making a save. This was cleared and a return by Jeffrey landed on top of the net.

Another long ball in by Jeffrey saw Quinn doing extremely well to control it right on the bye-line. He then cleverly beat Hyslop and put the ball inside to Crate who, *amidst the greatest of excitement from the home supporters*, scored to bring Newcastle right back into this game. No more than five minutes had elapsed since the restart.

Newcastle kept up their pressure and Law was desperately unlucky with a very fine effort as it grazed the crossbar and went out. The goal kick was immediately returned and Dowe was lucky in his intervention, robbing Law when he was getting close in. Not long after an effort from Graham went over the bar.

The defence of Newcastle once again came under some pressure and Rodger and Jeffrey performed well, as indeed they had to. Several advances from the visiting quintet were resisted by the pair.

As the game was drawing to a close, *there were about six minutes left to play*, a fine centre was put in by Gillespie which was missed by Millar but ran through to Scott who shot it past Lowery with great aplomb. However, there was controversy surrounding this goal as in the build up to it a foul by one of the Sunderland players was overruled with the referee ushering play to continue. The protestations were equally waved away by the referee and the point stood.

Play was then even until the final whistle. Neither side really pressing. The third goal, and by its nature, had deflated the Newcastle lads somewhat and the Sunderland players knew they had the game won. So when time was called Sunderland were victorious, albeit very luckily as Newcastle should have had two or three goals whilst Sunderland of course should not have had their third.

The Players

Newcastle United: Appearance & Goalscoring Statistics

Player	Total Apps	Total Goals	League Apps	League Goals	FA Cup Apps	FA Cup Goals	Friendly Apps	Friendly Goals
Crate, Thomas "Tom"	30	14	28	13	2	1	15	9
Creilly, Robert "Bobby"	30	1	28	1	2	-	14	1
Graham, William "Willie"	30	5	28	5	2	-	15	-
McKane, Joseph "Joe"	30	-	28	-	2	-	15	-
Lowery, William	28	-	26	-	2	-	11	-
Thompson, William Pringle "Willie"	28	10	26	10	2	-	9	6
Jeffrey, Harry	27	3	25	3	2	-	16	-
Wallace, Joseph "Joe"	27	17	25	15	2	2	14	3
Quinn, Charles "Charlie"	25	5	23	5	2	-	11	3
Rodger, Thomas "Tom"	18	-	16	-	2	-	11	-
Willis, Robert	16	5	16	5	-	-	10	5
Law, John	10	2	8	2	2	-	10	3
Miller, James	9	-	9	-	-	-	3	-
Gillespy, Toby	4	-	4	-	-	-	-	-
Bartlett, Thomas	3	3	3	3	-	-	-	-
Inglis, John	3	-	3	-	-	-	-	-
Laverick, J	3	-	3	-	-	-	1	-
Barr, John	1	-	1	-	-	-	2	-
Bowman, John	1	-	1	-	-	-	3	-
Keir, Matthew "Matt"	1	-	1	-	-	-	-	-
Patten, John Thomas "Jack"	1	-	1	-	-	-	-	-
Ramsay, George	1	-	1	-	-	-	3	-
Ryder, Isaac James	1	-	1	-	-	-	1	-
Ryder, Joseph "Joe"	1	-	1	-	-	-	2	-
Simm, William	1	-	1	-	-	-	-	-
Sorley, John "Jock"	1	1	1	1	-	-	1	-
Friendlies only…								
Campbell, Thomas "Tom"							2	1
Donaldson, A							1	-
McFarlane, George							1	1
Milne, William							1	1
Other, A.N.							1	-
Patterson							1	1
Thompson, William							1	-

Friendlies are included for informational purposes only; they **ARE NOT** included in any statistics for appearances and goals scored by a player.

Mass Dismissal

Sacked or accept wage reduction.

Before we move on to the players, we need to discuss the situation Newcastle United found themselves in during the early part of the season. As has been discussed the club was not on a very sound financial footing and there arose the need to reduce the wage bill. Controversy reigns as to whether this led to the dismissal of every first team player or not. There is a (very) wide difference between the various newspapers as to whether the players were sacked by the Newcastle United Committee or whether they took a greatly reduced wage voluntarily. *Some reports even go so far as to suggest that the reduction in wages was the idea of the players themselves*! It is indeed quite a bewildering situation when versions of the same story are so wildly different. The truth probably lays somewhere between the two extremes and with the following I will leave you to draw your own conclusions.

Two of the most prominent local newspapers, "The Newcastle Daily Journal" and "The Sunderland Daily Echo", carried the same article, no doubt due to the syndication method of reporting prevalent in those days, *but still common today*. In it they state:

> "Newcastle United Football Club: It will no doubt be very gratifying to followers of the Association game in Newcastle, and of the United Club in particular, to know that although at one time it was decided to abandon professionalism and to play amateurs only, yet better counsels have prevailed, and it has been agreed by the executive of the club to run the club as a professional and amateur team. As soon as it was known that there was a chance of the club going down, the majority of the professional players at once signified to the committee that they were prepared, with a view of helping the club, to play for a greatly reduced wage, whilst the whole of the amateurs at once consented to sign League forms, so as to help the team in the League games. The committee at once accepted both these generous offers, and they hope to place in the field in the course of the next few weeks a team as strong, if not stronger, than the team they started the season with. To show the saving that will be effected in the club's expenditure, it may be stated that the generous offer of the majority of the club's professionals will lead to a saving of over £600 for the rest of the season in wages alone. The players who have so generously come to the assistance of the club are Jeffrey, Miller, Creilly, Graham, McKane, Thompson, Crate, and Wallace. Ramsay has returned to Scotland, but his place will be filled by undoubtedly the most clever amateur of the North, who has consented to become a professional. The two vacant positions in the forward ranks will be filled by 'A' Team players, to whom the committee we understand will give every encouragement."

This then needs to be contrasted against the following:

The Evening Press. [Tuesday, 19/09/1893.] A friendly match was played about a week ago between Newcastle United and Middlesbrough and as the former could only bring off a drawn game with the amateurs the Committee of the Newcastle Club and their professionals had a conflict which ended in the lot being discharged. Sorley, their smart forward, has gone to the Blackburn Rovers, Ramsay and Bowman have returned to Dundee, and one or two of the others are expected to find a home at Middlesbrough, as they are in treaty with Ironopolis. The remainder have been re-engaged by the Newcastle club, but at a reduced wage, the committee declining to pay the £2 per week to each man as they have hitherto done.

The Evening Telegraph. [Wednesday, 20/09/1893.] The Committee of the Newcastle United Club and their players have already come into conflict and on Tuesday night the officials decided on sacking the lot, as they were not satisfied with their play against Middlesbrough. Ramsay and Bowman have returned home to Dundee, while the remaining players have agreed to continue in the service of the club, though at a reduced rate of payment.

There are numerous other reports, but they just reiterate the context of those above with a little mixture of the wording. As you can see, it is a bit of a nightmare to untangle and we will, in all likelihood, never know what the true story actually was. Just be aware of those differences.

Back Row: W. Golding; J. Willis; H. Jeffrey; W. Lowery; T. Rodgers; J. Pearce J. Graham
Middle Row: R. Creilly; W. Graham; J. McKain
Front Row: C. Quinn; T. Crate; W. Thompson J. Wallace; J. Law
(*Notice spelling of Rodgers and McKain*)

Picture Postcard of the 1893-94 squad, seen in black and white striped kit, which they never actually wore that season, they still played in the red of East End.

Barr, John W.

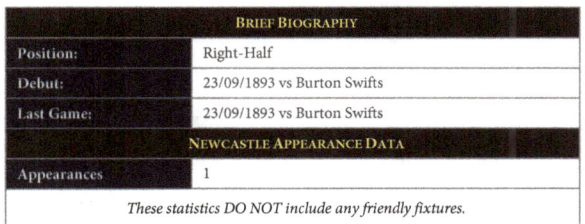

Barr was captain of Grantham Rovers, who played in the Midland League, prior to coming to Newcastle in the summer of 1893. He was however only to stay at St James's Park for the one season, and only to make the one league appearance, though he did appear alongside the likes of Quinn, the Ryder brothers and Rodger in the reserves, Newcastle "A". When he left Newcastle, he moved back to local amateur football with at first Ashington, then it was reported he went to Southwick.

Bartlett, Thomas

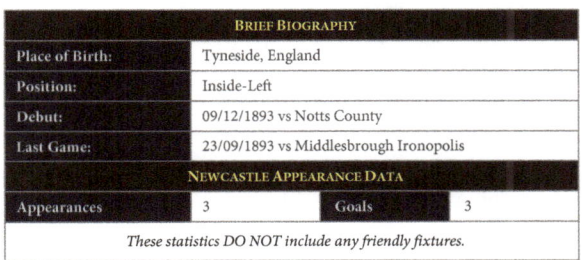

Bartlett was a local lad and described as a "lively inside-forward", and his bustling style of play earned him the nickname of 'Knocker' as apparently, he was not averse to knocking a player off the ball, nor of knocking the goalkeeper over the line as well as the ball! He had played in the local leagues and was well known, *indeed respected*, in local football. Whilst he only ever made the three senior appearances for Newcastle, covered in this book, he scored a hat-trick in one of them! That was in the New Years' Day fixture against Lincoln City, a game Newcastle went on to win 5-1. Whilst you may wonder as to why he had so few appearances with a record like that, the reason was that Joe Wallace was the preferred inside-left and Bartlett was always seen as his deputy. Bartlett returned local football with Willington Athletic. He had a period at Walsall Swifts before returning to Willington. He came back to Newcastle for the 1895-96 season, but did not make a first-team appearance, then went to Hebburn Argyle before finishing his playing career with Gateshead NER, circa1899.

Incidentally, all of Bartlett's games were at St James's Park, and all of them resulted in a win for Newcastle.

Bowman, John

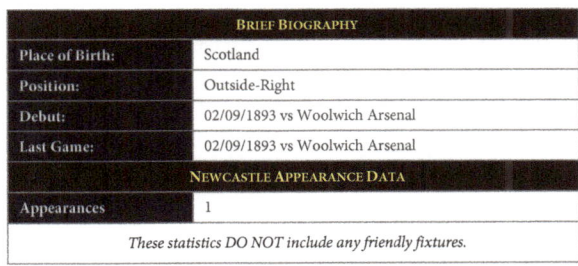

Bowman was a right winger who had built a fine reputation whilst with Dundee East End, being described as one of the best forwards on Tayside. Unfortunately for Bowman swapping Tayside for Tyneside was not a happy move. Always seen as an 'understudy' to both Crate and Quinn he only managed one official appearance and that was to be in United's first-ever game in the Football League, against Woolwich Arsenal. Bowman was involved in the friendly match against Middlesbrough mentioned previously. He point-blankly refused to take the pay cut and smartly returned to Scotland.

Campbell, Thomas "Tom"

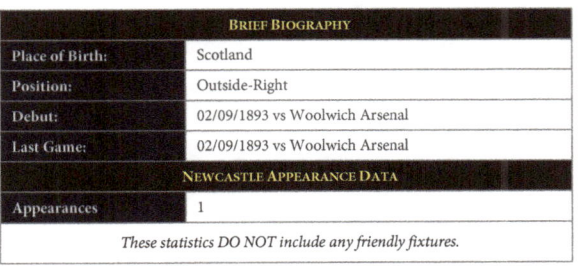

Campbell didn't make an appearance for the first team in a league game during the season covered by this book, he is included only as he played in the benefit match, against Willington Athletic, and in the friendly with Sunderland. However, for reference, he played in the first two games of Newcastle's second season in the Football League.

Some sources spell his surname as 'Cambell', however consensus is that it should be "Campbell". Other than that, very little is published about him.

Crate, Thomas "Tom"

BRIEF BIOGRAPHY	
Place of Birth:	Ayrshire, Scotland
Position:	Inside-Right
Debut:	24/09/1892 vs Sheffield United
Last Game:	05/01/1895 vs Burton Swifts
NEWCASTLE APPEARANCE DATA			
Appearances	50	Goals	18

The statistics above include Northern League fixtures for the 1892-93 season but DO NOT include any friendly fixtures.

Crate is one of Newcastle's early heroes. He has the distinction of being Newcastle East End's first ever goal scorer at St James's Park, this when he put through the opener against Sunderland on 07/09/1892, a friendly fixture which ended in a draw of two goals each. He was to unfortunately miss out on the opportunity of playing in "Newcastle United's" first ever game, due to the fact that he was suspended by the Football Association for one month, from December 22, 1892. This suspension arising from him having played during the "close season". However, he then went on to become Newcastle United's first ever goal scorer in the Football League, achieving this feat when he scored in the game against Woolwich Arsenal on 02/09/1893 at Plumstead. A game that what was itself quite historical, as it was the first Football League game to played in the capital, London. As with the Sunderland game that also ended in a draw of two goals each.

Crate was also part of the infamous "friendly" match against Middlesbrough mentioned previously. This incident being accredited as the overriding factor in his move away from St James's Park. He initially stayed in the North-East however, playing for a range of local sides but was to return home to his native Ayrshire where he worked in the coal mines.

Creilly, Robert "Bobby"

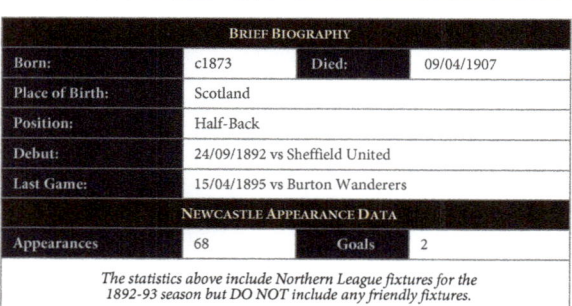

BRIEF BIOGRAPHY			
Born:	c1873	Died:	09/04/1907
Place of Birth:	Scotland		
Position:	Half-Back		
Debut:	24/09/1892 vs Sheffield United		
Last Game:	15/04/1895 vs Burton Wanderers		
NEWCASTLE APPEARANCE DATA			
Appearances	68	Goals	2

The statistics above include Northern League fixtures for the 1892-93 season but DO NOT include any friendly fixtures.

Creilly was a stalwart of the early Newcastle East End teams. Although ostensibly a half-back, Creilly was probably Newcastle's first ever 'utility man', having the ability to play "anywhere and everywhere" and doing so with great aplomb it must be said. He played in Newcastle East End's first game at St James's Park, the friendly v. Celtic. He also played in the "self-titled" United's first game at St James's Park, the Northern League fixture vs. Middlesbrough Ironopolis, on 10/12/1892, and he played in the now officially sanctioned entitled "Newcastle United" first game at St James's Park, a friendly encounter on 31/12/1892 vs. Corinthians. He also played in Newcastle United's  first game in the Football League, the aforementioned fixture vs. Woolwich Arsenal in 1893. Creilly was also involved in the "mass sacking" debacle.

Donaldson, A

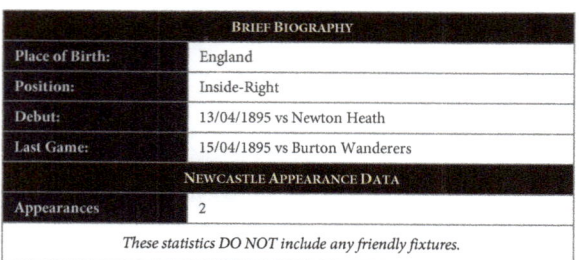

BRIEF BIOGRAPHY	
Place of Birth:	England
Position:	Inside-Right
Debut:	13/04/1895 vs Newton Heath
Last Game:	15/04/1895 vs Burton Wanderers
NEWCASTLE APPEARANCE DATA	
Appearances	2

These statistics DO NOT include any friendly fixtures.

Very little can be found regarding Donaldson, so little in fact that it has been impossible to even find out his forename. During the season covered by this book he only played in a friendly fixture, yes, 'that' fixture against Middlesbrough. He did however go on to make a couple of appearances in the 1984-85 season. One of these he would no doubt have preferred not to, it was Newcastle's record defeat, a 9-0 hammering by Burton Wanderers in April 1895.

Gillespy, Thomas "Toby"

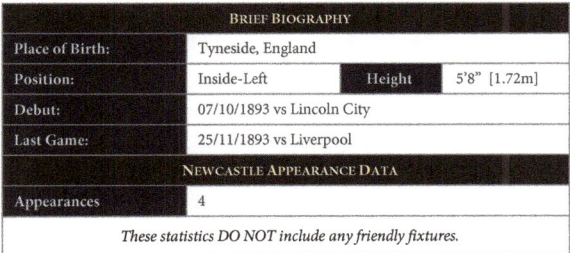

BRIEF BIOGRAPHY	
Place of Birth:	Tyneside, England
Position:	Inside-Left — Height 5'8" [1.72m]
Debut:	07/10/1893 vs Lincoln City
Last Game:	25/11/1893 vs Liverpool
NEWCASTLE APPEARANCE DATA	
Appearances	4

These statistics DO NOT include any friendly fixtures.

Geordie lad Gillespy was signed from local club Arthur's Hill as Newcastle made their entry into the Football League in 1893. He only ever played the four games for Newcastle however, and in truth very little else is known about him. Though not confirmed, it was said that he moved to Hebburn Argyle in 1894.

Graham, William "Willie"

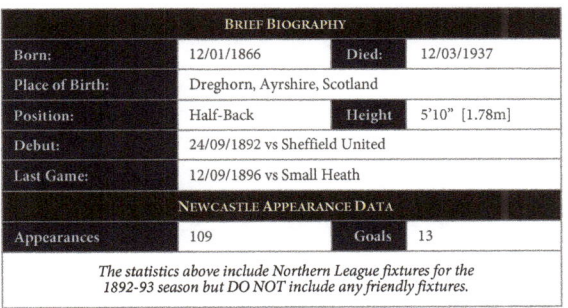

BRIEF BIOGRAPHY			
Born:	12/01/1866	Died:	12/03/1937
Place of Birth:	Dreghorn, Ayrshire, Scotland		
Position:	Half-Back — Height		5'10" [1.78m]
Debut:	24/09/1892 vs Sheffield United		
Last Game:	12/09/1896 vs Small Heath		
NEWCASTLE APPEARANCE DATA			
Appearances	109	Goals	13

The statistics above include Northern League fixtures for the 1892-93 season but DO NOT include any friendly fixtures.

Arriving at the beginning of the 1892-93 season, Graham was one of the first signings for Newcastle East End following their move into West End's old ground of St James's Park, and there he was to prove to be a mainstay in East End's transition from Northern League to Football Association League football. A coalminer by trade Graham was a strong half-back, preferring to be in the middle of the three, but prepared to play anywhere. He is a member of the "All Four Club" as he played in Newcastle East End's first game at St James's Park, the friendly vs. Celtic, he played in the first game of the self-entitled United at St James's Park, the Northern League fixture vs. Middlesbrough Ironopolis, on 10/12/1892, and he played in the first game of the now officially titled "United" at St James's Park, a friendly encounter vs. Corinthians on 31/12/1892. He also played in Newcastle United's first game in the Football Association League football, the fixture vs. Woolwich Arsenal in 1893. His natural leadership abilities made him club captain and he is widely accepted as being instrumental in shaping the fledgling United.

Graham played in all ten of the games in the Northern League, 1892-93 season, these games do not count in official statistics. The only official game of the 1892-93 season being the FA Cup tie v Middlesbrough (21/01/1893). NB: On the subject of Middlesbrough, Graham was also involved in the "mass sacking" debacle!

Inglis, John

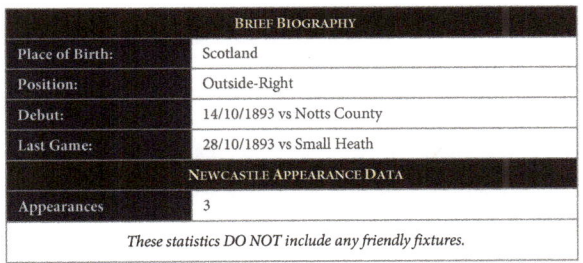

BRIEF BIOGRAPHY	
Place of Birth:	Scotland
Position:	Outside-Right
Debut:	14/10/1893 vs Notts County
Last Game:	28/10/1893 vs Small Heath
NEWCASTLE APPEARANCE DATA	
Appearances	3

These statistics DO NOT include any friendly fixtures.

Inglis, described as being "a lively and tricky" winger came on trial at Newcastle from Dalmuir Thistle in October 1893. His three games were all in that October. Whilst it was reported that he performed "moderately well" he was to soon lose his place. That obviously had a bearing on proceedings as though the trial period is not reported in any depth, therefore we have no idea of when it ended, what we do know is that he was not taken up by Newcastle. Whether this was because the trial period had indeed ended, or because Newcastle ended the trial early, is therefore up for debate. Whatever the outcome of the debate Inglis soon returned to Scotland and Dunlocher Harp.

Jeffrey, Harry

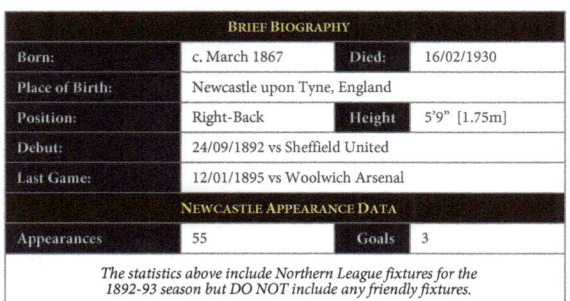

BRIEF BIOGRAPHY			
Born:	c. March 1867	Died:	16/02/1930
Place of Birth:	Newcastle upon Tyne, England		
Position:	Right-Back	Height	5'9" [1.75m]
Debut:	24/09/1892 vs Sheffield United		
Last Game:	12/01/1895 vs Woolwich Arsenal		
NEWCASTLE APPEARANCE DATA			
Appearances	55	Goals	3
The statistics above include Northern League fixtures for the 1892-93 season but DO NOT include any friendly fixtures.			

Jeffrey played for all three of the Newcastle teams, West End, East End and United. A local lad he played non-League football for various clubs in the area before joining Newcastle West End in 1886. At the demise of Newcastle West End he was retained by Newcastle East End and when Newcastle became United he was very much an integral part of the set-up already.

He played in East End's first ever game at St James's Park, vs Celtic, and he played in Newcastle United's first game in the Football Association League, vs Woolwich Arsenal in 1893, which incidentally was also the very first Football League game ever to be played in London. Unfortunately for Jeffrey, and Newcastle, just as he had established himself as the regular right-back he was forced to give up the game because of a leg injury sustained against Sunderland in a friendly fixture on 19/01/1895 at St James's Park. Jeffrey was trying to block an advance and in doing so received a very heavy kick on the leg, *totally accidental*, from Scott which saw him carried off the field.

In very fair play the Sunderland representatives made it known immediately that they would have no objection to Jeffrey being replaced, this at a time when there was no such thing as substitutes, even in friendlies under normal circumstances. Newcastle took advantage of their offer and after a few minutes William Beattie, the reserve, came on in place of Jeffrey.

At the time it was reported that the leg injury was not serious, but it later became known that he suffered damage to both his knee-cap and his ankle and after a lengthy period of being "very ill" he had to retire from the professional game, this after only three good seasons. [*So, there's a canny pub-quiz question for you. Was Jeffrey the first Newcastle United player to be substituted?*]

Keir, Matthew "Matt"

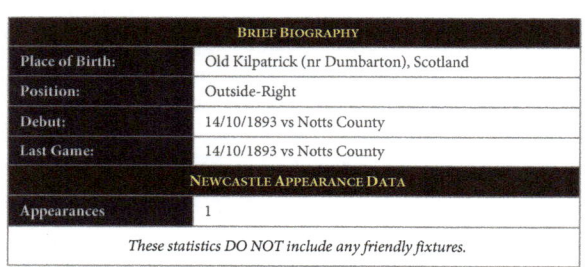

BRIEF BIOGRAPHY	
Place of Birth:	Old Kilpatrick (nr Dumbarton), Scotland
Position:	Outside-Right
Debut:	14/10/1893 vs Notts County
Last Game:	14/10/1893 vs Notts County
NEWCASTLE APPEARANCE DATA	
Appearances	1
These statistics DO NOT include any friendly fixtures.	

Keir, came to Newcastle East End prior to the beginning of the 1892-93 season. Arriving from Dalmuir Thistle (Clydebank) he had a reputation of being a lively and enthusiastic wing player, and together with the other new arrivals, fellow Scots J. Kirkland and William Graham, the management committee were happy to think that East End were in a much stronger position than last season.

Keir made no Northern League appearances in the 1892-93 season, playing only in 'friendly' and reserve games. His League debut came the following season in the Second Division game against Notts County (14/10/1893). It was to be the most unfortunate of debuts, however. Keir was deputising for injured Charles Quinn the 'regular' outside-right and picked up an injury himself. He was, again unfortunately, not selected again for the first team. Obviously unhappy with this situation he moved back to Scotland.

Laverick, J

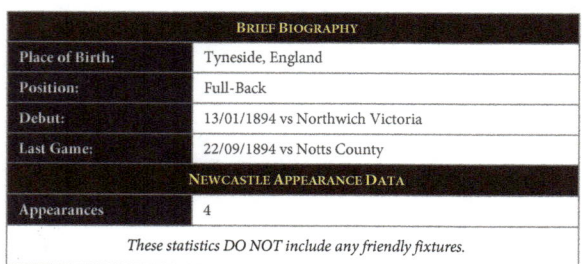

BRIEF BIOGRAPHY	
Place of Birth:	Tyneside, England
Position:	Full-Back
Debut:	13/01/1894 vs Northwich Victoria
Last Game:	22/09/1894 vs Notts County
NEWCASTLE APPEARANCE DATA	
Appearances	4
These statistics DO NOT include any friendly fixtures.	

Not a great deal is reported regarding Laverick. He is Tyneside born and noted by the Newcastle Daily Chronicle as being a "rugged" full-back and came to Newcastle from Trafalgar. In his four appearances he deputised at both right-back, *for Harry Jeffrey*, and left-back, *for Tom Rodger*, so he was certainly versatile too. He made appearances in the reserve team, Newcastle "A". Perhaps that versatility was his downfall, meaning he couldn't command either position, who knows. When he left Newcastle, after almost two seasons, he went to Hebburn Argyle.

Law, John

Brief Biography	
Place of Birth:	Scotland
Position:	Inside-Right
Debut:	26/12/1893 vs Walsall Town Swifts
Last Game:	24/03/1894 vs Burton Swifts
Newcastle Appearance Data	
Appearances	10	Goals:	2
These statistics DO NOT include any friendly fixtures.	

Law was drafted into the Newcastle ranks as they struggled to get to grips with life in the Football League. His arrival at St James's Park was a rather convoluted affair. Newcastle spotted him on Merseyside playing for Everton, however they could not transfer him as he was still registered with Rangers (Glasgow). The Newcastle directors had to get a 'release clause' from Everton before they could sign him. Worth the initial effort though as the record of the games he played in would suggest they were on to a very decent player, winning eight, drawing one and losing one. Unfortunately, the upturn in Newcastle's form was erratic and Law lost his place and soon returned to Scotland.

Lowery, William

Brief Biography			
Place of Birth:	Tyneside, England		
Position:	Goalkeeper	Height:	5'10" [1.77m]
Debut:	30/09/1893 vs Woolwich Arsenal		
Last Game:	27/10/1894 vs Ardwick		
Newcastle Appearance Data			
Appearances	30		
These statistics DO NOT include any friendly fixtures.			

Lowery was a goalkeeper of some renown within the Tyneside footballing community. He had built up an excellent reputation during his time with local amateur sides, most notably with Trafalgar. Perhaps it was his outstanding performance in the friendly fixture between Newcastle United and Trafalgar, on 04/09/1893, at Heaton Junction that persuaded the Newcastle committee to bring Lowery to St James's Park. Despite being beaten twice in that game his performance was otherwise exemplary, and no doubt if not for him Newcastle would have won that game by a handsome margin.

Whatever the eventual reason(s) may have been, it was very soon after that game that Lowery did take up his charge as custodian for United and he made his debut in their very first home game in the Football League. This was against Woolwich Arsenal and though it ended as an easy victory for Newcastle, 6-0, his performance in that match, and subsequent ones, ensured that he remained as the first-choice goalkeeper for the rest of that inaugural season.

The acquisition of Ward during the summer of 1894 saw Lowery losing his place in the senior squad and he eventually moved back into the local amateur game with sides such as Gateshead NER and Blyth.

McFarlane, George

Brief Biography	
Place of Birth:	Newcastle upon Tyne, England
Position:	Half-Back
Debut:	26/12/1893 vs Walsall Town Swifts
Last Game:	24/03/1894 vs Burton Swifts
Newcastle Appearance Data	
McFarlane only appeared in friendly fixtures.	

McFarlane was a local lad who played for Rosewood as a junior. Rosewood being the one of originating clubs of Newcastle United, as it was they and Stanley who formed Newcastle East End upon their merger. Though it is also variously quoted that Stanley absorbed Rosewood indicating it was not the mutual combining most think it was, I'm with the former in believing it was a true merger between the two clubs and done with the blessing of both.

Though he stayed at the club through its transition from Rosewood, to Newcastle East End and finally Newcastle United he never made a competitive appearance for either East End or United. Towards the twilight of his career, aged thirty, he did eventually make it into the Newcastle United first-team, in the friendly fixture against Dundee.

Standing in for Crate it would be a bitter-sweet debut for him. Whilst he scored a goal, starting a first half fight back that led to it being 2-2 at the break, Newcastle went on to concede no fewer than six goals in the second half and therefore lose 8-2! Bitter-sweet indeed.

McKane, Joseph

BRIEF BIOGRAPHY			
Place of Birth:	Scotland		
Position:	Half-Back	Height:	5'10" [1.77m]
Debut:	24/09/1892 vs Sheffield United		
Last Game:	15/12/1894 vs Rotherham Town		
NEWCASTLE APPEARANCE DATA			
Appearances	51		

The statistics above include Northern League fixtures for the 1892-93 season but DO NOT include any friendly fixtures.

You can't help it, but McKane will always be known as *"McKane who missed the train"*!

A riveter by trade, in the shipyards on the Tyne, McKane has a strong association with Newcastle. Described as being quick to the tackle he was to swiftly endear himself to the Newcastle faithful. He appeared in Newcastle East End's first appearance in the FA Cup proper, this against Nottingham Forest on January 16th, 1892 at Nottingham, a game East End were to lose 2-1. He also played in Newcastle East End's first ever game at St James's Park on Saturday, September 3rd 1892, against Celtic.

Add to this the fact that he also played in Newcastle United's first game in the Football League, against Woolwich Arsenal in 1893, which incidentally was also the very first Football League game ever to be played in London. An impressive list of firsts for him indeed.

He was an ever present in Newcastle's first season in the Football League (1893-94), playing in all 28 of their league games and their two FA Cup ties. A great regular in the first two seasons of United's League existence.

However, as alluded to, McKane has quite an anecdotal, and unfortunate, association with one of our North-East neighbours, Middlesbrough, and a train.

The day was Saturday, February 11, 1893, Newcastle were going to Middlesbrough for what would be their last ever fixture in the Northern League. In those days there were no such things as substitutes and money was very tight and Newcastle, like many other teams, when travelling away would usually only take with them the eleven players who would be in the team, and occasionally a reserve player. For Newcastle at the time though the funds were not there for them on this occasion.

As the story goes the team met at Newcastle Central Station to catch the train to Middlesbrough and for some reason McKane missed the train! There are various humorous stories about him getting locked in a toilet! How true these are it is impossible to say but it does put a smile on a desperate occasion as Newcastle had to play the whole match with only ten men and were soundly beaten 4-0!

NB: On the subject of Middlesbrough, McKane was also involved in the "mass sacking" debacle!

Miller, James

BRIEF BIOGRAPHY			
Place of Birth:	Scotland		
Position:	Right-Back	Height:	5'8" [1.72m]
Debut:	24/09/1892 vs Sheffield United		
Last Game:	18/11/1893 vs Northwich Victoria		
NEWCASTLE APPEARANCE DATA			
Appearances	20		

The statistics above include Northern League fixtures for the 1892-93 season but DO NOT include any friendly fixtures.

Miller was a right-back of some note and had captained Newcastle East End. When Newcastle became 'United' he remained part of the new team and switched to left-back during their first season in the Football League. Miller, apart from being a very credible player, was a bit of a character it has to be admitted. Whilst playing in a Newcastle 'Derby' match between West End and East End there was a fracas between Miller, then of East End, and John Barker then of West End, *soon to be team-mates in 'United'*, but for now very much in opposition to each other. The upshot of the incident was that Miller was suspended by the Football Association, on October 02, 1889 until November 17, 1889 for 'misconduct on the field of play'. The punishment for Barker was a suspension until November 03, 1889. On another occasion Miller was suspended by United, this after announcing that he didn't like training and refused to take part in such! This suspension basically ended his career at St James's Park as he never made another appearance.

Miller married a "local lass", the Newcastle Daily Chronicle (18/01/1893) carried the following:

"Followers of football in the North will universally tender their congratulations and best wishes for happiness and prosperity to James Miller, the clever popular back of the Newcastle United Club, on the occasion of his marriage, which took place on Monday to a young lady belonging to Heaton."

In April 1893, with 'canny' bit of forward thinking, he took over possession of the Wheat Sheaf Inn, which was on Lime Street in the Ouseburn area of Newcastle. **NB:** Miller was also involved in the game against Middlesbrough which led to the "mass sacking" debacle!

Milne, William

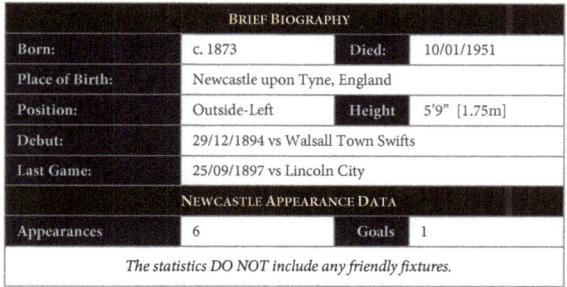

BRIEF BIOGRAPHY			
Born:	c. 1873	Died:	10/01/1951
Place of Birth:	Newcastle upon Tyne, England		
Position:	Outside-Left	Height	5'9" [1.75m]
Debut:	29/12/1894 vs Walsall Town Swifts		
Last Game:	25/09/1897 vs Lincoln City		
NEWCASTLE APPEARANCE DATA			
Appearances	6	Goals	1
The statistics DO NOT include any friendly fixtures.			

Milne had two spells at Newcastle, these being interspersed with a short stay at Sunderland. In his first spell, this season, 1893-94, he only made one friendly appearance. The following season (1894-95) he made 5 appearances, (*not counting friendlies*). When he returned the 1897-98 season saw one more appearance. The reasoning behind his meagre return, for his length of stay, could simply be that apart from football he was also a very talented cricketer, perhaps even preferring the 'willow' to the 'leather'. He was also keen to retain his 'amateur' status as a footballer. He was, incidentally, son of Mr George T. Milne, director, and chairman of Newcastle United.

Other, A.N.

As the moniker suggests nothing is known about the player who took to the field in the friendly fixture with Dipton Wanderers on December 2nd. No reports on the game, *which are scarce*, name this player in either the line-up or the text.

Patten, John Thomas "Jack"

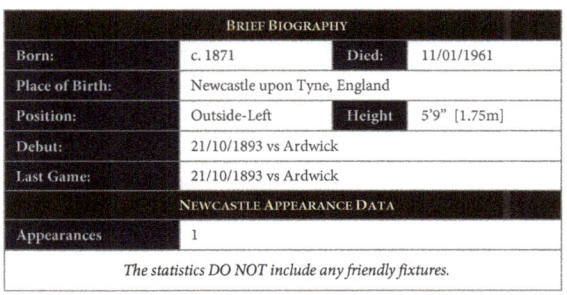

BRIEF BIOGRAPHY			
Born:	c. 1871	Died:	11/01/1961
Place of Birth:	Newcastle upon Tyne, England		
Position:	Outside-Left	Height	5'9" [1.75m]
Debut:	21/10/1893 vs Ardwick		
Last Game:	21/10/1893 vs Ardwick		
NEWCASTLE APPEARANCE DATA			
Appearances	1		
The statistics DO NOT include any friendly fixtures.			

Patten was with Trafalgar and Newcastle West End and was one of the players Newcastle East End took over the registration of at West End's demise. He played mainly in the reserves with Newcastle "A" but did manage the one appearance in the 1893-94 season against Ardwick. He left Newcastle and returned to non-league football with Hebburn Argyle. However, it is not as a player that he is best known to us for he was one of the stalwarts of Newcastle United's back-room staff. He served for many years as a secretary and reserve manager. He also was a FA Council member and served with the Northumberland FA for over forty-years.

Patterson

Other than the fact that he played, and scored, in the friendly against Trafalgar, nothing is known about Patterson, not even his first name! The man is a complete mystery, but my research continues, perhaps in vain, but continues…

Quinn, Charles "Charlie"

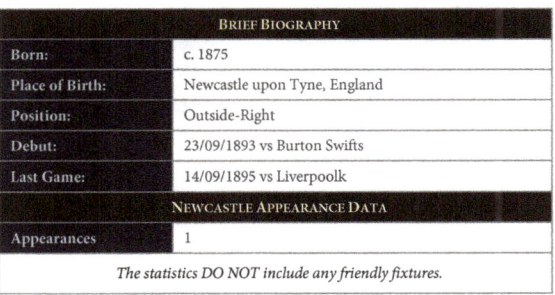

BRIEF BIOGRAPHY	
Born:	c. 1875
Place of Birth:	Newcastle upon Tyne, England
Position:	Outside-Right
Debut:	23/09/1893 vs Burton Swifts
Last Game:	14/09/1895 vs Liverpoolk
NEWCASTLE APPEARANCE DATA	
Appearances	1
The statistics DO NOT include any friendly fixtures.	

Quinn was a local lad who had two stints at St James's Park. In his first stint he made a single appearance, against Stockton, in the April 1893, but when Newcastle entered the Football League the following season, (1893-94), he was a regular team member. However, he was played in a variety of positions across the forward line. His very versatility had the detrimental side effect of him not being able to command any one position within the first-team. Whilst he appeared frequently for the reserves, he was in need of first-team action and this saw him move to the 'newly named' Manchester City, formerly Ardwick, in December 1894. His time there was unfortunately not a happy one as he once again failed to gain a place in the first-team so he moved back to St James's Park in 1895. His second stint at Newcastle though wasn't as successful as his first, as he made only one appearance, and that was in a 5-1 thrashing at the hands of Liverpool. Quinn subsequently went into non-league football with Blyth, Gateshead NER then Ashington.

Ramsay, George

BRIEF BIOGRAPHY	
Place of Birth:	Scotland
Position:	Goalkeeper
Debut:	02/09/1893 vs Woolwich Arsenal
Last Game:	02/09/1893 vs Woolwich Arsenal
NEWCASTLE APPEARANCE DATA	
Appearances	1
These statistics DO NOT include any friendly fixtures.	

Ramsey is variously reported as being either George or Andrew, however he is cited in official Football League records as being as George, though who is to say they cannot be wrong? In any event Ramsay was a Newcastle East End player who had moved to Stockton in May 1892. With the formation of the new "United" and entrance into the Football League he returned to Newcastle, *albeit now United*, in July 1893. It was certainly not to be a happy return for Ramsay, however.

His only official appearance was to be in United's first-ever game in the Football League, against Woolwich Arsenal, but then he was involved in the aforementioned friendly match against Middlesbrough, and he was one of those who refused to take the pay cut and he smartly returned home to Scotland.

Rodger, Thomas "Tom"

BRIEF BIOGRAPHY			
Born:	17/08/1871	Died:	13/03/1946
Place of Birth:	Perth, Scotland		
Position:	Left-Back	Height	5'9" [1.75m]
Debut:	25/11/1893 vs Liverpool		
Last Game:	20/10/1894 vs Leicester Fosse		
NEWCASTLE APPEARANCE DATA			
Appearances	24		
The statistics DO NOT include any friendly fixtures.			

Rodger, although originally from Perth, was another recruit from, as local newspapers quoted, *"the land o'cakes"*, Dundee to you and I.

He was playing as an amateur with Newcastle East End "A" and was described as being decidedly an acquisition to the club. Following some very good performances in the reserves he was to get an opportunity to appear for the senior team as a trialist in a friendly match with Notts County on February 18, 1893, this owing to the unavailability of Harry Jeffrey.

Whilst the game was a good, if narrow, win against top-flight opposition it still took him another while to get his full first-team debut, November 1893, but once he did, he remained the regular left-back for the rest of the season and into the beginning of the next.

There are varying stories as to what happened next with Rodger, some sources are quoted as saying that upon losing his place, *and owing to the fact that he never really settled in England*, that he returned to Scotland early in 1895. Other sources have him as remaining in Newcastle for over 40 years working as a print compositor for a local newspaper. As always, take your pick, but considering that when he made his unofficial debut, [*the aforementioned friendly against Notts County*], he was on the printing staff of the Newcastle Journal, and that he reportedly died in Newcastle in 1946, the latter of the two choices seems the more likely.

NB: You may see various references to the spelling of his surname as both Roger and/or Rogers, however the consensus is most definitely Rodger as presented here.

Ryder, Isaac

BRIEF BIOGRAPHY			
Born:	23/12/1871	Died:	26/05/1960
Place of Birth:	Newcastle upon Tyne, England		
Position:	Inside-Left		
Debut:	30/09/1893 vs Woolwich Arsenal		
Last Game:	30/09/1893 vs Woolwich Arsenal		
NEWCASTLE APPEARANCE DATA			
Appearances	1		
The statistics DO NOT include any friendly fixtures.			

Ryder, born in the Westgate area of Newcastle, was from a family of 14 children. He and his younger brother Joseph, a goalkeeper, were to be at St James's Park at the same time. Whilst they appeared in the A team together, they were never to appear in the same senior side.

Ryder made only one senior appearance, but what a historical match it was! Played at St James's Park against Woolwich Arsenal (now just plain old Arsenal) it was United's first-ever victory in the Football League, saw United's first ever hat-trick, and double hat-trick!

There are reports of an abhorrent incident involving Isaac Ryder following a Northern Alliance fixture between Shankhouse and Newcastle United A on Saturday December 30th, 1893. The referee for the match, Mr Glass, missed the train and therefore the match, so Ryder stepped in as referee. Some of his decisions did not go down too well with some of the spectators and as soon as he blew the final whistle those 'supporters', *and I use that term lightly as people like that are NOT supporters as I see supporters*, anyway, a 'group of people' shall we call them, stormed past the ropes and began to roughly handle Ryder. It was said that if not for the intervention of the Shankhouse committeemen, and a band of responsible supporters of the Shankhouse club, then Ryder would have doubtless fared badly. So, even in those days disgusting behaviour was evident from so-called football 'supporters'.

Ryder, Joseph "Joe"

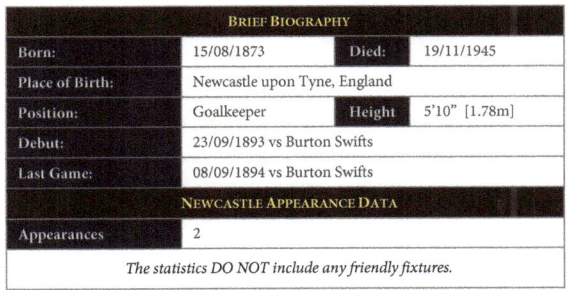

BRIEF BIOGRAPHY	
Born:	15/08/1873 Died: 19/11/1945
Place of Birth:	Newcastle upon Tyne, England
Position:	Goalkeeper Height: 5'10" [1.78m]
Debut:	23/09/1893 vs Burton Swifts
Last Game:	08/09/1894 vs Burton Swifts
NEWCASTLE APPEARANCE DATA	
Appearances	2

The statistics DO NOT include any friendly fixtures.

Ryder, as mentioned above, was born in the Westgate area of Newcastle, and was from a family of 14 children. He and his older brother, Isaac, were at St James's Park at the same time. Whilst they appeared in the "A" team together, they were never to appear in the same senior side.

Ryder had originally joined Newcastle West End, circa 1890, and upon their demise and incorporation was retained by Newcastle East End and was with them when they became United. However, now having to compete against the likes of Whitton, Lowery and Ward for the custodian's position chances were few and far between for him. He made his unofficial debut against Stoke in the friendly on 04/03/1893, and unfortunately conceded four goals in a seven-goal thriller.

His official debut came the season after, against Burton Swifts, 23/09/1893, and he had to wait for almost a full year before he made his next appearance, 08/09/1894, and again it was against Burton Swifts. On both occasions Ryder conceded three goals.

Ryder returned to non-league football and appeared for various local Tyneside clubs before ending up at Willington Athletic F.C. However, in the August of 1895 Ryder was to return to St James's Park, for the Alliance side, when Newcastle United starting paying their 'reserves', much to the chagrin of many amateur sides, not least Willington Athletic of course.

Simm, William

Only made the one appearance for Newcastle but was prominent within local non-league teams in the Tyneside area.

Sorley, John "Jock"

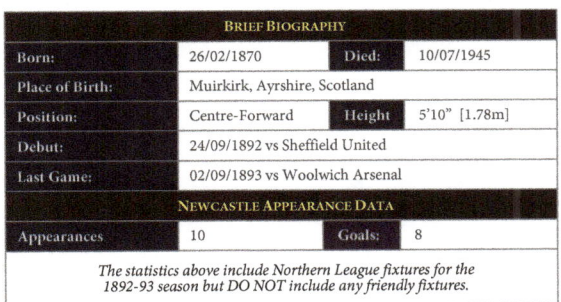

BRIEF BIOGRAPHY	
Born:	26/02/1870 Died: 10/07/1945
Place of Birth:	Muirkirk, Ayrshire, Scotland
Position:	Centre-Forward Height: 5'10" [1.78m]
Debut:	24/09/1892 vs Sheffield United
Last Game:	02/09/1893 vs Woolwich Arsenal
NEWCASTLE APPEARANCE DATA	
Appearances	10 Goals: 8

The statistics above include Northern League fixtures for the 1892-93 season but DO NOT include any friendly fixtures.

Sorley was captain of Newcastle East End and upon the formation of the new United he remained with the team. He therefore has the honour of playing in East End's first ever game at St James's Park, vs Celtic on 03/09/1892, the first game of the 'unofficially' entitled United against Middlesbrough Ironopolis, on 10/12/1892, in the Northern League, the first game of the now officially entitled United, a friendly against the Corinthian on 31/12/1892.

To complete the 'fantastic four' he played in United's first ever Football League game when they joined Division 2 in 1893 against Woolwich Arsenal, a game in which he scored the equalising goal to ensure United took a share of the points. You could indeed say it was a 'fabulous five' as the game against Woolwich Arsenal was the first Football League game to be played in London.

During the course of the 1892-93 season Sorley played eight of the ten Northern League fixtures and scored seven goals. He also appeared in twenty-four friendly fixtures and scored an amazing twenty goals, that is one heck of a return by anyone's standard! He was most certainly not going to be easily replaced.

Unfortunately, however the new United they were beset by financial problems, some saying that this being more a legacy of Newcastle West End than of their own making, but it meant Sorley moving from the Tyne to the Tees as he was sold to Middlesbrough. However, blink and you'll miss it, Sorley went straight from Middlesbrough to Blackburn Rovers without making an appearance for the Teesiders.

Thompson, William "Willie"

Brief Biography			
Born:	[c.] October 1867	Died:	[c.] September 1928
Place of Birth:	North Seaton, Northumberland, England		
Position:	Inside-Left	Height	5'7" [1.70m]
Debut:	24/09/1892 vs Sheffield United		
Last Game:	09/01/1897 vs Leicester City		
Newcastle Appearance Data			
Appearances	98	Goals:	46

The statistics above include Northern League fixtures for the 1892-93 season but DO NOT include any friendly fixtures.

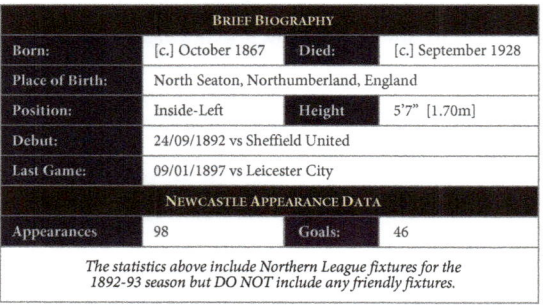

Thompson was a Blacksmith by trade and played football with local non-league sides such as Bedlington Burdon, Ashington Rising Sun and the famous Shankhouse Black Watch before moving to Newcastle East End circa 1889.

Thompson, though only 5 foot 7 inches tall, was once described as being a lanky individual one can only assume from that description that Thompson must have been of slim build! He was also described as possessing lightning-fast pace and was able to use either foot with extreme power and accuracy. His goalscoring record of 46 goals in only 98 matches is testament to that fact. It certainly made him an early crowd favourite at St James's Park.

He could play anywhere along the forward line but his preferred positions were inside-left or centre-forward. It was in the latter position that he became the first Newcastle United player to score a hat-trick. This being in the return League Division 2 fixture against Woolwich Arsenal on 03/09/1893. A very memorable game indeed, and one for the annals of history, as not only did Thompson score a hat-trick that day but so did his team-mate Joe Wallace, Thompson though notching the first.

As mentioned, that game was the return fixture against Woolwich Arsenal, the first match being the season opener at Arsenal's Manor Field ground in Plumstead making it Newcastle United's first ever Football Association League game and the first such game ever to played in London. Yes, Thompson is a definite history maker at Newcastle. It was reported that Thompson dropped back down to non-league football with Jarrow and then Ashington late in his career.

Was there a darker side of Thompson that we are not seeing? Perhaps so. Almost hidden within the columns of The Athletic News on Monday, 9th October, 1893 was the following:

"Thompson, their old centre forward, is playing with better judgement this season than ever, and if he could only keep his temper under proper control, he would be able to hold his own in any company."

Wallace, Joseph "Joe"

Brief Biography			
Born:	[c.] 1870	Died:	[c.] September 1941
Place of Birth:	Hurlford, Ayrshire, Scotland		
Position:	Inside-Left	Height	5'4" [1.62m]
Debut:	24/09/1892 vs Sheffield United		
Last Game:	12/04/1895 vs Burslem Port Vale		
Newcastle Appearance Data			
Appearances	98	Goals:	46

The statistics above include Northern League fixtures for the 1892-93 season but DO NOT include any friendly fixtures.

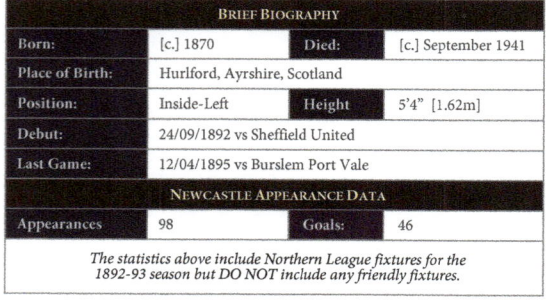

Wallace was a 'pocket dynamo' at only 5 foot 4 inches tall, making him one of the shortest players to have donned the colours of Newcastle United. Though being of diminutive stature he was credited with having great footballing acumen and was commonly termed *"clever wee Wallace"* in varying press circles.

Making a name for himself in local football, in Ayrshire, with the delightfully named Glenbuck Cherrypickers, Wallace was enticed south of the border and joined Newcastle East End around the same time as Peter Watson and Jock Sorley, circa 1891.

The name Glenbuck Cherrypickers, originally Glenbuck Athletic (circa 1870), was said to derive from either the fact that the local men, from Glenbuck and Muirkirk, served in the 11th Hussars in the Boer War who themselves were named the Cherry Pickers, or that almost all of the men associated with the club, be they players or officials, worked in the local pits where one of the jobs was sorting the good coal from stones, hence them being nicknamed "cherry-pickers".

In any event he very soon became a firm favourite at East End and the newly entitled United. He was a stalwart of Newcastle's first two seasons in the Football League. With his silky skills there was also a deep determination that saw him quite prepared to mix it up when the occasion warranted and was never shy of the tackle. Testament to this was the bruising Newcastle Derby of October 1891 when East End played West End and Wallace was injured, his shoulder being so badly put out that after consultation with a doctor he was laid up for some weeks.

Wallace only just missed out on being Newcastle United's first ever hat-trick scorer. 'Just' being the operative word as it was Willie Thompson who beat him to it, and both hat-tricks were scored in the same game, the six-nil thrashing of Woolwich Arsenal on 30/09/1893. Wallace though still gets his mention in the history books for the following:

a) He played in Newcastle End's first game at St James's Park the friendly against Celtic on 03/09/1892.
b) He played in Newcastle United's first game in the Football League, against Woolwich Arsenal on 02/09/1893.
c) The aforementioned fixture was at Woolwich's Manor Field ground in Plumstead, making it the first Football League game to be played in London.
d) He played in the game which saw Newcastle United record their first double hat-trick, and indeed being one of the hat-trick scorers himself.

Upon leaving United at the end of the 1894-95 season Wallace remained in Newcastle and joined local non-league club, Rendel, who were based in the Benwell area of Newcastle. It is very sadly reported that Wallace was to fall on hard times once he left football altogether and at one stage received financial assistance and was bought clothing by Newcastle United.

Willis, Robert "Bobby"

BRIEF BIOGRAPHY	
Born:	[c.] 1871
Place of Birth:	Shankhouse, Northumberland, England
Position:	Inside-Right — Height — 5'4" [1.62m]
Debut:	16/12/1893 vs Small Heath
Last Game:	16/02/1895 vs Aston Villa
NEWCASTLE APPEARANCE DATA	
Appearances: 36	Goals: 19
The statistics above DO NOT include any friendly fixtures.	

Willis joined Newcastle from local amateur club Shankhouse Black Watch during their first season in League football.

Making an immediate impact he scored on his debut against Small Heath, scored twice against Ironopolis and twice against Burton Swifts.

In fact, his first season was a roaring success. He played 16 times and during that Newcastle only lost once, at Rotherham, won 11 times and drew the remaining four. The following season saw him making 20 appearances, scoring a further 14 goals, thus helping Newcastle to establish themselves in the League.

His goal record was quite a remarkable, equivalent to scoring once in every two games.

He returned to Black Watch and amateur football after his successful spell at St James's Park.

Note...

For a comprehensive list of each, and every, game the players above have been involved outside of the season this book covers, then visit:

www.toon1892.com

Every player, every manager and every game are covered within the pages of that site.

About the Author

Born and bred in Newcastle and raised on a staple diet of stories of Hughie Gallacher from my Grandfather and Jackie Milburn from my Father there was never any doubt about where my football loyalties would lay. Going to St James's Park for the first time as a child and seeing Newcastle play a goalless draw with Everton, which if memory serves me correctly was an instantly forgettable game from a football point of view - but to me it was just amazing. I'd never seen so many people in the same place at the same time before, almost 30,000 - I was hooked straight away. Now, after more years than I care to remember, it's all about sharing the history of, to me, the greatest football club in the world with all you good people out there.

Also available from this Author:

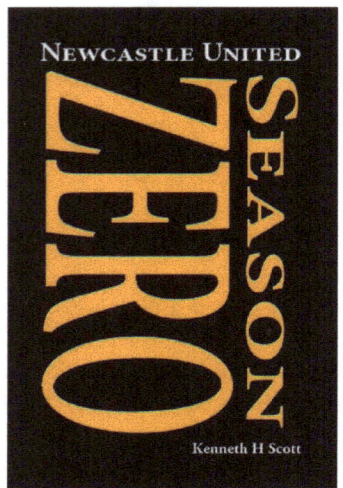

Newcastle United Season ZERO

Available in both Hardback and Paperback
ISBN: 978-0-9934201-5-3
ISBN: 978-0-9934201-6-0

At the beginning of the 1892-93 season Newcastle West End no longer existed, Newcastle East End had moved across the city into West End's ground, St James's Park, and mid-season changed their name to Newcastle United. This was a season of change; this was Season ZERO. This book is the game-by-game account of that season, (1892-93), detailing all the Northern League games, the unfortunate early exit from the FA Cup and the 33 friendlies too. Read all about the six times Newcastle notched up five goals, the three times they scored seven goals and yes, the time they scored eight goals!

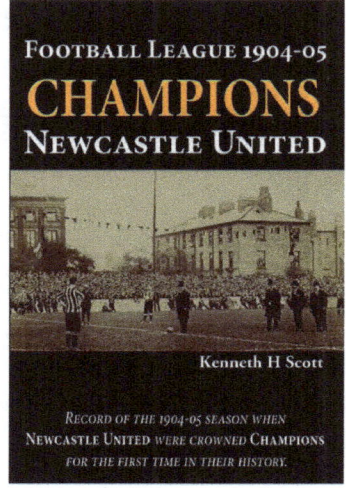

Football League 1904-05 Champions Newcastle United

Available in both Hardback and Paperback
ISBN: 978-0-9934201-4-6
ISBN: 978-0-9934201-3-9

Newcastle United, Football League Champions what a wonderful sound that is, and it was first heard at the end of the 1904-05 season. In a title race that went down to the very last game of the season Newcastle United were crowned Champions of the Football League and this book chronicles their passage through the Football League First Division, the 'top-tier' of English football, and the title.

If you're a fan of Newcastle United, then this is a "must read" book giving you the facts and figures for each of the steps it took to take the title. If you're a football fan in general, then this book is for you too as it details game by game the 1904-05 season in all its glory.

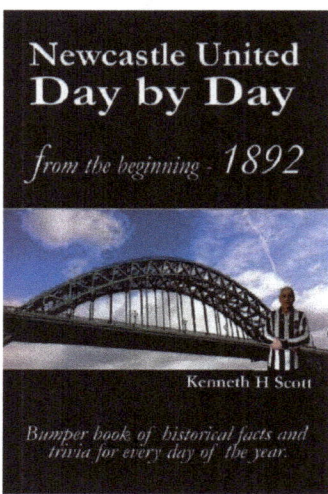

Newcastle United Day by Day

Available in both Hardback and Paperback
ISBN: 978-0-9934201-0-8
ISBN: 978-0-9934201-2-2

Think of the great games, think of the great players, and even think of those players who, for whatever reason, only appeared on a single occasion (*as their contribution is equally valued*) this book has them all. Plotting its way through the history of Newcastle United on a day-by-day basis this book delivers and highlights some of the interesting facts, figures anecdotes, and trivia that may have occurred on that day. This book includes every debut, every first meeting against every opposition faced, each scoring debut, and much, much more...

Bibliography

Newcastle Daily Chronicle. (1893). The Football Association, Newcastle Daily Chronicle, Wednesday, August 9th, 1893. [p7b]. Newcastle upon Tyne, England.
Newcastle Daily Chronicle. (1893). Football. Association, Newcastle Daily Chronicle, Thursday, August 10th, 1893. [p7d]. Newcastle upon Tyne, England.
Newcastle Daily Chronicle. (1893). Football. Association, Newcastle Daily Chronicle, Friday, August 11th, 1893. [p7d]. Newcastle upon Tyne, England.
Newcastle Daily Chronicle. (1893). Newcastle United Football Club, Newcastle Daily Chronicle, Saturday, August 12th, 1893. [p7d]. Newcastle upon Tyne, England.
Newcastle Daily Chronicle. (1893). Football. Association. Newcastle United Football Club, Newcastle Daily Chronicle, Saturday, August 12th, 1893. [p7d]. Newcastle upon Tyne, England.
Newcastle Daily Chronicle. (1893). Football. Newcastle United, Newcastle Daily Chronicle, Saturday, August 26th, 1893. [p7d]. Newcastle upon Tyne, England.
Newcastle Daily Chronicle. (1893). Football. Association, Newcastle Daily Chronicle, Tuesday, August 29th, 1893. [p7e]. Newcastle upon Tyne, England.
Newcastle Daily Chronicle. (1893). Football. Association, Newcastle Daily Chronicle, Thursday, August 31st, 1893. [p7e]. Newcastle upon Tyne, England.
Newcastle Daily Chronicle. (1893). Newcastle United Football Club, Newcastle Daily Chronicle, Saturday, September 2nd, 1893. [p7d]. Newcastle upon Tyne, England.
Nottingham Evening Post. (1893). League Division II., Saturday, September 2nd, 1893, England.
Newcastle Daily Chronicle. (1893). Woolwich Arsenal v. Newcastle United, Newcastle Daily Chronicle, Monday, September 4th, 1893. [p6d]. Newcastle upon Tyne, England.
Sporting Life. (1893). Woolwich Arsenal v. Newcastle United, Sporting Life, Monday, September 4th, 1893. [p4b]. London, England.
Sunderland Daily Echo. (1893). The Second League, Sunderland Daily Echo, Monday, September 4th, 1893. [p4b]. Sunderland, England.
Birmingham Daily Post. (1893). Second Division, The Birmingham Daily Post, Monday, September 4th, 1893. [p7g]. Birmingham, England.
Shields Gazette. (1893). Association. League - Second Division, Shields Daily Gazette and Shipping Telegraph, Monday, September 4th, 1893. [p4d]. South Shields, England.
Manchester Courier. (1893). Royal Arsenal v. Newcastle United, Manchester Courier and Lancashire General Advertiser, Monday, September 4th, 1893. [p7c]. Manchester, England.
Liverpool Echo. (1893). Liverpool v. Middlesbrough Ironopolis, Liverpool Echo, Monday, September 4th, 1893
Shields Daily News. (1893). Rendel v. Newcastle United A, The Shields Daily News, Monday, September 4th, 1893. [p4e]. South Shields, England.
Newcastle Daily Chronicle. (1893). Newcastle United v. Trafalgar, Newcastle Daily Chronicle, Tuesday, September 5th, 1893. [p7a]. Newcastle upon Tyne, England.
Newcastle Daily Chronicle. (1893). Newcastle United v Sunderland, Newcastle Daily Chronicle, Thursday, September 7th, 1893. [p7e]. Newcastle upon Tyne, England.
Sunderland Echo. (1893). Sunderland v. Newcastle United, Sunderland Daily Echo, Thursday, September 7th, 1893. [p4c]. Sunderland, England.
Kentish Mercury. (1893). Football: Woolwich Arsenal v. Newcastle United, Kentish Mercury, Friday, September 8th, 1893. [p6c], Merritt & Hatcher. London, England.
Newcastle Daily Chronicle. (1893). Middlesbrough v. Newcastle United, Newcastle Daily Chronicle, Monday, September 11th, 1893. [p6d]. Newcastle upon Tyne, England.
Northern Echo. (1893). Middlesbrough v. Newcastle United, The Northern Echo, Monday, September 11th, 1893. [p4c]. Middlesbrough, England.
Shields Gazette. (1893). Association. Newcastle United v Middlesbro, The Shields Daily Gazette and Shipping Telegraph, Monday, September 11th, 1893. [p4e]. South Shields, England.
Daily Express. (1893). Teams For Today. League No.2. Burton Swifts v. Newcastle United, The Nottingham Daily Express, Saturday, September 23rd, 1893. [p7e]. Nottingham, England.
Lloyds Weekly. (1893). Second Division. Burton Swifts v. Newcastle United, Lloyd's Weekly Newspaper, Sunday, September 24th, 1893. [p1c]. London, England.
Lincolnshire Echo. (1893). Burton Swifts v. Newcastle United, The Lincolnshire Echo, Monday, September 25th, 1893. [p3c]. Lincolnshire, England.
Athletic News. (1893). Burton Swifts Improving, The Athletic News, Monday, September 25th, 1893. [p2b]. London, England.
Sporting Life. (1893). The Football League. Burton Swifts v Newcastle United, The Sporting Life, Monday, September 25th, 1893. [p4c]. London, England.
Sunderland Echo. (1893). The Northern Alliance, Sunderland Daily Echo, Monday, September 25th, 1893. [p4c]. Sunderland, England.
Sheffield Independent. (1893). The league. - Division II, The Sheffield and Rotherham Independent, Monday, September 25th, 1893. [p7d], England.
Newcastle Daily Chronicle. (1893). Burton Swifts v. Newcastle United, The Newcastle Daily Chronicle, Monday, September 25th, 1893. [p6f]. Newcastle upon Tyne, England.
Nottingham Express. (1893). Burton Swifts v. Newcastle United, The Nottingham Daily Express, Monday, September 25th, 1893. [p6f], England.
Northern Echo. (1893). Football, Brief Results, Northern Echo, Monday, October 2nd, 1893. Darlington, England.
Birmingham Daily Post. (1893). Notes on Sport, Birmingham Daily Post, Monday, October 2nd, 1893. Birmingham, England.
Glasgow Herald. (1893). Saturday's Football, Glasgow Herald, Monday, October 2nd, 1893. Glasgow, Scotland.
Newcastle Daily Chronicle. (1893). Newcastle United v. Woolwich Arsenal, Newcastle Daily Chronicle, Monday, October 2nd, 1893. [p6d]. Newcastle upon Tyne, England.
Lloyd's Weekly. (1893). Second Division. Lincoln City v. Newcastle United, Lloyd's Weekly Newspaper, Sunday, October 8th, 1893. [p16b], Edward Llyod (Limited). London, England.
Northern Echo. (1893). Brief Results, The Northern Echo, Monday, October 9th, 1893. [p4e], Northern Echo Company (Limited). Darlington, England.
Newcastle Daily Chronicle. (1893). Lincoln City v. Newcastle United, Newcastle Daily Chronicle, Monday, October 9th, 1893. [p6e]. Newcastle upon Tyne, England.
Big Tom. (1893). Lincolnshire Echoes, The Athletic News, Monday, October 9th, 1893. [p5d]. Manchester, England.
Tynesider. (1893). Notes from the North. Tyneside, Athletic News, Monday, October 9th, 1893. [p7e], Edward Hulton. Steam Printing Office. Manchester, England.
Sporting Life. (1893). Lincoln City v. Newcastle United, The Sporting Life, Monday, October 9th, 1893. [p4f], John Lake. No.148 Fleet-street. London, England.
Free Kick. (1893). Football Notes, The Lincolnshire Echo, Monday, October 9th, 1893. [p4a], Lincolnshire Publishing Company Limited. Lincolnshire, England.
Lincolnshire Chronicle. (1893). Lincoln City v. Newcastle United, The Lincolnshire Chronicle, Tuesday, October 10th, 1893. [p3c]. Lincoln, England.
Half-back. (1893). Association Matches, The Ipswich Journal, Saturday, October 14th, 1893. [p3]. Ipswich, England.
Llyod's Weekly. (1893). Football Yesterday, Lloyd's Weekly Newspaper, Sunday, October 15th, 1893. [p16]. London, England.
Reynolds. (1893). Yesterday's Sport, Reynolds Newspaper, Sunday, October 15th, 1893. [p8]. London, England.
Glasgow Herald. (1893). The Association Game in England, Glasgow Herald, Monday, October 16th, 1893. [p10]. Glasgow, Scotland.
Northern Echo. (1893). Brief Results, Northern Echo, Monday, October 16th, 1893. [p4]. Darlington, England.
Newcastle Daily Chronicle. (1893). Newcastle United v. Notts County, Newcastle Daily Chronicle, Monday, October 16th, 1893. [p6e]. Newcastle upon Tyne, England.
Nottingham Express. (1893). Notts v. Newcastle United, The Nottingham Daily Express, Monday, October 16th, 1893. [p6e], England.
Anon. (1893). Notes on Sport, Birmingham Daily Post, Monday, October 23rd, 1893. Birmingham, England.
Sheffield Telegraph. (1893). Ardwick v. Newcastle United, The Sheffield Daily Telegraph, Monday, October 23rd, 1893. [p6f]. Sheffield, England.
Nottingham Express. (1893). Ardwick v. Newcastle United, The Nottingham Daily Express, Monday, October 23rd, 1893. [p7a]. Nottingham, England.
Newcastle Daily Chronicle. (1893). Newcastle United A v. Berwick Rangers, Newcastle Daily Chronicle, Monday, October 23rd, 1893. [p6e]. Newcastle upon Tyne, England.
Newcastle Daily Chronicle. (1893). Ardwick v. Newcastle United, Newcastle Daily Chronicle, Monday, October 23rd, 1893. [p6f]. Newcastle upon Tyne, England.
Examiner. (1893). Ardwick v. Newcastle United, The Examiner & Times, Monday, October 23rd, 1893. [p7b]. Manchester, England.
Manchester Courier. (1893). Ardwick v. Newcastle United, Manchester Copurier and Lancashire General Advertiser, Monday, October 23rd, 1893. [p3c]. Manchester, England.
Newcastle Daily Chronicle. (1893). Newcastle United v. Small Heath, Newcastle Daily Chronicle, Monday, October 23rd, 1893. [p6e]. Newcastle upon Tyne, England.
Birmingham Daily Post. (1893). Notes On Sport, The Birmingham Daily Post, Monday, October 30th, 1893. [p7g]. Birmingham, England.
Loiterer, The. (1893). Association, The Athletic News, Monday, November 6th, 1893. [p3f]. Manchester, England.
Sheffield Daily Telegraph. (1893). Second Division. Liverpool v Newcastle, Sheffield Daily Telegraph, Monday, November 6th, 1893. [p6f]. Sheffield, England.
Northern Echo. (1893). Football. Liverpool v Newcastle United, Northern Echo, Monday, November 6th, 1893. [p4d]. Durham, England.
Evening Telegraph. (1893). Sheffield United v. Newcastle United, The Evening Telegraph and Star, Saturday, November 11th, 1893. [p4e]. Sheffield, England.
Sheffield Independent. (1893). Newcastle United v. Sheffield United, The Sheffield and Rotherham Independent, Monday, November 13th, 1893. [p8a], England.
Newcastle Daily Chronicle. (1893). Sheffield United v. Newcastle United, The Newcastle Daily Chronicle, Monday, November 13th, 1893. [p6e]. Newcastle upon Tyne, England.
Lancashire Post. (1893). Division II. Northwich Victoria v. Newcastle United, The Lancashire Daily Post, Saturday, November 18th, 1893. [p3c]. Lancashire, England.
Nottingham Evening Post. (1893). Football League Referees, Nottingham Evening Post, The, Saturday, November 18th, 1893. [p4f]. Nottingham, England.
Nottingham Express. (1893). Northwich Victoria v. Newcastle United, The Nottingham Daily Express, Monday, November 20th, 1893. [p7c]. Nottingham, England.
Sheffield Independent. (1893). Northwich Victoria v. Newcastle United, The Sheffield and Rotherham Independent, Monday, November 20th, 1893. [p7e]. Sheffield, England.
Northwich Guardian. (1893). Second Division. Northwich Victoria v. Newcastle United, The Guardian, Wednesday, November 22nd, 1893. [p2f]. Northwich, England.
Liverpool Mercury. (1893). Newcastle United v. Liverpool, Liverpool Mercury, The, Monday, November 27th, 1893. [p7d]. Liverpool, England.
Newcastle Daily Chronicle. (1893). Newcastle United v. Liverpool, Newcastle Daily Chronicle, The, Monday, November 27th, 1893. [p7a]. Newcastle upon Tyne, England.
Weekly Chronicle. (1893). Popular Pastimes, Newcastle Weekly Chronicle, The, Saturday, December 2nd, 1893. [p7e]. Newcastle upon Tyne, England.

Newcastle United 1893-94 – Season One

Newcastle Daily Chronicle. (1893). Newcastle United v. Dipton Wanderers, The Newcastle Daily Chronicle, Monday, December 4th, 1893. [p6d]. Newcastle upon Tyne, England.
Evening Telegraph. (1893). This Day's Football. Newcastle United v. Notts County, The Evening Telegraph and Star, Saturday, December 9th, 1893. [p4d]. Sheffield, England.
Nottingham Post. (1893). The League - Division II. Notts v. Newcastle United, The Nottingham Evening Post, Saturday, December 9th, 1893. [p3d]. Nottingham, England.
Evening Chronicle. (1893). Newcastle United v. Notts County, Evening Chronicle, The, Saturday, December 9th, 1893. [p4c]. Newcastle upon Tyne, England.
Nottingham Express. (1893). League - Division II. Newcastle United v. Notts, The Nottingham Daily Express, Monday, December 11th, 1893. [p7a]. Nottingham, England.
Newcastle Daily Chronicle. (1893). Newcastle United v. Notts County, Newcastle Daily Chronicle, The, Monday, December 11th, 1893. [p6d]. Newcastle upon Tyne, England.
Evening Telegraph. (1893). League No.2 Small Heath v. Newcastle United, The Evening Telegraph and Star, Saturday, December 16th, 1893. [p4c]. Sheffield, England.
Nottingham Evening Post. (1893). The Football League, Nottingham Evening Post, The, Saturday, December 16th, 1893. [p4f]. Nottingham, England.
Brum. (1893). Midland Notes. A Disappointing Show, The Athletic News, Monday, December 18th, 1893. [p6d]. Lancashire, England.
Sporting Life. (1893). Division 2. Newcastle United v. Small Heath, The Sporting Life, Monday, December 18th, 1893. [p4c]. London, England.
Newcastle Daily Chronicle. (1893). Newcastle United v. Small Heath, Newcastle Daily Chronicle, The, Monday, December 18th, 1893. [p6d]. Newcastle upon Tyne, England.
Referee. (1893). The League Matches, The Referee, Sunday, December 24th, 1893. [p5b]. London, England.
Newcastle Daily Chronicle. (1893). Newcastle United v. First Royal Scots, Newcastle Daily Chronicle, Monday, December 25th, 1893. [p6c]. Newcastle upon Tyne, England.
Sporting Life. (1893). The Football League, The Sporting Life, Monday, December 25th, 1893. [p4c]. London, England.
Newcastle Daily Chronicle. (1893). Saturday's Football. Association, Newcastle Daily chronicle, Monday, December 25th, 1893. [pp6a-d]. Newcastle upon Tyne, England.
Northern Echo. (1893). Christmas Day Games. Ironopolis v. Newcastle United, Northern Echo, Tuesday, December 26th, 1893. [p4e], England.
Birmingham Post. (1893). Yesterday's Football. Middlesbrough Ironopolis v. Newcastle United, The Birmingham Daily Post, Tuesday, December 26th, 1893. [p7f]. Birmingham, England.
Athletic News. (1893). League - Second Division. Middlesbrough Ironopolis v. Newcastle United, The Athletic News, Tuesday, December 26th, 1893. [p6e]. Lancashire, England.
Evening Press. (1893). Second Division. Middlesbrough Ironopolis v. Newcastle United, The Evening Press, Tuesday, December 26th, 1893. [p4d]. Yorkshire, England.
Evening Telegraph. (1893). This Day's Football. Walsall v. Newcastle United, The Evening Telegraph and Star, Tuesday, December 26th, 1893. [p4d]. Sheffield, England.
Sportsman. (1893). The League Championships. Second Division, The Sportsman, Tuesday, December 26th, 1893. [p4d], England.
Evening Telegraph. (1893). The Football League. League No.2., The Evening Telegraph and Star, Tuesday, December 26th, 1893. [p4d]. Sheffield, England.
Sunderland Echo. (1893). The Northern Alliance, Sunderland Daily Echo, Tuesday, December 26th, 1893. [p4b]. Sunderland, England.
Sporting Life. (1893). The Football League. Division 2., The Sporting Life, Tuesday, December 26th, 1893. [p4c]. London, England.
Northern Guardian. (1893). Walsall v Newcastle United, The Northern Guardian, Tuesday, December 26th, 1893. [p4e]. Hartlepool, England.
Newcastle Daily Chronicle. (1893). Middlesbrough Ironopolis v. Newcastle United, Newcastle Daily Chronicle, The, Tuesday, December 26th, 1893. [p7a]. Newcastle upon Tyne, England.
Birmingham Evening Post. (1893). Yesterday's football, Division II, Birmingham Daily Post, Wednesday, December 27th, 1893. [p7d]. Birmingham, England.
Nottingham Post. (1893). This Day's Football. Newcastle United v. Crewe Alexandra, The Nottingham Evening Post, Wednesday, December 27th, 1893. [p3f]. Nottingham, England.
Newcastle Daily Chronicle. (1893). Yesterday's Football, The Newcastle Daily Chronicle, Wednesday, December 27th, 1893. [p6b]. Newcastle upon Tyne, England.
Shields Daily News. (1893). Newcastle United v Walsall, The Shields Daily News, Wednesday, December 27th, 1893. [p4e]. North Shields, England.
Sporting Life. (1893). Division 2. Newcastle United v. Crewe Alexandra, The Sporting Life, Friday, December 29th, 1893. [p4b]. London, England.
Evening Post. (1893). Division II. Newcastle United v. Burslem Port Vale, The Lancashire Evening Post, Saturday, December 30th, 1893. [p3c]. Lancashire, England.
Nottingham Post. (1893). Newcastle United v. Burslem Port Vale, The Nottingham Evening Post, Saturday, December 30th, 1893. [p3d]. Nottingham, England.
Newcastle Daily Chronicle. (1893). Newcastle United v. Burslem Port Vale, The Newcastle Daily Chronicle, Saturday, December 30th, 1893. [p7e]. Newcastle upon Tyne, England.
Crewe Guardian. (1893). Crewe Alexandra v. Newcastle United, The Crewe Guardian, Saturday, December 30th, 1893. [p5b]. Mackie & Co. Limited. Crewe, England.
Walsall Advertiser. (1893). Walsall v. Newcastle United, The Walsall Advertiser, Saturday, December 30th, 1893. [p3b]. Walsall, England.
Referee. (1894). Second Division, Scottish Referee, Monday, January 1st, 1894. [p1b]. Glasgow, Scotland.
Newcastle Daily Chronicle. (1894). Newcastle United v. Burslem Port Vale, Newcastle Daily Chronicle, Monday, January 1st, 1894. [p6f]. Newcastle upon Tyne, England.
Evening Chronicle. (1894). Newcastle United v. Lincoln City, Evening Chronicle, Monday, January 1st, 1894. [p4d]. Newcastle upon Tyne, England.
Lincolnshire Echo. (1894). Football. The League. Division II., The Lincolnshire Echo, Tuesday, January 2nd, 1894. [p3e]. Lincoln, England.
Newcastle Journal. (1894). Newcastle United v. Lincoln City, The Newcastle Daily Journal, Tuesday, January 2nd, 1894. [p7d]. Newcastle upon Tyne, England.
Newcastle Daily Chronicle. (1894). Newcastle United v. Lincoln City, The Newcastle Daily Chronicle, Tuesday, January 2nd, 1894. [p6f]. Newcastle upon Tyne, England.
Captain. (1894). Football Notes. Association, The Newcastle Daily Chronicle, Wednesday, January 3rd, 1894. [p7e]. Newcastle upon Tyne, England.
Daily Journal. (1894). Newcastle United v. Middlesbrough Ironopolis, The Newcastle Daily Journal, Wednesday, January 3rd, 1894. [p7e]. Newcastle upon Tyne, England.
Newcastle Daily Chronicle. (1894). Football Notes. Association, The Newcastle Daily Chronicle, Wednesday, January 3rd, 1894. [p7e]. Newcastle upon Tyne, England.
The Referee. (1894). Football League, Second Division, The Referee, Sunday, January 7th, 1894. [p6a]. London, England.
Manchester Courier. (1894). Newcastle United v. Ardwick, The Manchester Courier, and Lancashire General Advertiser, Monday, January 8th, 1894. [p3b]. Manchester, England.
Newcastle Journal. (1894). Newcastle United v. Ardwick, The Newcastle Daily Journal, Monday, January 8th, 1894. [p7d]. Newcastle upon Tyne, England.
Newcastle Daily Chronicle. (1894). Newcastle United v. Ardwick, The Newcastle Daily Chronicle, Monday, January 8th, 1894. [p7a]. Newcastle upon Tyne, England.
Sheffield Independent. (1894). Newcastle United v. Northwich Victoria, The Sheffield and Rotherham Independent, Monday, January 15th, 1894. [p7c]. Sheffield, England.
Newcastle Journal. (1894). Newcastle United v. Northwich Victoria, The Newcastle Daily Journal, Monday, January 15th, 1894. [p7d]. Newcastle upon Tyne, England.
Newcastle Daily Chronicle. (1894). Newcastle United v. Northwich Victoria, The Newcastle Daily Chronicle, Monday, January 15th, 1894. [p6c]. Newcastle upon Tyne, England.
Sheffield Independent. (1894). The League. Division II., The Sheffield and Rotherham Independent, Monday, January 22nd, 1894. [p7c]. Sheffield, England.
Newcastle Journal. (1894). Rotherham Town v. Newcastle United, The Newcastle Daily Journal, Monday, January 22nd, 1894. [p7d]. Newcastle upon Tyne, England.
Newcastle Daily Chronicle. (1894). Rotherham Town v. Newcastle United, The Newcastle Daily Chronicle, Monday, January 22nd, 1894. [p6c]. Newcastle upon Tyne, England.
Evening Chronicle. (1894). Newcastle United v Sheffield United, Evening Chronicle, The, Saturday, January 27th, 1894. [p4c]. Newcastle upon Tyne, England.
Newcastle Daily Chronicle. (1894). Newcastle United v. Sheffield United, Newcastle Daily Chronicle, The, Monday, January 29th, 1894. [p6d]. Newcastle upon Tyne, England.
Sheffield Independent. (1894). Newcastle United v. Sheffield United, Sheffield and Rotherham Independent, The, Monday, January 29th, 1894. [p7d]. Sheffield, England.
Sheffield Daily Telegraph. (1894). Sheffield United v. Newcastle United, Sheffield Daily Telegraph, The, Monday, January 29th, 1894. [p6d]. Sheffield, England.
Evening Chronicle. (1894). Newcastle United v Burslem Port Vale, Evening Chronicle, The, Saturday, February 3rd, 1894. [p4c]. Newcastle upon Tyne, England.
Newcastle Daily Chronicle. (1894). Newcastle United v. Burslem Port Vale, Newcastle Daily Chronicle, The, Monday, February 5th, 1894. [p6b]. Newcastle upon Tyne, England.
Evening Post. (1894). This Day's Football. Association Cup, The Nottingham Evening Post, Saturday, February 10th, 1894. [p3b]. Nottingham, England.
Newcastle Daily Chronicle. (1894). Newcastle United v. Bolton Wanderers, The Newcastle Daily Chronicle, Monday, February 12th, 1894. [p6d]. Newcastle upon Tyne, England.
Free Critic. (1894). A Close Shave at Newcastle, Athletic News, The, Monday, February 12th, 1894. [p4e]. Manchester, England.
Manchester Courier. (1894). English Cup - Second Round, Manchester Courier, The, Monday, February 12th, 1894. [p3a]. Manchester, England.
Evening Post. (1894). The League - Division II, The Nottingham Evening Post, Saturday, February 24th, 1894. [p3f]. Nottingham, England.
Glasgow Herald. (1894). Saturday's Football, The League, Glasgow Herald, Monday, February 26th, 1894. [p9]. Glasgow, Scotland.
Newcastle Daily Chronicle. (1894). Newcastle United v. Grimsby Town, Newcastle Daily Chronicle, The, Monday, February 26th, 1894. [p6d]. Newcastle upon Tyne, England.
Newcastle Daily Chronicle. (1894). Newcastle United v. Walsall Town Swifts, The Newcastle Daily Chronicle, Saturday, March 10th, 1894. [p6e]. Newcastle upon Tyne, England.
Newcastle Daily Chronicle. (1894). League No. 2. Newcastle United v. Walsall Town Swifts, The Newcastle Daily Chronicle, Monday, March 12th, 1894. [p6e]. Newcastle upon Tyne, England.
Newcastle Journal. (1894). Newcastle United v. Walsall Town Swifts, The Newcastle Daily Journal, Monday, March 12th, 1894. [p7b]. Newcastle upon Tyne, England.
Newcastle Daily Chronicle. (1894). Chief Matches To-Day, The Newcastle Daily Chronicle, Saturday, March 17th, 1894. [p7d]. Newcastle upon Tyne, England.
Birmingham Daily Post. (1894). Saturday's Football, The Birmingham Daily Post, Monday, March 19th, 1894. [p7c], England.
Athletic News. (1894). Notes from the North, The Athletic News, Monday, March 19th, 1894. [p6a]. London, England.
Newcastle Daily Chronicle. (1894). Newcastle United v. Burslem Port Vale, The Newcastle Daily Chronicle, Monday, March 19th, 1894. [p9a]. Newcastle upon Tyne, England.
Newcastle Daily Chronicle. (1894). Football. Association, The Newcastle Daily Chronicle, Friday, March 23rd, 1894. [p7d]. Newcastle upon Tyne, England.
Newcastle Journal. (1894). Newcastle United v. Crewe Alexandra, The Newcastle Daily Journal, Friday, March 23rd, 1894. [p7d]. Newcastle upon Tyne, England.
Evening Chronicle. (1894). To-Day's Football. Association, The Evening Chronicle, Friday, March 23rd, 1894. [p3f]. Newcastle upon Tyne, England.
Newcastle Daily Chronicle. (1894). League 2., The Newcastle Daily Chronicle, Saturday, March 24th, 1894. [p6d]. Newcastle upon Tyne, England.
Newcastle Daily Chronicle. (1894). Newcastle United v. Burton Swifts, The Newcastle Daily Chronicle, Monday, March 26th, 1894. [p6c]. Newcastle upon Tyne, England.

Bibliography

Leicester Daily Post. (1894). Leicester Fosse v. Newcastle United, The Leicester Daily Post, Tuesday, March 27th, 1894. [p3c]
Newcastle Daily Chronicle. (1894). Leicester Fosse v. Newcastle United, The Newcastle Daily Chronicle, Tuesday, March 27th, 1894. [p6c]. Newcastle upon Tyne, England.
Northern Echo. (1894). Newcastle United v. Middlesbrough Ironopolis, The Northern Echo, Monday, April 2nd, 1894. [p4f]. Hartlepool, England.
Newcastle Daily Chronicle. (1894). Newcastle United v. Ironopolis, The Newcastle Daily Chronicle, Monday, April 2nd, 1894. [p6d]. Newcastle upon Tyne, England.
Daily Journal. (1894). Newcastle United v. Middlesbrough Ironopolis, The Newcastle Daily Journal, Monday, April 2nd, 1894. [p7b]. Newcastle upon Tyne, England.
Newcastle Daily Chronicle. (1894). Newcastle United v. Sunderland, Newcastle Daily Chronicle, Thursday, April 5th, 1894. [p7c]. Newcastle upon Tyne, England.
Newcastle Daily Chronicle. (1894). Newcastle United v. Sunderland, Newcastle Daily Chronicle, Friday, April 6th, 1894. [p7d]. Newcastle upon Tyne, England.
Sunderland Echo. (1894). Sunderland v. Newcastle United, Sunderland Daily Echo, Friday, April 6th, 1894. [p4a]. Sunderland, England.
Dundee Courier. (1894). Dundee v. Newcastle United, The Dundee Courier, Monday, April 9th, 1894. [p5d]. Ireland.
Newcastle Daily Chronicle. (1894). Newcastle United v. Dundee, The Newcastle Daily Chronicle, Monday, April 9th, 1894. [p6b]. Newcastle upon Tyne, England.
Lloyd's Weekly. (1894). Grimsby v. Newcastle United, Lloyd's Weekly Newspaper, Sunday, April 15th, 1894. [p16b], Edward Llyod (Limited). London, England.
Newcastle Daily Chronicle. (1894). Saturday's Football. Association, The Newcastle Daily Chronicle, Monday, April 16th, 1894. [p6b]. Newcastle upon Tyne, England.
Shields Daily News. (1894). Saturday's Football Matches, The Shields Daily News, Monday, April 16th, 1894. [p4e]. South Shields, England.
Sporting Life. (1894). The Football League. Division 2, The Sporting Life, Monday, April 16th, 1894. [p4c]. London, England.
Sheffield Independent. (1894). The League. Division II., The Sheffield and Rotherham Independent, Monday, April 16th, 1894. [p7d]. Sheffield, England.
The Linesman. (1894). Notes from the North. Tyneside, The Athletic News, Monday, April 16th, 1894. [p2f]. Manchester, England.
Yorkshire Herald. (1894). The Football League. Second Division, The Yorkshire Herald, Monday, April 16th, 1894. [p7e]. York, England.
Manchester Courier. (1894). Grimsby Town v. Newcastle United, Manchester Courier and Lancashire General Advertiser, Monday, April 16th, 1894. [p3c]. Manchester, England.
Newcastle Journal. (1894). Grimsby Town v. Newcastle United, The Newcastle Daily Journal, Monday, April 16th, 1894. [p7c]. Newcastle upon Tyne, England.
Newcastle Daily Chronicle. (1894). Newcastle United v. Sunderland, Newcastle Daily Chronicle, Saturday, April 21st, 1894. [p7d]. Newcastle upon Tyne, England.
Newcastle Daily Chronicle. (1894). Sunderland v. Newcastle United, Newcastle Daily Chronicle, Monday, April 23rd, 1894. [p6c]. Newcastle upon Tyne, England.
Sunderland Echo. (1894). Sunderland v. Newcastle United, Sunderland Daily Echo, Monday, April 23rd, 1894. [p4a]. Sunderland, England.
Newcastle Daily Chronicle. (1894). Newcastle United v. Shankhouse, Newcastle Daily Chronicle, Tuesday, April 24th, 1894. [p7d]. Newcastle upon Tyne, England.
Newcastle Daily Chronicle. (1894). Newcastle United v. Willington Athletic, Newcastle Daily Chronicle, Tuesday, April 24th, 1894. [p7d]. Newcastle upon Tyne, England.
Newcastle Daily Chronicle. (1894). Newcastle United v. Shankhouse, Newcastle Daily Chronicle, Wednesday, April 25th, 1894. [p7d]. Newcastle upon Tyne, England.
Newcastle Daily Chronicle. (1894). Newcastle United v. Shankhouse, Newcastle Daily Chronicle, Thursday, April 26th, 1894. [p7e]. Newcastle upon Tyne, England.
Newcastle Daily Chronicle. (1894). Ironopolis v. Newcastle United, Newcastle Daily Chronicle, The, Monday, April 30th, 1894. [p6c]. Newcastle upon Tyne, England.
Newcastle Daily Chronicle. (1894). Newcastle United v. Sunderland, Newcastle Daily Cronicle, Tuesday, May 1st, 1894. [p7d]. Newcastle upon Tyne, England.
Sunderland Echo. (1894). Sunderland v. Newcastle United, Sunderland Daily Echo, Tuesday, May 1st, 1894. [p4a]. Sunderland, England.

www.ingramcontent.com/pod-product-compliance
Lightning Source LLC
Chambersburg PA
CBHW061154010526
44118CB00027B/2973